DISCOVERING THE
AMERICAN PAST

DISCOVERING THE AMERICAN PAST

A Look at the Evidence

FIFTH EDITION

✳ **VOLUME ONE: to 1877** ✳

William Bruce Wheeler
University of Tennessee

Susan D. Becker
University of Tennessee, Emerita

Houghton Mifflin Company   BOSTON   NEW YORK

Editor-in-Chief: Jean L. Woy
Sponsoring Editor: Colleen Shanley Kyle
Associate Editor: Leah Strauss
Project Editor: Carla Thompson
Editorial Assistant: Christian Downey
Associate Production/Design Coordinator: Lisa Jelly Smith
Manufacturing Manager: Florence Cadran
Senior Marketing Manager: Sandra McGuire
Marketing Assistant: Jim David

Cover Design: Jonathan Wallen/National Archives
Cover Image: Pennsylvania German Fraktur Birth and Family Register, early nineteenth
century

*For permission to use copyrighted material, grateful acknowledgment is made to the
copyright holders listed on pages 305–306, which are hereby considered an extension of
the copyright page.*

Printed in the U.S.A.

Library of Congress Control Number: 2001131560

ISBN: 0-618-10224-8

10 11 12 13 14 15-QF-09 08 07 06 05

Contents

❈ CHAPTER SIX ❈

Land, Growth, and Justice:
The Removal of the Cherokees

❈ CHAPTER SEVEN ❈

Away from Home:
The Working Girls of Lowell

❋ CHAPTER EIGHT ❋

The "Peculiar Institution": Slaves Tell Their Own Story

❋ CHAPTER NINE ❋

Slavery and Territorial Expansion: The Wilmot Proviso Debate, February 1847

Preface

The presidential election of 2000 was an incredibly exciting, confusing, and frustrating experience for our country. But as commentator after commentator noted, the election was also "a history teacher's dream." Millions of students—and a surprising number of adult Americans—were suddenly, somewhat painfully, educated about the origins, role, and assumptions of the electoral college. The previously obscure, even unknown, disputed election of 1876 between Rutherford Hayes and Samuel Tilden took on new relevance. Both state and federal judges sought precedents in the past to help them make important decisions in the present. And finally, questions about the evidence of the votes and the methods by which they were counted simply could not be settled completely and to everyone's satisfaction.

We live in a complex world, and we strongly believe that students need help in developing the skills of critical thinking so essential for coping with life in the twenty-first century. How can we rely on statements made by a president of the United States, any other world leader, the chairman of the Federal Reserve Board, a member of Congress, a radio talk show host, a TV newscaster, or a professor unless we are able to examine and analyze the available evidence to understand how it is being used? How can we ourselves learn to use evidence intelligently when we write a report, make a public address, or participate in a debate? The subject of this volume is American history, but the important skills of examination, analysis, and proper use of evidence are important to every person in every vocation.

In *Discovering the American Past: A Look at the Evidence,* we show students the importance of acquiring and sharpening these skills. Moreover, as they acquire or hone these skills, students generally discover that they enjoy "doing history," welcome the opportunity to become active learners, retain more historical knowledge, and are eager to solve a series of historical problems themselves rather than simply being told about the past. Unlike a source reader, this book prompts students actually to *analyze* a wide variety of authentic primary-source material, make inferences, and draw conclusions based on the available evidence, much in the same way that historians do.

As in previous editions, we try to expose students to the broad scope of the American experience by providing a mixture of types of historical problems and a balance among political, social, diplomatic, economic, intellectual, and cultural history. This wide variety of historical topics and events engages students' interest and rounds out their view of American history.

✳ FORMAT OF THE BOOK ✳

Historians are fully aware that everything that is preserved from the past can be used as evidence to solve historical problems. In that spirit, we have included as many different *types* of historical evidence as we could. Almost every chapter gives students the opportunity to work with a different type of evidence: works of art, first-person accounts, trial transcripts, statistics, maps, letters, charts, biographical sketches, court decisions, music lyrics, prescriptive literature, newspaper accounts, congressional debates, speeches, diaries, proclamations and laws, political cartoons, photographs, architectural plans, advertisements, posters, film reviews, fiction, memoirs, and oral interviews. In this book, then, we have created a kind of historical sampler that we believe will help students learn the methods and skills historians use, as well as help them learn historical content.

Each type of historical evidence is combined with an introduction to the appropriate methodology in an effort to teach students a wide variety of research skills. As much as possible, we have tried to let the evidence speak for itself and have avoided leading students to one particular interpretation or another. This approach is effective in many different classroom situations, including seminars, small classes, discussion sections, and large lecture classes. Indeed, we have found that the previous editions of *Discovering the American Past* have proven themselves equally stimulating and effective in very large classes as well as very small ones.

Each chapter is divided into six parts: The Problem, Background, The Method, The Evidence, Questions to Consider, and Epilogue. Each of the parts relates to or builds upon the others, creating a uniquely integrated chapter structure that helps guide the reader through the analytical process. "The Problem" section begins with a brief discussion of the central issues of the chapter and then states the questions students will explore. A

"Background" section follows, designed to help students understand the historical context of the problem. The section called "The Method" gives students suggestions for studying and analyzing the evidence. "The Evidence" section is the heart of the chapter, providing a variety of primary source material on the particular historical event or issue described in the chapter's "Problem" section. The section called "Questions to Consider" focuses students' attention on specific evidence and on linkages among different evidence material. The "Epilogue" section gives the aftermath or the historical outcome of the evidence—what happened to the people involved, who won the election, the results of a debate, and so on.

❋ CHANGES IN THE FIFTH EDITION ❋

In response to student evaluations and faculty reviews, we have made significant alterations in the content of this edition. There are five new chapters, three in Volume I and two in Volume II.

In Volume I, we have rewritten Chapter 3 to give students a broader, more diverse view of Americans in the late colonial period. Demographic and statistical material from both the Chesapeake and New England colonies allows students to make regional comparisons as well as learn to use such data to describe people who were not famous. Chapter 9 focuses on the reintroduction of the Wilmot Proviso and the subsequent congressional debates of 1847 about the westward expansion of slavery. Chapter 11 utilizes the political cartoons of Thomas Nast and Matthew Morgan as a window into the important Reconstruction issues of the election of 1872.

Although the hard-fought battle for woman suffrage was won in 1920 with the passage of the Nineteenth Amendment, many social, economic, and political questions about women's place remained. In Volume II, Chapter 6 looks at women's issues during the crucial period of the 1920s. Chapter 11 emphasizes immigration as one of the main themes of American history, examining the "fourth wave" of immigrants in California during the latter part of the twentieth century.

❋ INSTRUCTOR'S RESOURCE MANUAL ❋

Because we value the teaching of American history and yet fully understand how difficult it is to do it well, we have written our own Instructor's Resource Manual to accompany *Discovering the American Past*. In this manual, we explain our specific content and skills objectives for each chapter, and we include an expanded discussion of the method and evidence sections. We also answer some of the questions that students often ask about the material in each problem. Our suggestions for various ways of teaching and for evaluating the students' learning draw not only upon our own experiences but also upon the experiences of those of you who have shared your classroom ideas with us. Finally, we wrote brief, updated bibliographic essays for each problem.

❋ ACKNOWLEDGMENTS ❋

We would like to thank all the students and instructors who have helped us in developing and refining our ideas for the fifth edition. In addition to our colleagues across the United States, we would like to thank especially our colleagues at the University of Tennessee who offered suggestions and read chapter drafts, along with Penny Hamilton and Kim Harrison who helped in preparing the manuscript. At Houghton Mifflin, we are indebted to Colleen Kyle, Leah Strauss, and Carla Thompson for their editorial assistance. Finally, colleagues at other institutions who reviewed chapter drafts made significant contributions to this edition, and we would like to thank them for their generosity, both in time and in helpful ideas and specific suggestions:

Jamie Bronstein, *New Mexico State University*
Eliga H. Gould, *University of New Hampshire*
Donna Cooper Graves, *University of Tennessee—Martin*
Gaylen Lewis, *Bakersfield College*
Linda Przybyszewski, *University of Cincinnati*
Elizabeth Rose, *Trinity College*
Clarice Stasz, *Sonoma State University*
Michael Topp, *University of Texas—El Paso*
Lynn Y. Weiner, *Roosevelt University*
Robert S. Wolff, *Central Connecticut State University*

As with our four previous editions, we dedicate these volumes to all our colleagues who seek to offer a challenging and stimulating academic experience to their students, and to those students themselves, who make all our work worthwhile.

W. B. W.
S. D. B.

1

First Encounters: The Confrontation Between Cortés and Montezuma (1519–1521)

❋ THE PROBLEM ❋

In 1492, Christopher Columbus became the first European to meet Indians[1] and record his observations. In the next few years, Europeans became increasingly fascinated with the New World and its inhabitants. Explorers' accounts were published and widely circulated, as were artistic renderings of the Indians by European artists, many of whom had never traveled to the New World or met a single Indian.

In turn, Native Americans doubtless recorded their own impressions of Europeans. Since most Indian cultures had not developed forms of writing, these impressions were preserved orally, largely through stories and songs. In central Mexico, however, the Aztecs and other peoples did record their observations of Europeans in writing and art. And although the Spanish *conquistadores* (conquerors) attempted to destroy all such records, a few of the written and artistic renderings have survived to tell the Indians' side of the story of the first encounters.

There is little doubt that the impressions created by these written and artistic works fostered perceptions that made Indian-white relations confusing, difficult, and ultimately tragic. The European hunger for land and treasure as well as a forced labor supply may have made the tragedies that followed almost inevitable, and yet

1. Although Europeans quickly realized that the name Columbus conferred on Native Americans was inaccurate, the word *Indian* continued to be used. Alternative names have never replaced it.

[1]

CHAPTER 1

FIRST
ENCOUNTERS:
THE
CONFRONTATION
BETWEEN
CORTÉS AND
MONTEZUMA
(1519–1521)

Europeans' early perceptions of Indians were an important factor in how explorers and early colonists dealt with Native American peoples and, in the end, subdued them. At the same time, the early impressions that Indians gained of Europeans (whether passed down orally or by other means) offered to many Native Americans a clear message concerning how they should respond to white encroachment.

In this chapter, you will be concentrating on the conquest of Mexico by Hernando Cortés, which took place between 1519 and 1521. In many ways, that confrontation was typical of the "first encounters" between Europeans and Native Americans. You will be examining and analyzing two separate sets of evidence: (1) selections written by Cortés to King Charles I of Spain, together with some artistic representations of Native Americans by European artists, and (2) selected written and artistic impressions of Cortés and his *conquistadores* by Aztecs and other Native Americans of central Mexico created within a few years of the events they described. Your task is twofold. First, you must use written and artistic accounts to determine the impressions that each side created of the other. Second, you must reach some conclusions about how those impressions (whether totally accurate or inaccurate) might have influenced how Europeans and

early colonists dealt with Native Americans and how Native Americans dealt with them.

Before you begin, we would like to issue a note of caution. When dealing with the evidence provided by European conquerors such as Cortés or by European artists, you will *not* be trying to determine what the Native Americans the Europeans encountered were really like, but only what Cortés and selected European artists perceived them to be like. To find out what the diverse peoples collectively known as Indians were really like, you would have to consult the works of archaeologists, cultural anthropologists, and cultural geographers. And yet, if we want to determine how Europeans perceived Indians, Cortés's letters and selected European works of art can provide excellent clues.

This chapter also will give you a revealing look at how historical evidence is created and how the availability— and unavailability—of that evidence influences the ways in which a past event or person is depicted by historians. For example, Cortés and his soldiers attempted to destroy as many of the Native American historical records as they could, for obvious reasons. But some pieces of that evidence survived. Without those pieces of evidence, historians' accounts of the "first encounters" very likely would be dramatically different.

✳ BACKGROUND ✳

By the time Europeans first encountered the various peoples they collec-

tively called Indians, Native Americans had inhabited the Western Hemisphere for approximately 20,000 to 40,000 years.[2] Although there is considerable disagreement about when these people first appeared in the Americas, it is reasonable to assume that they first migrated to the Western Hemisphere sometime in the middle of the Pleistocene Age. During that period, roughly from 75,000 to 8000 B.C.E., huge glaciers covered a large portion of North America, the ice cap extending southward to the approximate present border of the United States and Canada. These glaciers, which in some places were more than 9,000 feet thick, interrupted the water cycle because moisture falling as rain or snow was caught by the glaciers and frozen and was thus prevented from draining back into the seas or evaporating into the atmosphere.

This process lowered ocean levels 250 to 300 feet, exposing a natural land bridge spanning the Bering Strait (between present-day Alaska and the former Soviet Union) across which people from Asia could easily migrate, probably in search of game. It is probable that various peoples from Asia did exactly that and then followed an ice-free corridor along the base of the Rocky Mountains southward into the more temperate areas of the American Southwest and then either eastward into other areas of North America or even farther southward into Central and South America. Recent discoveries suggest that other migrants may have arrived by a sea route. These migrations took thousands of years, and

some Indian peoples were still moving when Europeans first encountered them.

About 8000 B.C.E., the glacial cap began to retreat fairly rapidly, raising ocean levels to approximately their present-day levels and cutting off further migration from Asia, thus isolating America's first human inhabitants from other peoples for thousands of years. This isolation was almost surely the cause of the inhabitants' extraordinarily high susceptibility to the diseases that Europeans later brought with them, such as measles, tuberculosis, and smallpox, to which the peoples of other continents had built up natural resistance. The glacial retreat also caused large portions of the American Southwest to become hot and arid, thus scattering Indian peoples in almost all directions. Nevertheless, for thousands of years a strong oral tradition enabled Indians to preserve stories of their origins and subsequent isolation. Almost all Indian peoples retained accounts of a long migration from the west and of a flood.

The original inhabitants of the Western Hemisphere obtained their food principally by hunting and gathering, killing mammoths, huge bison, deer, elk, antelope, camels, horses, and other game with stone weapons and picking wild fruits and grasses. Beginning about 5000 B.C.E., however, Indians in present-day Mexico began practicing agriculture. By the time Europeans arrived, most Indians were domesticating plants and raising crops, although their levels of agricultural sophistication were extremely diverse.

The development of agriculture, which occurred about the same time

2. Other estimates run as high as 70,000 years. Whatever the case, it is almost certain that Indians were not native to the Western Hemisphere because no subhuman remains have ever been found.

CHAPTER 1

FIRST
ENCOUNTERS:
THE
CONFRONTATION
BETWEEN
CORTÉS AND
MONTEZUMA
(1519–1521)

in Europe and the Americas, profoundly affected Indian life. Those peoples who adopted agriculture abandoned their nomadic ways and lived in settled villages (some of the Central American ones became magnificent cities). This more sedentary life permitted them to erect permanent housing, create and preserve pottery and art, and establish more complex political and social institutions. Agriculture also led to a sexual division of labor, with women planting, raising, and harvesting crops and men hunting to supplement their villages' diets with game. With more and better food, it is likely that Indian populations grew more rapidly, thus furthering the need for more complex political and social structures. The development of agriculture also affected these peoples' religious beliefs and ceremonies, increasing the homage to sun and rain gods who could bring forth good harvests. Contact with other Indian peoples led to trading, a practice with which Indians were quite familiar by the time of European intrusion.

Those Indian cultures that made the transition from food gathering to food producing often attained an impressive degree of economic, political, social, and technological sophistication. In Central America, the Mayas of present-day Mexico and Guatemala built great cities, fashioned elaborate gold and silver jewelry, devised a form of writing, were proficient in mathematics and astronomy, and constructed a calendar that could predict solar eclipses and was more accurate than any system in use in Europe at the time. The conquerors of the Mayas, the Aztecs (a scholarly term

for the Mexica and other Nahua-speaking Indians), built on the achievements of their predecessors, extending their political and economic power chiefly by subjugating other Indian peoples. By the time Cortés and his army of 400 men, 16 horses, and a few cannon landed at Vera Cruz in 1519, the Aztecs had constructed the magnificent city of Tenochtitlán (the site of present-day Mexico City), which rivaled European cities in both size (approximately 300,000 people) and splendor.

Tenochtitlán contained magnificent pyramids and public buildings, a fresh water supply brought to the city by complex engineering, causeways that connected the island city to other islands and the mainland, numerous skilled craftsmen, and even a compulsory education system for all male children (no state in the United States would have such a system for more than 300 years). Raw materials and treasure flowed into Tenochtitlán from all over the Aztec empire, which stretched from the Pacific Ocean to the Gulf of Mexico and from central Mexico to present-day Guatemala. Little wonder that the *conquistadores* with Hernando Cortés were awed and enchanted when they saw it.

In many ways, Cortés was the typical Spanish *conquistador.* Born in 1485 to a respected but poor family (his father had been a career military officer but never rose above the rank of captain), Cortés spent two unsuccessful years studying for the law. Abandoning that goal, he became a soldier and was determined to gain fame and fortune through a military career. In 1504, when he was only nineteen years old, he boarded a ship bound for the Spanish possessions in the New World. After fourteen years of military service, Cortés finally got his big break in 1518, when he was chosen to command a new armada whose purpose was to conquer Mexico. Earlier, unsuccessful expeditions had given some indications of gold in Mexico, and Cortés was sent to find it as well as to try to locate members of the earlier expeditions who might still be alive. Since Cortés himself financed a good portion of the new armada (he had to borrow money to do so), he had the opportunity to realize his dreams of wealth if his men found treasure. When Cortés landed at Vera Cruz, he was thirty-four years old.

✳ THE METHOD ✳

In this chapter, you will be working with two distinct types of evidence: (1) written accounts and (2) artistic representations. In addition, the evidence has been divided into two sets: (1) Hernando Cortés's and European artists' perceptions of Indians and (2) Indians' written and artistic accounts of Cortés's invasion of the Aztec capital, Tenochtitlán (1519–1521). As noted previously, Cortés's account comes from letters he wrote to the Spanish king soon after the events he described took place. As for the European artists, some of them undoubtedly used their active imaginations to construct their images of Indians, whereas others relied on explorers' accounts or word-of-mouth reports from those who had seen Native Americans whom the explorers had brought to Europe.

The Indians' accounts of Europeans pose something of a problem. We cannot be sure that all (or any) of the written or artistic representations were done by eyewitnesses to the events they describe. We do know,

however, that most of the written selections were completed by 1528, only seven years after Cortés's conquest of Tenochtitlán, and that all the written and artistic representations were created within the normal lifetimes of eyewitnesses. Therefore, if the writers and artists themselves were not eyewitnesses, they doubtless knew of eyewitnesses who could have reported to them what they saw. Thanks to Roman Catholic missionaries who preserved these accounts, we have what we can assume are firsthand reactions by Native Americans to European intruders.

Even so, the Native American accounts of Cortés's conquest pose some problems for historians. In addition to the difficulty that Native American place and people names present to non-Indians who attempt to pronounce them, it is not always clear in these accounts precisely what is being described. For example, remember that the Native Americans at first believed that Cortés and his party were some form of gods ("As for their food,

CHAPTER 1

FIRST
ENCOUNTERS:
THE
CONFRONTATION
BETWEEN
CORTÉS AND
MONTEZUMA
(1519–1521)

it is like human food"), which explains their sacrifices before Cortés, their offering of gifts, and their preparations to "celebrate their god's fiesta." Precisely when they abandoned this notion is unclear, for at the same time that they were conducting their celebration, they simultaneously posted guards at the Eagle Gate. It will take some care and thought to determine exactly what was taking place.

Also, occasionally historical evidence can be contradictory. For instance, Cortés claimed that he attacked the Aztecs only after learning that they were plotting to kill him and his men. Yet the Native American account suggests that no such plot existed and that Cortés's attack was unprovoked. Can you determine from the accounts which explanation is the more nearly correct? Read carefully through both Cortés's and the Native American accounts, and you will see that determining what actually happened is not so difficult as it first appears to be. Also, you will see that both Cortés and the Native American chroniclers occasionally describe the same events, which can make for some fascinating comparisons.

The two types of evidence in this chapter (written accounts and artistic representations) must be dealt with differently. As you read the written accounts, think of some adjectives that, after reading these accounts, Europeans who read Cortés's letters, some of which were published and widely distributed, might have used to describe Indians. For the Native American written accounts, imagine what adjectives Native Americans who shared the accounts might have used to describe Europeans. How do those

adjectives present a collective image of Indians? Of Europeans? How do the stories each author tells reinforce that image? As you read each written account, make a list of adjectives for each set of evidence, then combine them to form a collective image. Be willing to read between the lines. Sometimes, for example, Cortés may simply have been trying to explain a specific incident or practice of the Indians. Yet, intentionally or unintentionally, he was creating an image in the minds of readers. Be equally cautious and sensitive when reading the Indians' written accounts.

The second type of evidence, artistic representations, is quite different from the written accounts. If you think of art as words made into pictures, you will see that you can approach this type of evidence as you did the written accounts. Study each picture carefully, looking especially for how Native Americans or Europeans are portrayed. How are they portrayed physically? How is their supposed nature or character portrayed in their behavior in the works of art? Again, as with the written accounts, create a list of adjectives and deduce the images Europeans would have had of Indians and the images Indians would have had of Europeans. As you analyze the evidence in this chapter, keep two central questions in mind: (1) What images do the written and artistic accounts create of Native Americans and of Europeans? (2) How might those images or impressions have influenced how European explorers and early colonists dealt with Native Americans and how Native Americans dealt with them?

✳ THE EVIDENCE ✳

EUROPEAN ACCOUNTS

Source 1 from Francis Augustus MacNutt, *Fernando Cortés: His Five Letters of Relation to the Emperor Charles V* (Cleveland: Arthur H. Clark Co., 1908), Vol. I, pp. 161–166, 211–216.

1. Selections from Cortés's First Letter to King Charles I of Spain, July 10, 1519.

. . . According to our judgment, it is credible that there is everything in this country which existed in that from whence Solomon is said to have brought the gold for the Temple, but, as we have been here so short a time, we have not been able to see more than the distance of five leagues inland, and about ten or twelve leagues of the coast length on each side, which we have explored since we landed; although from the sea it must be more, and we saw much more while sailing.

The people who inhabit this country, from the Island of Cozumel, and the Cape of Yucatan to the place where we now are, are a people of middle size, with bodies and features well proportioned, except that in each province their customs differ, some piercing the ears, and putting large and ugly objects in them, and others piercing the nostrils down to the mouth, and putting in large round stones like mirrors, and others piercing their under lips down as far as their gums, and hanging from them large round stones, or pieces of gold, so weighty that they pull down the nether lip, and make it appear very deformed. The clothing which they wear is like long veils, very curiously worked. The men wear breech-cloths about their bodies, and large mantles, very thin, and painted in the style of Moorish draperies. The women of the ordinary people wear, from their waists to their feet, clothes also very much painted, some covering their breasts and leaving the rest of the body uncovered. The superior women, however, wear very thin shirts of cotton, worked and made in the style of *rochets* [blouses with long, straight sleeves]. Their food is maize and grain, as in the other Islands, and *potuyuca*, as they eat it in the Island of Cuba, and they eat it broiled, since they do not make bread of it; and they have their fishing, and hunting, and they roast many chickens, like those of the Tierra Firma, which are as large as peacocks.[3]

There are some large towns well laid out, the houses being of stone, and mortar when they have it. The apartments are small, low, and in the Moorish style, and, when they cannot find stone, they make them of adobes,

---

3. These were turkeys, which were unknown in Europe.

CHAPTER 1

FIRST
ENCOUNTERS:
THE
CONFRONTATION
BETWEEN
CORTÉS AND
MONTEZUMA
(1519–1521)

whitewashing them, and the roof is of straw. Some of the houses of the principal people are very cool, and have many apartments, for we have seen more than five courts in one house, and the apartments very well distributed, each principal department of service being separate. Within them they have their wells and reservoirs for water, and rooms for the slaves and dependents, of whom they have many. Each of these chiefs has at the entrance of his house, but outside of it, a large court-yard, and in some there are two and three and four very high buildings, with steps leading up to them, and they are very well built; and in them they have their mosques[4] and prayer places, and very broad galleries on all sides, and there they keep the idols which they worship, some being of stone, some of gold, and some of wood, and they honour and serve them in such wise, and with so many ceremonies, that much paper would be required to give Your Royal Highnesses an entire and exact description of all of them. These houses and mosques, wherever they exist, are the largest and best built in the town, and they keep them very well adorned, decorated with feather-work and well-woven stuffs, and with all manner of ornaments. Every day, before they undertake any work, they burn incense in the said mosques, and sometimes they sacrifice their own persons, some cutting their tongues and others their ears, and some hacking the body with knives; and they offer up to their idols all the blood which flows, sprinkling it on all sides of those mosques, at other times throwing it up towards the heavens, and practising many other kinds of ceremonies, so that they undertake nothing without first offering sacrifice there.

They have another custom, horrible, and abominable, and deserving punishment, and which we have never before seen in any other place, and it is this, that, as often as they have anything to ask of their idols, in order that their petition may be more acceptable, they take many boys or girls, and even grown men and women, and in the presence of those idols they open their breasts, while they are alive, and take out the hearts and entrails, and burn the said entrails and hearts before the idols, offering that smoke in sacrifice to them. Some of us who have seen this say that it is the most terrible and frightful thing to behold that has ever been seen. So frequently, and so often do these Indians do this, according to our information, and partly by what we have seen in the short time we are in this country, that no year passes in which they do not kill and sacrifice fifty souls in each mosque; and this is practised, and held as customary, from the Isle of Cozumel to the country in which we are now settled. Your Majesties may rest assured that, according to the size of the land, which to us seems very

4. Temples.

considerable, and the many mosques which they have, there is no year, as far as we have until now discovered and seen, when they do not kill and sacrifice in this manner some three or four thousand souls. Now let Your Royal Highnesses consider if they ought not to prevent so great an evil and crime, and certainly God, Our Lord, will be well pleased, if, through the command of Your Royal Highnesses, these peoples should be initiated and instructed in our Very Holy Catholic Faith, and the devotion, faith, and hope, which they have in their idols, be transferred to the Divine Omnipotence of God; because it is certain, that, if they served God with the same faith, and fervour, and diligence, they would surely work miracles.

It should be believed, that it is not without cause that God, Our Lord, has permitted that these parts should be discovered in the name of Your Royal Highnesses, so that this fruit and merit before God should be enjoyed by Your Majesties, of having instructed these barbarian people, and brought them through your commands to the True Faith. As far as we are able to know them, we believe that, if there were interpreters and persons who could make them understand the truth of the Faith, and their error, many, and perhaps all, would shortly quit the errors which they hold, and come to the true knowledge; because they live civilly and reasonably, better than any of the other peoples found in these parts.

To endeavour to give to Your Majesties all the particulars about this country and its people, might occasion some errors in the account, because much of it we have not seen, and only know it through information given us by the natives; therefore we do not undertake to give more than what may be accepted by Your Highnesses as true. Your Majesties may, if you deem proper, give this account as true to Our Very Holy Father, in order that diligence and good system may be used in effecting the conversion of these people, because it is hoped that great fruit and much good may be obtained; also that His Holiness may approve and allow that the wicked and rebellious, being first admonished, may be punished and chastised as enemies of Our Holy Catholic Faith, which will be an occasion of punishment and fear to those who may be reluctant in receiving knowledge of the Truth; thereby, that the great evils and injuries they practise in the service of the Devil, will be forsaken. Because, besides what we have just related to Your Majesties about the men, and women, and children, whom they kill and offer in their sacrifices, we have learned, and been positively informed, that they are all sodomites,[5] and given to that abominable sin. In all this, we beseech Your Majesties to order such measures taken as are most

---

5. People who practice anal or oral copulation with members of the opposite (or same) gender or who have sex with animals.

CHAPTER 1

FIRST
ENCOUNTERS:
THE
CONFRONTATION
BETWEEN
CORTÉS AND
MONTEZUMA
(1519–1521)

profitable to the service of God, and to that of Your Royal Highnesses, and so that we who are here in your service may also be favoured and recompensed. . . .

. . . Along the road we encountered many signs, such as the natives of this province had foretold us, for we found the high road blocked up, and another opened, and some pits, although not many, and some of the city streets were closed, and many stones were piled on the house tops. They thus obliged us to be cautious, and on our guard.

I found there certain messengers from Montezuma, who came to speak with those others who were with me, but to me they said nothing, because, in order to inform their master, they had come to learn what those who were with me had done and agreed with me. These latter messengers departed, therefore, as soon as they had spoken with the first, and even the chief of those who had formerly been with me also left.

During the three days which I remained there I was ill provided for, and every day was worse, and the lords and chiefs of the city came rarely to see and speak to me. I was somewhat perplexed by this, but the interpreter whom I have, an Indian woman of this country whom I obtained in Putunchan, the great river I have already mentioned in the first letter to Your Majesty, was told by another woman native of this city, that many of Montezuma's people had gathered close by, and that those of the city had sent away their wives, and children, and all their goods, intending to fall upon us and kill us all; and that, if she wished to escape, she should go with her, as she would hide her. The female interpreter told it to that Geronimo de Aguilar, the interpreter whom I obtained in Yucatan, and of whom I have written to Your Highness, who reported it to me. I captured one of the natives of the said city, who was walking about there, and took him secretly apart so that no one saw it, and questioned him; and he confirmed all that the Indian woman and the natives of Tascaltecal had told me. As well on account of this information as from the signs I had observed, I determined to anticipate them, rather than be surprised, so I had some of the lords of the city called, saying that I wished to speak with them, and I shut them in a chamber by themselves. In the meantime I had our people prepared, so that, at the firing of a musket, they should fall on a crowd of Indians who were near to our quarters, and many others who were inside them. It was done in this wise, that, after I had taken these lords, and left them bound in the chamber, I mounted a horse, and ordered the musket to be fired, and we did such execution that, in two hours, more than three thousand persons had perished.

In order that Your Majesty may see how well prepared they were, before I went out of our quarters, they had occupied all the streets, and stationed all their men, but, as we took them by surprise, they were easily overcome, especially as the chiefs were wanting, for I had already taken them prisoners. I ordered fire to be set to some towers and strong houses, where they defended themselves, and assaulted us; and thus I scoured the city fighting during five hours, leaving our dwelling place which was very strong, well guarded, until I had forced all the people out of the city at various points, in which those five thousand natives of Tascaltecal and the four hundred of Cempoal gave me good assistance. . . .

CHAPTER 1

FIRST
ENCOUNTERS:
THE
CONFRONTATION
BETWEEN
CORTÉS AND
MONTEZUMA
(1519–1521)

Sources 2 through 5 from Hugh Honor, *The European Vision of America* (Cleveland: Cleveland Museum of Art, 1975), plates 3, 8, 64, 65. Source 2 photo: The British Library.

2. German Woodcut, 1509.

Source 3: Museo National de Arte Antiga, Lisbon.

3. Portuguese Oil on Panel, 1550.

Source 4: Library of Congress/Rare Book Division.

4. German Engraving, 1590.

CHAPTER 1

FIRST
ENCOUNTERS:
THE
CONFRONTATION
BETWEEN
CORTÉS AND
MONTEZUMA
(1519–1521)

Source 5: Library of Congress/Rare Book Division.

5. German Engraving, 1591.

Sources 6 and 7 from Stefan Lorant, ed., *The New World: The First Pictures of America* (New York: Duell, Sloan & Pearce, 1946), pp. 51, 119. Photos: Metropolitan Museum of Art.

6. German Engraving, 1591.

7. German Engraving, 1591.

Sources 8 and 9 from Honor, *The European Vision of America,* plates 85, 91.
Photos: New York Historical Society.

8. French Engraving, 1575.

CHAPTER 1

FIRST
ENCOUNTERS:
THE
CONFRONTATION
BETWEEN
CORTÉS AND
MONTEZUMA
(1519–1521)

9. French Engraving, 1579–1600.

NATIVE AMERICAN ACCOUNTS

Source 10 from Miguel Leon-Portilla, ed., *The Broken Spears: The Aztec Account of the Conquest of Mexico,* trans. Lysander Kemp (Boston: Beacon Press, 1962), pp. viii–ix, 30, 92–93, 128–144.

10. Cortés's Conquest of Tenochtitlán.

Year 1-Canestalk. The Spaniards came to the palace at Tlayacac. When the Captain[6] arrived at the palace, Motecuhzoma[7] sent the Cuetlaxteca[8] to greet him and to bring him two suns as gifts. One of these suns was made of the yellow metal, the other of the white.[9] The Cuetlaxteca also brought him a mirror to be hung on his person, a gold collar, a great gold pitcher, fans and ornaments of quetzal feathers[10] and a shield inlaid with mother-of-pearl.

The envoys made sacrifices in front of the Captain. At this, he grew very angry. When they offered him blood in an "eagle dish," he shouted at the man who offered it and struck him with his sword. The envoys departed at once. . . .

When the sacrifice was finished, the messengers reported to the king. They told him how they had made the journey, and what they had seen, and what food the strangers ate. Motecuhzoma was astonished and terrified by their report, and the description of the strangers' food astonished him above all else.

He was also terrified to learn how the cannon roared, how its noise resounded, how it caused one to faint and grow deaf. The messengers told him: "A thing like a ball of stone comes out of its entrails: it comes out shooting sparks and raining fire. The smoke that comes out with it has a pestilent odor, like that of rotten mud. This odor penetrates even to the brain and causes the greatest discomfort. If the cannon is aimed against a mountain, the mountain splits and cracks open. If it is aimed against a tree, it shatters the tree into splinters. This is a most unnatural sight, as if the tree had exploded from within."

The messengers also said: "Their trappings and arms are all made of iron. They dress in iron and wear iron casques[11] on their heads. Their swords are iron; their bows are iron; their shields are iron; their spears are iron.

6. Cortés.
7. Montezuma.
8. The Cuetlaxteca were an Indian people allied with the Aztecs.
9. Gold and silver.
10. Quetzal: A type of bird native to Central America; the male has tail feathers up to 2 feet in length.
11. Helmets.

CHAPTER 1

FIRST
ENCOUNTERS:
THE
CONFRONTATION
BETWEEN
CORTÉS AND
MONTEZUMA
(1519–1521)

Their deer[12] carry them on their backs wherever they wish to go. These deer, our lord, are as tall as the roof of a house.

"The strangers' bodies are completely covered, so that only their faces can be seen. Their skin is white, as if it were made of lime. They have yellow hair, though some of them have black. Their beards are long and yellow, and their moustaches are also yellow. Their hair is curly, with very fine strands.

"As for their food, it is like human food. It is large and white, and not heavy.[13] It is something like straw, but with the taste of a cornstalk, of the pith of a cornstalk. It is a little sweet, as if it were flavored with honey; it tastes of honey, it is sweet-tasting food.

"Their dogs are enormous, with flat ears and long, dangling tongues. The color of their eyes is a burning yellow; their eyes flash fire and shoot off sparks. Their bellies are hollow, their flanks long and narrow. They are tireless and very powerful. They bound here and there, panting, with their tongues hanging out. And they are spotted like an ocelot."

When Motecuhzoma heard this report, he was filled with terror. It was as if his heart had fainted, as if it had shriveled. It was as if he were conquered by despair. . . .

Then the Captain marched to Tenochtitlán. He arrived here during the month called Bird, under the sign of the day 8-Wind. When he entered the city, we gave him chickens, eggs, corn, tortillas and drink. We also gave him firewood, and fodder for his deer. Some of these gifts were sent by the lord of Tenochtitlán, the rest by the lord of Tlatelolco.

Later the Captain marched back to the coast, leaving Don Pedro de Alvarado—The Sun—in command.

During this time, the people asked Motecuhzoma how they should celebrate their god's fiesta. He said: "Dress him in all his finery, in all his sacred ornaments."

During this same time, The Sun commanded that Motecuhzoma and Itzcohuatzin, the military chief of Tlatelolco, be made prisoners. The Spaniards hanged a chief from Acolhuacan named Nezahualquentzin. They also murdered the king of Nauhtla, Cohualpopocatzin, by wounding him with arrows and then burning him alive.

For this reason, our warriors were on guard at the Eagle Gate. The sentries from Tenochtitlán stood at one side of the gate, and the sentries from Tlatelolco at the other. But messengers came to tell them to dress the

12. Horses.
13. Probably pasta.

figure of Huitzilopochtli.[14] They left their posts and went to dress him in his sacred finery: his ornaments and his paper clothing.

When this had been done, the celebrants began to sing their songs. That is how they celebrated the first day of the fiesta. On the second day they began to sing again, but without warning they were all put to death. . . . They ran in among the dancers, forcing their way to the place where the drums were played. They attacked the man who was drumming and cut off his arms. Then they cut off his head, and it rolled across the floor.

They attacked the celebrants, stabbing them, spearing them, striking them with their swords. They attacked some of them from behind, and these fell instantly to the ground with their entrails hanging out. Others they beheaded: they cut off their heads, or split their heads to pieces.

They struck others in the shoulders, and their arms were torn from their bodies. They wounded some in the thigh and some in the calf. They slashed others in the abdomen, and their entrails all spilled to the ground. Some attempted to run away, but their intestines dragged as they ran; they seemed to tangle their feet in their own entrails. No matter how they tried to save themselves, they could find no escape. . . .

The Sun treacherously murdered our people on the twentieth day after the Captain left for the coast. We allowed the Captain to return to the city in peace. But on the following day we attacked him with all our might, and that was the beginning of the war.

The Spaniards attempted to slip out of the city at night, but we attacked furiously at the Canal of the Toltecs, and many of them died. This took place during the fiesta of Tecuilhuitl. The survivors gathered first at Mazatzintamalco and waited for the stragglers to come up.

Year 2-Flint. This was the year in which Motecuhzoma died. Itzcohuatzin of Tlatelolco died at the same time.

The Spaniards took refuge in Acueco, but they were driven out by our warriors. They fled to Teuhcalhueyacan and from there to Zoltepec. Then they marched through Citlaltepec and camped in Temazcalapan, where the people gave them hens, eggs and corn. They rested for a short while and marched on to Tlaxcala.

Soon after, an epidemic broke out in Tenochtitlán. . . . It began to spread during the thirteenth month and lasted for seventy days, striking everywhere in the city and killing a vast number of our people. Sores erupted on our faces, our breasts, our bellies; we were covered with agonizing sores from head to foot.

14. The mythical founder of the Aztec people and their supreme god.

CHAPTER 1

FIRST
ENCOUNTERS:
THE
CONFRONTATION
BETWEEN
CORTÉS AND
MONTEZUMA
(1519–1521)

The illness was so dreadful that no one could walk or move. The sick were so utterly helpless that they could only lie on their beds like corpses, unable to move their limbs or even their heads. They could not lie face down or roll from one side to the other. If they did move their bodies, they screamed with pain.

A great many died from this plague, and many others died of hunger. They could not get up to search for food, and everyone else was too sick to care for them, so they starved to death in their beds.[15]

Some people came down with a milder form of the disease; they suffered less than the others and made a good recovery. But they could not escape entirely. Their looks were ravaged, for wherever a sore broke out, it gouged an ugly pockmark in the skin. And a few of the survivors were left completely blind. . . .

[*Here the account describes Cortés's siege of Tenochtitlán, a siege that was successful due in part to bickering among the Aztecs themselves (in which several leaders were put to death), in part to the panic caused by Cortés's cannon and in part to a number of nearby Indian peoples whom the Aztecs had dominated, turning on their former masters and supporting the Spanish. Of course, the devastating smallpox epidemic and general starvation due to the siege also played important roles.*]

Broken spears lie in the roads;
we have torn our hair in our grief.
The houses are roofless now, and their walls
are red with blood.

Worms are swarming in the streets and plazas,
and the walls are splattered with gore.
The water has turned red, as if it were dyed,
and when we drink it,
it has the taste of brine.

We have pounded our hands in despair
against the adobe walls,
for our inheritance, our city, is lost and dead.
The shields of our warriors were its defense,
but they could not save it.

We have chewed dry twigs and salt grasses;
we have filled our mouths with dust and bits of adobe;
we have eaten lizards, rats and worms. . . .

---

15. The epidemic probably was smallpox.

Cuauhtemoc was taken to Cortes along with three other princes. The Captain was accompanied by Pedro de Alvarado and La Malinche.

When the princes were made captives, the people began to leave, searching for a place to stay. Everyone was in tatters, and the women's thighs were almost naked. The Christians searched all the refugees. They even opened the women's skirts and blouses and felt everywhere: their ears, their breasts, their hair. Our people scattered in all directions. They went to neighboring villages and huddled in corners in the houses of strangers.

The city was conquered in the year 3-House. The date on which we departed was the day 1-Serpent in the ninth month. . . .

[*The account next describes Cortés's torture of the remaining Aztec leaders in an attempt to find where the Aztecs' treasures were hidden.*]

When the envoys from Tlatelolco had departed, the leaders of Tenochtitlán were brought before the Captain, who wished to make them talk. This was when Cuauhtemoc's feet were burned. They brought him in at daybreak and tied him to a stake.

They found the gold in Cuitlahuactonco, in the house of a chief named Itzpotonqui. As soon as they had seized it, they brought our princes—all of them bound—to Coyoacan.

About this same time, the priest in charge of the temple of Huitzilopochtli was put to death. The Spaniards had tried to learn from him where the god's finery and that of the high priests was kept. Later they were informed that it was being guarded by certain chiefs in Cuauhchichilco and Xaltocan. They seized it and then hanged two of the chiefs in the middle of the Mazatlan road. . . .

They hanged Macuilxochitl, the king of Huitzilopochco, in Coyoacan. They also hanged Pizotzin, the king of Culhuacan. And they fed the Keeper of the Black House, along with several others, to their dogs.

And three wise men of Ehecatl, from Tezcoco, were devoured by the dogs. They had come only to surrender; no one brought them or sent them there. They arrived bearing their painted sheets of paper. There were four of them, and only one escaped; the other three were overtaken, there in Coyoacan. . . .

CHAPTER 1

FIRST
ENCOUNTERS:
THE
CONFRONTATION
BETWEEN
CORTÉS AND
MONTEZUMA
(1519–1521)

Sources 11 through 14 are present-day adaptations of Aztec artistic works that were created not long after the events they depict took place. The modern adaptations can be found in Leon-Portilla, *The Broken Spears,* pp. 21, 82, 75, 143. Illustrations by Alberto Beltran.

11. Native Americans Greet Cortés and His Men.

12. Spanish Response to Native American Greeting.

13. The Massacre at the Fiesta.

CHAPTER 1

FIRST
ENCOUNTERS:
THE
CONFRONTATION
BETWEEN
CORTÉS AND
MONTEZUMA
(1519–1521)

14. Fate of the Wise Men of Ehecatl.

❉ QUESTIONS TO CONSIDER ❉

As you read Cortés's account (Source 1), it helps to look for five factors:

1. Physical appearance (bodies, hair, clothing, jewelry, and so on). This description can provide important clues about Cortés's attitude toward the Indians he confronted.
2. Nature or character (childlike, bellicose, cunning, honest, intellectual, lazy, and so on). Be sure to note the examples Cortés used to provide his analysis of the Indians' nature or character.
3. Political, social, and religious practices (behavior of women, ceremonies, eating habits, government, and so on). Descriptions of these practices can provide excellent insight into the explorer's general perception of the Indians he encountered. Be especially sensitive to Cortés's use of descriptive adjectives.
4. Overall impression of the Indians. What was Cortés's collective image or impression?
5. What did Cortés think should be done with the Indians?

Once you have analyzed Cortés's account using points 1 through 4, you should be able to explain how, based on his overall impression of the Indians, he thought the Indians should be dealt with (point 5). Sometimes Cortés comes right out and tells you, but in other cases you will have to use a little imagination. Ask yourself the following question: If I had been living in Spain in 1522 and read Cortés's account, what would my perception of Native Americans have been? Based on that perception, how would I have thought those peoples should be dealt with?

You can handle the artistic representations (Sources 2 through 9) in the same way. Each artist tried to convey his notion of the Indians' nature or character. Some of these impressions are obvious, but others are less so. Think of the art as words made into pictures. How are the Indians portrayed? What are they doing? How are they dealing with Europeans? On the basis of these artistic representations, decide how the various artists believed Indians should be dealt with. For example, the Indian woman with child in Source 4 depicts Native Americans in a particular way. What is it? On the basis of this depiction, what would you say was the artist's perception of Indians? Moreover, how would that perception have affected the artist's—and viewer's—opinion of how Indians should be treated? Follow these steps for all the artistic representations (Sources 2 through 9).

Finally, put together the two types of evidence. Is there more than one "image" of Native Americans? How might each perception have affected the ways Europeans and early colonists dealt with Indians?

On the surface, the Native Americans' perception of Europeans was one-dimensional and is easily discovered: the Aztec writers and artists portrayed Cortés and his men as brutal and sadistic murderers who were driven mad by their lust for gold.

CHAPTER 1

FIRST
ENCOUNTERS:
THE
CONFRONTATION
BETWEEN
CORTÉS AND
MONTEZUMA
(1519–1521)

Closer examination of the early section of the written account (Source 10) and of one of the artistic representations (Source 11), however, reveals other perceptions as well. In the written account, when Montezuma's envoys reported back to him, how did they describe the Europeans (you may use points 1 through 4 above)? What was Montezuma's reaction to the report? The other artistic accounts (Sources 12–14) are quite direct, and you should have no difficulty discovering the Indians' overall perception of Europeans. You will, however, have to infer from the accounts how Indians believed Europeans should be dealt with in the future, since none of the written or artistic accounts deals with that question.

�֎ EPILOGUE ✖

In many respects, the encounter between Cortés and the native peoples of Mexico was typical of many first encounters between Europeans and Native Americans. For one thing, the Indian peoples were terribly vulnerable to the numerous diseases that Europeans unwittingly brought with them. Whether warlike or peaceful, millions of Native Americans fell victim to smallpox, measles, and other diseases against which they had no resistance. Whole villages were wiped out and whole nations decimated as (in the words of one Roman Catholic priest who traveled with Cortés) "they died in heaps."

In addition, although the Indians had brave warriors who fought fiercely in hand-to-hand combat, their swords and other weapons were no match for European muskets and cannons. Battles between Indian peoples were often fought to gain captives, most of whom were later sacrificed to the gods. The Spanish, sometimes greatly outnumbered, tried to kill their enemies in battle rather than take captives. By no means passive peoples in what ultimately would become a contest for a hemisphere, Indians nevertheless had not developed the military technology and tactics to hold Europeans permanently at bay.

Nor were the Indians themselves united against their European intruders. All the explorers and early settlers were able to pit one Indian people against another, thus dividing the opposition and in the end conquering them all. In this practice Cortés was particularly adept; he found a number of villages ready to revolt against Montezuma and used those schisms to his advantage. Brief attempts at Indian unity against European intruders generally proved temporary and therefore unsuccessful.

Sometimes the Native Americans' initial misperceptions of Europeans worked to their own disadvantage. As we have seen, some Central American Indians, including the mighty Aztecs, thought Cortés's men were the "white gods" from the east whom prophets predicted would appear. Cortés's actions quickly disabused them of this notion, but by then much damage had been done. In a somewhat similar vein, Indians of the Powhatan Confederacy in Virginia at first thought the Europeans were indolent because they could not grow their own food. Like the Aztecs' misperception, this mistaken image was soon shattered. In sum, Native Americans' perceptions of Europeans often worked against any notions that they were a threat— until it was too late.

Finally, once Europeans had established footholds in the New World, the Indians often undercut their own positions. For one thing, they rarely were able to unite against the Europeans, fractured as they so often were by intertribal conflicts and jealousies. Therefore, Europeans often were able to enlist Indian allies to fight against those Native Americans who opposed them. Also, after the Indians in North America came to recognize the value of European manufactured goods, they increasingly engaged in wholesale hunting and trapping of animals with the skins and furs Europeans wanted in exchange for those goods. Before the arrival of Europeans, Native Americans saw themselves as part of a complete ecosystem that could sustain all life so long as it was kept in balance. In contrast, Europeans saw the environment as a series of commodities to be exploited, a perception that Indians who desired European goods were quickly forced to adopt. Thus not only did the Indians lose their economic and cultural independence, but they also nearly eliminated certain animal species that had sustained them for so long. An ecological disaster was in the making, driven by the European view of the environment as something to conquer and exploit.

For a number of reasons, Native Americans were extremely vulnerable to the European "invasion" of America. At the same time, however, a major biological "event" was in process that would change life in both the Old World and the New. Called by historians the Columbian exchange, the process involved the transplantation to the New World (sometimes accidentally) of various plants (cabbages, radishes, bananas, wheat, onions, sugar cane), animals (horses, pigs, cattle, sheep, cats), and diseases. At the same time, Europeans returned home with maize, peanuts, squash, sweet potatoes, pumpkins, pineapples, tomatoes, and cocoa. Less beneficial was the possible transportation from the New World to the Old of venereal syphilis. Indeed, some five hundred years later, the Columbian exchange is still going on. In the Great Smoky Mountains of North Carolina and Tennessee, wild boars, imported from Germany in the nineteenth century for sportsmen, threaten the plants, grasses, and small animals of the region. The zebra mussel, released by accident into the Great Lakes in ballast water from Eastern Europe, has spread into the Illinois, Mississippi, Ohio, and Tennessee rivers. An Asian variety of the gypsy moth is chewing its way through the forests of the Pacific Northwest. A recent survey in Olympic National Park has identified 169 species of plants and animals not indigenous to the Western Hemisphere. In the South, the kudzu vine, imported from Japan

CHAPTER 1

FIRST
ENCOUNTERS:
THE
CONFRONTATION
BETWEEN
CORTÉS AND
MONTEZUMA
(1519–1521)

to combat erosion, was dubbed by the *Los Angeles Times* (July 21, 1992) "the national plant of Dixie." Whether purposeful or by accident, whether beneficial or detrimental, the Columbian exchange continues.

Because Europeans ultimately were victorious in their "invasion" of the Western Hemisphere, it is their images of Native Americans that for the most part have survived. Christopher Columbus, who recorded the Europeans' first encounter, depicted Native Americans as innocent, naive children. But he also wrote, "I could conquer the whole of them with fifty men, and govern them as I pleased." For his part, Amerigo Vespucci was less kind, depicting Native Americans as barbarous because "they have no regular time for their meals . . . [and] in making water they are dirty and without shame, for while talking with us they do such things." By placing this badge of inferiority on Indian peoples, most Europeans could justify a number of ways Indians could be dealt with (avoidance, conquest, "civilizing," trading, removal, extermination). Ultimately for the Indian peoples, all methods proved disastrous. Although

different European peoples (Spanish, French, English) often treated Indians differently, in the end the results were the same.

Hernando Cortés returned to Spain in 1528 a fabulously wealthy man. But the ultimate *conquistador* lost most of his fortune in ill-fated expeditions and died in modest circumstances in 1547. In his will, he recognized the four children he had fathered by Native American women while in Mexico (Cortés was married at the time) and worried about the morality of what he had done. In 1562, his body was taken to Mexico to be reburied, but for Hernando Cortés's remains, there would be no rest. In 1794, they were moved again, this time to the chapel of a Mexican hospital that he had endowed. In 1823, Cortés's remains disappeared for good, perhaps as the result of an effort to protect them from politically oriented grave robbers after Mexico declared its independence from Spain. Rumors abound that they were secretly carried back across the Atlantic, this time to Italy. The ultimate *conquistador* has vanished, but his legacy lives on.

2

The Threat of
Anne Hutchinson

✳ THE PROBLEM ✳

In the cold, early spring of 1638, Anne Hutchinson and her children left Massachusetts to join her husband and their many friends who had moved to an island in Narragansett Bay near what is now Rhode Island. Just a year before, in 1637, Hutchinson and her family had been highly respected, prominent members of a Puritan church in Boston. But then she was put on trial and sentenced to banishment from the Massachusetts Bay colony and excommunication from her church—next to death, the worst punishment that could befall a Puritan in the New World.

What had Anne Hutchinson done? Why was she such a threat to the Massachusetts Bay colony? You will be reading the transcript of her trial in 1637 to find the answers to these questions.

✳ BACKGROUND ✳

The English men and women who came to the New World in the seventeenth and early eighteenth centuries did so for a variety of reasons. Many who arrived at Jamestown colony were motivated by the promise of wealth; at one point, Virginians grew tobacco in the streets and even threatened their own existence by favoring tobacco (a crop they could sell) over food crops. In contrast, the majority of the early settlers of Pennsylvania were Friends (Quakers) in search of religious freedom. In short, the American colonies represented for thousands of English men and women a chance to make significant changes in their lives.

Such was the case with the Puritans who settled and dominated the colony of Massachusetts Bay, founded in 1630. Although technically still members of the Church of England, the Puritans were convinced that many of that church's beliefs and practices were wrong and that the Church of England needed to be thoroughly purified (hence their name). Puritans were convinced that the Church of England, which had broken away from the Roman Catholic Church and the pope during the reign of Henry VIII, was still encumbered with unnecessary ceremony, rituals, and hierarchy—things they called "popery." Popery, the Puritans believed, actually obstructed the ties between God and human beings, and therefore should be eliminated.

Believing it impossible to effect their reforms in England, many Puritans sought "voluntary banishment," as one of them called it, to the New World. Fired by the sense that God was using them to revolutionize human history, more than one thousand men, women, and children arrived during the first decades of the founding of New England to form their model community based on the laws of God and his commandments. "We shall be as a city upon a hill," exulted Puritan leader and colonial governor John Winthrop, "the eyes of all people are upon us."

There were at least five central characteristics of American Puritanism. First, the idea that Massachusetts Bay should be a "city upon a hill" implied that the New World experiment was a kind of holy mission. Its success could be a very important stimulus to religious reformers back home in England. Failure of the mission, however, would be a disaster. The Massachusetts settlers thus carried with them a double responsibility: to create a successful, orderly, godly community in the New World and to serve as a perfect, shining example to the rest of the Protestant world, especially to England.

Belief in a "covenant of grace" was a second important aspect of the New England Way. American Puritans did not believe that human salvation could be earned by individual effort, such as going to church, leading a good life, or helping one's neighbors. The Puritans called the idea that one could *earn* salvation a "covenant of works," a notion they believed was absolutely wrong. They insisted that salvation came only as a free gift from God (a "covenant of grace"), and those few who received it were the true "saints," full members of the church.

Yet there was a paradox at the heart of this distinction between the covenant of grace and the covenant of works. Puritans believed that God expected everyone to lead a good life and behave themselves. Those who were not yet saved would be preparing for the possibility of God's grace, while those who were already saints would naturally live according to God's laws. Some ministers, like John Cotton, deemphasized the idea of preparation, maintaining that God's grace could be granted instantaneously to anyone. Other ministers put more emphasis on preparing to receive God's grace.

The third significant characteristic of Puritanism was the belief that the community, as well as the individual, entered into a contract, or covenant, with God. Seeing themselves as the modern version of the ancient Israelites, Puritans believed that God had made a specific contract with the Puritans of New England. As Winthrop explained, "Thus stands the cause between God and us: we are entered into covenant with Him. . . . The God of Israel is among us." To Puritans, the covenant meant that the entire community must follow God's laws as interpreted by Puritan leaders. If they did, God would reward them; if not, the community would be punished. Therefore, community solidarity was essential, and individual desires and thoughts had to be subjugated to those of the community.

Thus, although Puritans sought religious freedom for themselves, they were not really willing to grant it to others. Dissent and discord, they reasoned, would lead to the breakdown of community cohesion, the inevitable violation of the covenant, and the punishment of the community in the same way God had punished the ancient Israelites when they had broken their covenant. Non-Puritans who migrated to the Massachusetts Bay colony were required to attend the Puritan church, although they could not become members and hence could not vote in either church or civil elections. Those who refused to abide by these rules were banished from the colony. Moreover, those Puritans who were not saints also had to obey these regulations and

similarly could not be church members or vote.

Thus, there was a hierarchy of authority in Massachusetts that controlled both the colony's church and the government. Within this hierarchy, the ministers played a very important role. Expected to be highly educated and articulate, the ministers of each Puritan church were to be the teachers and leaders of their respective congregations. Of course, the civil officials of Massachusetts Bay, such as the governor and his council, were good Puritans and full members of their churches. Their job was to ensure that the laws and practices of civil government were in accord with the requirements of living in a godly community. Civil authorities, then, were expected to support the religious authorities, and vice versa.

Finally, New England Puritans placed more emphasis than English Puritans on the importance of having a conversion experience—an experience when you knew that you had been "saved." Young people and adults prayed, tried to live according to biblical precepts, and often kept diaries in which they reflected on their shortcomings and "sinfulness." Only a conversion experience would admit a person into full church membership. To become a saint, one had to be examined by a church committee and demonstrate that he or she had experienced the presence of God and the Holy Spirit. There was no agreement among the ministers about the exact nature of this revelation, although people sometimes reported a physical sensation. For most, it simply meant that individuals would recognize the Holy Spirit moving within themselves. Some ministers urged their congregations not to fear, and even to seek out, more direct contact with God. This was far more controversial, as you will see in Anne Hutchinson's trial.

In fact, there was a good deal of dissension in Massachusetts Bay colony. Religious squabbles were common, often arising between saints over biblical interpretation, the theological correctness of one minister or another, or the behavior of certain fellow colonists. Indeed, to a limited extent, Puritans actually welcomed these disputes because they seemed to demonstrate that religion was still a vital part of the colonists' lives. As John Winthrop said, "The business of religion is the business of the Puritans." Participants of weeknight gatherings at various church members' homes often engaged in these religious debates, tolerated by both the ministers and the colony's civil leaders as long as the squabbles did not get out of control.

By the mid-1630s, however, one of the disputes had grown to such an extent that it threatened the religious and secular unity of the colony. Some Puritans in both England and Massachusetts Bay had begun to espouse an extreme version of the covenant of grace: they believed that, having been assured of salvation, an individual was virtually freed from the man-made laws of both church and state, taking commands only from God, who communicated his wishes to the saints. Called Antinomians (from *anti*, "against," and *nomos*, "law"), these Puritan extremists attacked what one of them called the "deadness" of religious services and charged that several

ministers were preaching the covenant of works. This charge was extremely offensive to these ministers, who did not at all believe they were teaching salvation through good behavior but rather preparation for the possibility of God's grace. Carried to its logical extension, of course, Antinomianism threatened to overthrow the authority of the ministers and even the power of the colonial government itself. Growing in number and intensity, the Antinomians in 1636 were able to elect one of their followers to replace Winthrop as colonial governor, although Winthrop managed to return to office the next year.

Into this highly charged atmosphere stepped Anne Hutchinson, age forty-three, who arrived in Massachusetts Bay in 1634 and soon became embroiled in the Antinomian controversy, or, as other Puritans called it, the "Antinomian heresy." The daughter of a clergyman who had been imprisoned twice for his religious unorthodoxy, Anne had married prosperous businessman William Hutchinson in 1612, when she was twenty-one years old. Before arriving in Massachusetts Bay, she had given birth to fourteen children, eleven of whom were alive in 1634.

In a society that emphasized the greater good of the community rather than the concept of individual happiness, relationships between men and women were complementary and complex. New England "goodwives," as married women were called, performed a variety of tasks essential to their families and communities. Spiritually, they were equal to their husbands in the eyes of God, but economically and politically, wives were expected to help with and supplement their husbands' public activities. In other words, both men and women had rights and responsibilities with respect to each other, their children, their neighbors, their communities, and their church. In carrying out these responsibilities, male and female roles sometimes overlapped, but more often they were divided into public (male) and private (female) spheres.

As in any other society, there were some unhappy marriages, cases of domestic violence and desertion, and even what we would call divorce. But the shared ideals and sense of mission of so many of the immigrants ensured that such dysfunctional relationships were relatively uncommon. Although building a new society in a wilderness was a difficult and dangerous undertaking, most women fulfilled their roles willingly and competently.

Anne Hutchinson's many duties at home did not prevent her from remaining very active in the church. Extremely interested in religion and theological questions, she was particularly influenced by John Cotton, a Puritan minister who had been forced to flee from England to Massachusetts Bay in 1633 because of his religious ideas. Upon arrival in the colony, Cotton said he was shocked by the extent to which colonists had been "lulled into security" by their growing belief that they could earn salvation through good works. Attacking this in sermons and in letters to other clergymen, Cotton helped fuel the Antinomian cause as well as Anne Hutchinson's religious ardor.

At first the Hutchinsons were seen as welcome additions to the community, largely because of William's prosperity and Anne's expertise in herbal medicines, nursing the sick, and midwifery. Soon, however, Anne Hutchinson began to drift into religious issues. She began to hold weeknight meetings in her home, at first to expand upon the previous Sunday's sermons and later to expound her own religious notions—ideas very close to those of the Antinomians. In November 1637, Anne's brother-in-law (John Wheelwright, another Puritan minister) was banished from the colony because of his radical sermons, and Anne was brought to trial before the General Court of Massachusetts Bay. With Governor Winthrop presiding, the court met to decide the fate of Anne Hutchinson. Privately, Winthrop called Hutchinson a person of "nimble wit and active spirit and a very voluble [fluent] tongue." Winthrop himself, however, believed that women should be submissive and supportive, like his wife and sister, and there was ample support for his position in the Bible.[1] No matter what he thought of Hutchinson's abilities, publicly the governor was determined to be rid of her.

Why were Winthrop and other orthodox Puritans so opposed to Hutchinson? What crime had she committed? Some of Wheelwright's followers had been punished for having signed a petition supporting him, but Hutchinson had not signed the petition. Many other Puritans had held religious discussions in their homes, and more than a few had opposed the views of their ministers. Technically,

---

1. Genesis 1:28–3:24; the First Letter of Paul to the Corinthians 11:1–16; the Letter of Paul to the Ephesians, Chapters 5 and 6, all verses.

Hutchinson had broken no law. Why, then, was she considered such a threat that she was brought to trial and ultimately banished from the colony?

THE METHOD

For two days, Anne Hutchinson stood before the General Court, presided over by the unsympathetic Governor John Winthrop. Fortunately, a fairly complete transcript of the proceedings has been preserved. In that transcript are the clues that you as the historian-detective will need to answer the questions previously posed. Although spelling and punctuation have been modernized in most cases, the portions of the transcript you are about to read are reproduced verbatim. At first, some of the seventeenth-century phraseology might seem a bit strange. As are most spoken languages, English is constantly changing (think of how much English has changed since Chaucer's day). Yet if you read slowly and carefully, the transcript should give you no problem.

Before you begin studying the transcript, keep in mind two additional instructions:

1. Be careful not to lose sight of the central question: Why was Anne Hutchinson such a threat to Massachusetts Bay colony? The transcript raises several other questions, some of them so interesting that they might pull you off the main track. As you read through the transcript, make a list of the various ways you think Hutchinson might have threatened Massachusetts Bay.
2. Be willing to read between the lines. As you read each statement, ask yourself what is being said. Then try to deduce what is actually meant by what is being said in the context of the early 1600s. Sometimes people say exactly what they mean, but often they do not. They might intentionally or unintentionally disguise the real meaning of what they are saying, but the real meaning can usually be found. In conversation with a person face to face, voice inflection, body language, and other visual clues often provide the real meaning to what is being said. In this case, where personal observation is impossible, you must use both logic and imagination to read between the lines.

THE EVIDENCE

Source 1 from an excerpt of the examination from Thomas Hutchinson (Anne's great-grandson), *The History of the Colony and Province of Massachusetts-Bay,* ed. Lawrence Shaw Mayo (Cambridge, Mass.: Harvard University Press, 1936), Vol. II, pp. 366–391.

1. The Examination of Mrs. Anne Hutchinson at the Court of Newton, November 1637.[2]

CHARACTERS

Mrs. Anne Hutchinson, the accused

General Court, consisting of the governor, deputy governor, assistants, and deputies

Governor, John Winthrop, chair of the court

Deputy Governor, Thomas Dudley

Assistants, Mr. Bradstreet, Mr. Nowel, Mr. Endicott, Mr. Harlakenden, Mr. Stoughton

Deputies, Mr. Coggeshall, Mr. Bartholomew, Mr. Jennison, Mr. Coddington, Mr. Colborn

Clergymen and Ruling Elders:

Mr. Peters, minister in Salem

Mr. Leveret, a ruling elder in a Boston church

Mr. Cotton, minister in Boston

Mr. Wilson, minister in Boston, who supposedly made notes of a previous meeting between Anne Hutchinson, Cotton, and the other ministers

Mr. Sims, minister in Charlestown

MR. WINTHROP, GOVERNOR. Mrs. Hutchinson, you are called here as one of those that have troubled the peace of the commonwealth and the churches here; you are known to be a woman that hath had a great share in the promoting and divulging of those opinions that are causes of this trouble, and to be nearly joined not only in affinity and affection with some of those the court had taken notice of and passed censure upon, but you have spoken divers things as we have been informed very prejudicial to the honour of the churches and ministers thereof, and you have maintained a meeting and an assembly in your house that hath been condemned by the general assembly as a thing not tolerable nor comely in the sight of God nor fitting for your sex, and notwithstanding that was cried down you have continued the same. Therefore we have thought good to send for you to understand how things are, that if you be in an erroneous way we may reduce you so that you may become a profitable member here among us. Otherwise if you be obstinate in your course that then the court may take such course that you

---

2. Normally the trial would have been held in Boston, but Anne Hutchinson had numerous supporters in that city, so the proceedings were moved to the small town of Newton, where she had few allies.

may trouble us no further. Therefore I would intreat you to express whether you do assent and hold in practice to those opinions and factions that have been handled in court already, that is to say, whether you do not justify Mr. Wheelwright's sermon and the petition.

MRS. HUTCHINSON. I am called here to answer before you but I hear no things laid to my charge.

GOV. I have told you some already and more I can tell you.

MRS. H. Name one, Sir.

GOV. Have I not named some already?

MRS. H. What have I said or done?

[Here, in a portion of the transcript not reproduced, Winthrop accused Hutchinson of harboring and giving comfort to a faction that was dangerous to the colony.]

MRS. H. Must not I then entertain the saints because I must keep my conscience?

GOV. Say that one brother should commit felony or treason and come to his brother's house. If he knows him guilty and conceals him he is guilty of the same. It is his conscience to entertain him, but if his conscience comes into act in giving countenance and entertainment to him that hath broken the law he is guilty too. So if you do countenance those that are transgressors of the law you are in the same fact.

MRS. H. What law do they transgress?

GOV. The law of God and of the state.

MRS. H. In what particular?

GOV. Why in this among the rest, whereas the Lord doth say honour thy father and thy mother.[3]

MRS. H. Ey, Sir, in the Lord.

GOV. This honour you have broke in giving countenance to them.

MRS. H. In entertaining those did I entertain them against any act (for there is the thing) or what God hath appointed?

GOV. You knew that Mr. Wheelwright did preach this sermon and those that countenance him in this do break a law?

MRS. H. What law have I broken?

GOV. Why the fifth commandment.[4]

MRS. H. I deny that for he [Wheelwright] saith in the Lord.

GOV. You have joined with them in the faction.

MRS. H. In what faction have I joined with them?

3. Exodus 20:12. Anne Hutchinson's natural father was in England and her natural mother was dead. To what, then, was Winthrop referring?
4. "Honour thy father and thy mother: that thy days may be long upon the land which the Lord thy God giveth thee." Exodus 20:12.

GOV. In presenting the petition.

MRS. H. Suppose I had set my hand to the petition. What then?

GOV. You saw that case tried before.

MRS. H. But I had not my hand to the petition.

GOV. You have councelled them.

MRS. H. Wherein?

GOV. Why in entertaining them.

MRS. H. What breach of law is that, Sir?

GOV. Why dishonouring of parents.

MRS. H. But put the case, Sir, that I do fear the Lord and my parents. May not I entertain them that fear the Lord because my parents will not give me leave?

GOV. If they be the fathers of the commonwealth, and they of another religion, if you entertain them then you dishonour your parents and are justly punishable.

MRS. H. If I entertain them, as they have dishonoured their parents I do.

GOV. No but you by countenancing them above others put honour upon them.

MRS. H. I may put honour upon them as the children of God and as they do honour the Lord.

GOV. We do not mean to discourse with those of your sex but only this: you do adhere unto them and do endeavour to set forward this faction and so you do dishonour us.

MRS. H. I do acknowledge no such thing. Neither do I think that I ever put any dishonour upon you.

GOV. Why do you keep such a meeting at your house as you do every week upon a set day? . . .

MRS. H. It is lawful for me so to do, as it is all your practices, and can you find a warrant for yourself and condemn me for the same thing? The ground of my taking it up was, when I first came to this land because I did not go to such meetings as those were, it was presently reported that I did not allow of such meetings but held them unlawful and therefore in that regard they said I was proud and did despise all ordinances. Upon that a friend came unto me and told me of it and I to prevent such aspersions took it up, but it was in practice befo｀ ᵓ I came. Therefore I was not the first.

GOV. For this, that you appeal to our practice you need no confutation. If your meeting had answered to the former it had not been offensive, but I will say that there was no meeting of women alone, but your meeting is of another sort for there are sometimes men among you.

MRS. H. There was never any man with us.

GOV. Well, admit there was no man at your meeting and that you was sorry for it, there is no warrant for your doings, and by what warrant do you continue such a course?

MRS. H. I conceive there lies a clear rule in Titus[5] that the elder women should instruct the younger and then I must have a time wherein I must do it.

GOV. All this I grant you, I grant you a time for it, but what is this to the purpose that you Mrs. Hutchinson must call a company together from their callings to come to be taught of you?

MRS. H. Will it please you to answer me this and to give me a rule for then I will willingly submit to any truth. If any come to my house to be instructed in the ways of God what rule have I to put them away?

GOV. But suppose that a hundred men come unto you to be instructed. Will you forbear to instruct them?

MRS. H. As far as I conceive I cross a rule in it.

GOV. Very well and do you not so here?

MRS. H. No, Sir, for my ground is they are men.

GOV. Men and women all is one for that, but suppose that a man should come and say, "Mrs. Hutchinson, I hear that you are a woman that God hath given his grace unto and you have knowledge in the word of God. I pray instruct me a little." Ought you not to instruct this man?

MRS. H. I think I may. Do you think it is not lawful for me to teach women and why do you call me to teach the court?

GOV. We do not call you to teach the court but to lay open yourself.

[*In this portion of the transcript not reproduced, Hutchinson and Winthrop continued to wrangle over specifically what law she had broken.*]

GOV. Your course is not to be suffered for. Besides that we find such a course as this to be greatly prejudicial to the state. Besides the occasion that it is to seduce many honest persons that are called to those meetings and your opinions being known to be different from the word of God may seduce many simple souls that resort unto you. Besides that the occasion which hath come of late hath come from none but such as have frequented your meetings, so that now they are flown off from magistrates and ministers and since they have come to you. And besides that it will not well stand with the commonwealth that families should be neglected for so many neighbours and dames and so much time spent. We see no rule of God for this. We see not that any should have

---

5. A reference to The Epistle of Paul to Titus in the Bible, probably the section stating that older women "may teach the young women to be sober, to love their husbands, to love their children," etc.

authority to set up any other exercises besides what authority hath already set up and so what hurt comes of this you will be guilty of and we for suffering you.

MRS. H. Sir, I do not believe that to be so.

GOV. Well, we see how it is. We must therefore put it away from you or restrain you from maintaining this course.

MRS. H. If you have a rule for it from God's word you may.

GOV. We are your judges, and not you ours and we must compel you to it.

[Here followed a discussion of whether men as well as women attended Hutchinson's meetings. In response to one question, Hutchinson denied that women ever taught at men's meetings.]

DEPUTY GOVERNOR. I would go a little higher with Mrs. Hutchinson. About three years ago we were all in peace. Mrs. Hutchinson from that time she came hath made a disturbance, and some that came over with her in the ship did inform me what she was as soon as she was landed. I being then in place dealt with the pastor and teacher of Boston and desired them to enquire of her, and then I was satisfied that she held nothing different from us. But within half a year after, she had vented divers of her strange opinions and had made parties in the country, and at length it comes that Mr. Cotton and Mr. Vane[6] were of her judgment, but Mr. Cotton had cleared himself that he was not of that mind. But now it appears by this woman's meeting that Mrs. Hutchinson hath so forestalled the minds of many by their resort to her meeting that now she hath a potent party in the country. Now if all these things have endangered us as from that foundation and if she in particular hath disparaged all our ministers in the land that they have preached a covenant of works,[7] and only Mr. Cotton a covenant of grace,[8] why this is not to be suffered, and therefore being driven to the foundation and it being found that Mrs. Hutchinson is she that hath depraved all the ministers and hath been the cause of what is falled out, why we must take away the foundation and the building will fall.

MRS. H. I pray, Sir, prove it that I said they preached nothing but a covenant of works.

DEP. GOV. Nothing but a covenant of works. Why a Jesuit[9] may preach truth sometimes.

6. Henry Vane, supported by the Antinomians and merchant allies, was elected governor of Massachusetts Bay colony in 1636 and lost that office to Winthrop in 1637.
7. For an explanation of the covenant of works, see the "Background" section.
8. For an explanation of the covenant of grace, see the "Background" section.
9. The Society of Jesus (Jesuits) is a Roman Catholic order that places special emphasis on missionary work. The Jesuits were known at this time for combating Protestantism and were particularly detested by many Protestants, including the Puritans.

MRS. H. Did I ever say they preached a covenant of works then?

DEP. GOV. If they do not preach a covenant of grace clearly, then they preach a covenant of works.

MRS. H. No, Sir. One may preach a covenant of grace more clearly than another, so I said.

DEP. GOV. We are not upon that now but upon position.

MRS. H. Prove this then Sir that you say I said.

DEP. GOV. When they do preach a covenant of works do they preach truth?

MRS. H. Yes, Sir. But when they preach a covenant of works for salvation, that is not truth.

DEP. GOV. I do but ask you this: when the ministers do preach a covenant of works do they preach a way of salvation?

MRS. H. I did not come hither to answer to questions of that sort.

DEP. GOV. Because you will deny the thing.

MRS. H. Ey, but that is to be proved first.

DEP. GOV. I will make it plain that you did say that the ministers did preach a covenant of works.

MRS. H. I deny that.

DEP. GOV. And that you said they were not able ministers of the New Testament, but Mr. Cotton only.

MRS. H. If ever I spake that I proved it by God's word.

COURT. Very well, very well.

MRS. H. If one shall come unto me in private, and desire me seriously to tell then what I thought of such an one, I must either speak false or true in my answer.

[*In this lengthy section, Hutchinson was accused of having gone to a meeting of ministers and accusing them all—except John Cotton—of preaching a covenant of works rather than a covenant of grace. The accusation, if proved, would have been an extremely serious one. Several of the ministers testified that Hutchinson had made this accusation.*]

DEP. GOV. I called these witnesses and you deny them. You see they have proved this and you deny this, but it is clear. You said they preached a covenant of works and that they were not able ministers of the New Testament; now there are two other things that you did affirm which were that the scriptures in the letter of them held forth nothing but a covenant of works and likewise that those that were under a covenant of works cannot be saved.

MRS. H. Prove that I said so.

GOV. Did you say so?

MRS. H. No, Sir. It is your conclusion.

DEP. GOV. What do I do charging of you if you deny what is so fully proved?

GOV. Here are six undeniable ministers who say it is true and yet you deny that you did say that they did preach a covenant of works and that they were not able ministers of the gospel, and it appears plainly that you have spoken it, and whereas you say that it was drawn from you in a way of friendship, you did profess then that it was out of conscience that you spake and said, "The fear of man is a snare. Wherefore shall I be afraid, I will speak plainly and freely."

MRS. H. That I absolutely deny, for the first question was thus answered by me to them: They thought that I did conceive there was a difference between them and Mr. Cotton. At the first I was somewhat reserved. Then said Mr. Peters, "I pray answer the question directly as fully and as plainly as you desire we should tell you our minds. Mrs. Hutchinson we come for plain dealing and telling you our hearts." Then I said I would deal as plainly as I could, and whereas they say I said they were under a covenant of works and in the state of the apostles why these two speeches cross one another. I might say they might preach a covenant of works as did the apostles, but to preach a covenant of works and to be under a covenant of works is another business.

DEP. GOV. There have been six witnesses to prove this and yet you deny it.

MRS. H. I deny that these were the first words that were spoken.

GOV. You make the case worse, for you clearly shew that the ground of your opening your mind was not to satisfy them but to satisfy your own conscience.

[*There was a brief argument here about what Hutchinson actually said at the gathering of ministers, after which the court adjourned for the day.*]

The next morning

GOV. We proceeded the last night as far as we could in hearing of this cause of Mrs. Hutchinson. There were divers things laid to her charge: her ordinary meetings about religious exercises, her speeches in derogation of the ministers among us, and the weakening of the hands and hearts of the people towards them. Here was sufficient proof made of that which she was accused of in that point concerning the ministers and their ministry, as that they did preach a covenant of works when others did preach a covenant of grace, and that they were not able ministers of the New Testament, and that they had not the seal of the spirit, and this was spoken not as was pretended out of private conference, but out of conscience and warrant from scripture alleged the fear of man is a snare and seeing God had given her a calling to it she would freely speak. Some other speeches she used, as that the letter of the scripture held forth a covenant of works, and this is offered to be proved by probable grounds. If there be any thing else that the court hath to say they may speak.

[*At this point, a lengthy argument erupted when Hutchinson demanded that the ministers who testified against her be recalled as witnesses, put under oath, and repeat their accusations. One member of the court said that "the ministers are so well known unto us, that we need not take an oath of them."*]

GOV. I see no necessity of an oath in this thing seeing it is true and the substance of the matter confirmed by divers. Yet that all may be satisfied, if the elders will take an oath they shall have it given them. . . .

MRS. H. I will prove by what Mr. Wilson hath written[10] that they [the ministers] never heard me say such a thing.

MR. SIMS. We desire to have the paper and have it read.

MR. HARLAKENDEN. I am persuaded that is the truth that the elders do say and therefore I do not see it necessary now to call them to oath.

GOV. We cannot charge any thing of untruth upon them.

MR. HARLAKENDEN. Besides, Mrs. Hutchinson doth say that they are not able ministers of the New Testament.

MRS. H. They need not swear to that.

DEP. GOV. Will you confess it then?

MRS. H. I will not deny it or say it.

DEP. GOV. You must do one.

[*More on the oath followed.*]

DEP. GOV. Let her witnesses be called.

GOV. Who be they?

MRS. H. Mr. Leveret and our teacher and Mr. Coggeshall.

GOV. Mr. Coggeshall was not present.

MR. COGGESHALL. Yes, but I was. Only I desired to be silent till I should be called.

GOV. Will you, Mr. Coggeshall, say that she did not say so?

MR. COGGESHALL. Yes, I dare say that she did not say all that which they lay against her.

MR. PETERS. How dare you look into the court to say such a word?

10. Wilson had taken notes at the meeting between Hutchinson and the ministers. Hutchinson claimed that these notes would exonerate her. They were never produced and are now lost.

MR. COGGESHALL. Mr. Peters takes upon him to forbid me. I shall be silent.

MR. STOUGHTON. Ey, but she intended this that they say.

GOV. Well, Mr. Leveret, what were the words? I pray, speak.

MR. LEVERET. To my best remembrance when the elders did send for her, Mr. Peters did with much vehemency and intreaty urge her to tell what difference there was between Mr. Cotton and them, and upon his urging of her she said, "The fear of man is a snare, but they that trust upon the Lord shall be safe." And being asked wherein the difference was, she answered that they did not preach a covenant of grace so clearly as Mr. Cotton did, and she gave this reason of it: because that as the apostles were for a time without the spirit so until they had received the witness of the spirit they could not preach a covenant of grace so clearly.

[Here Hutchinson admitted that she might have said privately that the ministers were not able ministers of the New Testament.]

GOV. Mr. Cotton, the court desires that you declare what you do remember of the conference which was at the time and is now in question.

MR. COTTON. I did not think I should be called to bear witness in this cause and therefore did not labour to call to remembrance what was done; but the greatest passage that took impression upon me was to this purpose. The elders spake that they had heard that she had spoken some condemning words of their ministry, and among other things they did first pray her to answer wherein she thought their ministry did differ from mine. How the comparison sprang I am ignorant, but sorry I was that any comparison should be between me and my brethren and uncomfortable it was. She told them to this purpose that they did not hold forth a covenant of grace as I did. . . . I told her I was very sorry that she put comparisons between my ministry and theirs, for she had said more than I could myself, and rather I had that she had put us in fellowship with them and not have made the discrepancy. She said she found the difference. . . . And I must say that I did not find her saying they were under a covenant of works, not that she said they did preach a covenant of works.

[Here John Cotton tried to defend Hutchinson, mostly by saying he did not remember most of the events in question.]

MRS. H. If you please to give me leave I shall give you the ground of what I know to be true. Being much troubled to see the falseness of the constitution of the Church of England, I had like to have turned Separatist. Whereupon I kept a day of solemn humiliation and pondering of the thing, the scripture was brought unto me—he that denies Jesus Christ to be come in the flesh is antichrist. This I considered of and in considering found that the papists[11] did not deny him to come in the flesh, nor we did not deny him. Who then was antichrist? Was the Turk antichrist only? The Lord knows that I could not open scripture; he must by his prophetical office open it unto me. So after that being unsatisfied in the thing, the Lord was pleased to bring this scripture out of the Hebrews. He that denies the testament denies the testator, and in this did open unto me and give me to see that those which did not teach the new covenant had the spirit of antichrist, and upon this he did discover the ministry unto me, and ever since, I bless the Lord. He hath let me see which was the clear ministry and which the wrong. Since that time I confess I have been more choice and he hath left me to distinguish between the voice of my beloved and the voice of Moses, the voice of John Baptist and the voice of antichrist, for all those voices are spoken of in scripture. Now if you do condemn me for speaking what in my conscience I know to be truth I must commit myself unto the Lord.

MR. NOWEL. How do you know that that was the spirit?

MRS. H. How did Abraham know that it was God that bid him offer his son, being a breach of the sixth commandment?

DEP. GOV. By an immediate voice.

MRS. H. So to me by an immediate revelation.

DEP. GOV. How! an immediate revelation.

MRS. H. By the voice of his spirit to my soul. . . .

[*In spite of the general shock that greeted her claim that she had experienced an immediate revelation from God, Hutchinson went on to state that God had compelled her to take the course she had taken and that God had said to her, as He had to Daniel of the Old Testament, that "though I should meet with affliction, yet I am the same God that delivered Daniel out of the lion's den, I will also deliver thee."*]

MRS. H. You have power over my body but the Lord Jesus hath power over my body and soul, and assure yourselves thus much: you go on in this course you begin you will bring a curse upon you and your posterity, and the mouth of the Lord hath spoken it.

DEP. GOV. What is the scripture she brings?

11. *Papists* is a Protestant term for Roman Catholics, referring to the papacy.

MR. STOUGHTON. Behold I turn away from you.

MRS. H. But now having seen him which is invisible I fear not what man can do unto me.

GOV. Daniel was delivered by miracle. Do you think to be deliver'd so too?

MRS. H. I do here speak it before the court. I took that the Lord should deliver me by his providence.

MR. HARLAKENDEN. I may read scripture and the most glorious hypocrite may read them and yet go down to hell.

MRS. H. It may be so.

[Hutchinson's "revelations" were discussed among the stunned court.]

MR. BARTHOLOMEW. I speak as a member of the court. I fear that her revelations will deceive.

[More on Hutchinson's revelations followed.]

DEP. GOV. I desire Mr. Cotton to tell us whether you do approve of Mrs. Hutchinson's revelations as she hath laid them down.

MR. COTTON. I know not whether I do understand her, but this I say: If she doth expect a deliverance in a way of providence, then I cannot deny it.

DEP. GOV. No, sir. We did not speak of that.

MR. COTTON. If it be by way of miracle then I would suspect it.

DEP. GOV. Do you believe that her revelations are true?

MR. COTTON. That she may have some special providence of God to help her is a thing that I cannot bear witness against.

DEP. GOV. Good Sir, I do ask whether this revelation be of God or no?

MR. COTTON. I should desire to know whether the sentence of the court will bring her to any calamity, and then I would know of her whether she expects to be delivered from that calamity by a miracle or a providence of God.

MRS. H. By a providence of God I say I expect to be delivered from some calamity that shall come to me.

[Hutchinson's revelations were further discussed.]

DEP. GOV. These disturbances that have come among the Germans[12] have been all grounded upon revelations, and so they that have vented them have stirred up their hearers to take up arms against their prince and

12. This reference is to the bloody and violent fighting that took place between orthodox Protestants and the followers of the radical Anabaptist John of Leiden in 1534 and 1535.

to cut the throats of one another, and these have been the fruits of them, and whether the devil may inspire the same into their hearts here I know not, for I am fully persuaded that Mrs. Hutchinson is deluded by the devil, because the spirit of God speaks truth in all his servants.

GOV. I am persuaded that the revelation she brings forth is delusion.

[All the court but some two or three ministers cried out, "We all believe—we all believe it." Hutchinson was found guilty. Coddington made a lame attempt to defend Hutchinson but was silenced by Governor Winthrop.]

GOV. The court hath already declared themselves satisfied concerning the things you hear, and concerning the troublesomeness of her spirit and the danger of her course amongst us, which is not to be suffered. Therefore if it be the mind of the court that Mrs. Hutchinson for these things that appear before us is unfit for our society, and if it be the mind of the court that she shall be banished out of our liberties and imprisoned till she be sent away, let them hold up their hands.

[All but three did so.]

GOV. Those that are contrary minded hold up yours.

[Only Mr. Coddington and Mr. Colborn did so.]

MR. JENNISON. I cannot hold up my hand one way or the other, and I shall give my reason if the court require it.

GOV. Mrs. Hutchinson, the sentence of the court you hear is that you are banished from out of our jurisdiction as being a woman not fit for our society, and are to be imprisoned till the court shall send you away.

MRS. H. I desire to know wherefore I am banished?

GOV. Say no more. The court knows wherefore and is satisfied.

✵ QUESTIONS TO CONSIDER ✵

Now that you have examined the evidence, at least one point is very clear: the political and religious authorities of Massachusetts Bay were determined to get rid of Anne Hutchinson, whether or not she actually had broken any law. They tried to bait her, force admissions of guilt from her, confuse her, browbeat her. Essentially, they had already decided on the verdict before the trial began. So we know that Anne Hutchinson was a threat—and a serious one—to the colony.

And yet the colony had dealt quite differently with Roger Williams, a Puritan minister banished in 1635 because of his extreme religious beliefs. Williams was given every chance to mend his ways, Governor Winthrop remained his friend throughout Williams's appearances before the General Court, and it was only with great reluctance that the court finally decided to send him out into the "wilderness."

Why, then, was Anne Hutchinson such a threat, and why was her trial such an ordeal? Obviously, she did pose a religious threat. As you look back through the evidence, try to clarify the exact points of difficulty between Hutchinson and the ministers. What was the basis of the argument over covenants of grace and works? What was Hutchinson supposed to have said? Under what circumstances had she allegedly said this? To whom? What was the role of her own minister, John Cotton, in the trial?

Remember that Hutchinson's trial took place in the midst of the divisive Antinomian controversy. What threat did the Antinomians pose to Massachusetts Bay and Puritanism? Did Hutchinson say anything in her testimony that would indicate she was an Antinomian? How would you prove whether or not she was?

Hutchinson's place or role in the community also seems to have come into question during the trial. What do the questions about the meetings she held in her home reveal? Look beyond what the governor and members of the court are actually saying. Try to imagine what they might have been thinking. How might Hutchinson's meetings have eventually posed a threat to the larger community?

Finally, look through the transcript one more time. It provides some clues, often subtle ones, about the relationships between men and women in colonial Massachusetts. Puritan law and customs gave women approximately equal status with men, and of course women could join the church, just as men could. But in every society, there are unspoken assumptions about how men and women should behave. Can you find any evidence that Hutchinson violated these assumptions? If so, what did she do? Again, why would this be dangerous?

In conclusion, try to put together all you know from the evidence to answer the central question: Why was Anne Hutchinson such a threat to Massachusetts Bay colony?

✳ EPILOGUE ✳

Even after banishment, misfortune continued to plague the Hutchinson family. After moving to Narragansett Bay, Hutchinson once again became pregnant. By then she was more than forty-five years old and had begun menopause. The fetus did not develop naturally and was aborted into a hydatidiform mole (resembling a cluster of grapes), which was expelled with considerable pain and difficulty. Many believed that the "birth" of this "monster baby" was proof of Hutchinson's religious heresy.

In 1642, Hutchinson's husband died, and she moved with her six youngest children to the Dutch colony of New Netherland in what is now the Bronx borough of New York City. The next year, she and all but one of her children were killed by Indians.

Ten years after Hutchinson was banished from Massachusetts Bay, John Winthrop died. Winthrop believed to the end of his life that he had had no choice other than to expel Hutchinson and her family. However, even Winthrop's most sympathetic biographer, historian Edmund S. Morgan, describes the Hutchinson trial and its aftermath as "the least attractive episode" in Winthrop's long public career.

Massachusetts Bay continued to try to maintain community cohesion for years after Anne Hutchinson and her family were expelled. Quakers who tried to convert Puritans were especially persecuted, even executed. But as the colony grew and prospered, change ultimately did come. New generations seemed unable to embrace the original zeal of the colony's founders. New towns increased the colony's size and made uniformity more difficult. Growth and prosperity also seemed to bring an increased interest in individual wealth and a corresponding decline in religious fervor. Reports

of sleeping during sermons, fewer conversions of young people, blasphemous language, and growing attention to physical pleasures were numerous, as were reports of election disputes, intrachurch squabbling, and community bickering.

To those who remembered the old ways of Massachusetts Bay, such straying from the true path was more than unfortunate. The Puritans believed that as the ancient Israelites had been punished by God when they broke their covenant, so they would have to pay for their indiscretions. As one Puritan minister said, "In the time of their prosperity, see how the Jews turn their backs and shake off the authority of the Lord." The comparison was lost on almost no one.

Jeremiads—stories that predicted disasters because of the decline in religious zeal and public morality—were especially popular in the 1660s. The minister and physician Michael Wigglesworth's poem "The Day of Doom" (specifically written for the general public) was "read to pieces," according to historian Perry Miller. Wigglesworth's more sophisticated but heartfelt poem "God's Controversy with New England" was equally popular among more educated readers. Hence it is not surprising that by the late 1680s (more than forty years after Anne Hutchinson's death), a wave of religious hysteria swept across Massachusetts Bay colony. Convinced that they had broken their covenant with God, many Puritans grimly awaited their punishment, spending long hours in churches listening to sermons. When in 1692 a few young girls in Salem Village began accusing some of their neighbors of being possessed by Satan, many were convinced that the day of punishment had arrived. Before that incident had run its course, twenty people had been killed, nineteen of them by hanging, and many more had been temporarily imprisoned. Although the Puritans' congregational church remained the official established church of Massachusetts until 1822, the original community cohesion had been altered long before that.

3

Rhythms of Colonial Life: The Statistics of Colonial Chesapeake Bay and Massachusetts Bay

❋ THE PROBLEM ❋

In 1759, a young English clergyman visiting Great Britain's North American colonies was struck by how different each colony was from one another. Reverend Andrew Burnaby observed that "fire and water are not more heterogeneous than the different colonies," and went on to say that

> . . . such is the difference of character of manners, of religion, of interest of the different colonies [that] were they left to themselves, there would soon be civil war . . . while the Indians and Negroes would . . . impatiently watch the opportunity of exterminating them all together.[1]

1. Andrew Burnaby, *Travels Through the Middle Settlements in North America,* quoted in Ronald Hoffman and Peter J. Albert, eds., *Sovereign States in an Age of Uncertainty* (Charlottesville, Va.: University Press of Virginia, 1981), pp. 226–227.

Burnaby was not the only person to remark on the differences—sometimes profound—from one colony to another. Although most colonists did not travel very far from their own farms or villages, when they did so they too were surprised by the differences they encountered. Indeed, decades after the War of Independence an elderly John Adams was still amazed that thirteen clocks so different from one another "were made to strike together—a perfection of mechanism, which no artist had ever before effected."[2]

Some of the differences between the various colonies were present from the moments of settlement, results of *en-*

2. John Adams to Hezekiah Niles, February 13, 1818, in Charles Francis Adams, ed., *The Works of John Adams* (Boston: Little, Brown & Co., 1856), Vol. X, p. 283.

vironmental factors (geography, climate, soil) as well as *volitional*[3] factors (goals of the founders, decisions concerning land ownership and labor systems, religious practices, and the like). Thus combinations of environmental and volitional factors made Great Britain's North American colonies different from one another at the times of their very beginnings.

In the years between settlement and the War of Independence, however, most colonies experienced important demographic and economic changes. In some cases, the changes were so profound that the colonies' respective founders would have scarcely recognized them.[4] And while to us these demographic and economic changes took place at an extremely slow pace, to the colonists they occurred with what to them must have seemed like startling speed. Indeed, a child born in one of the colonies in 1650, whether male or female, experienced a dramatically different life from that of a child born in 1750. Thus as the colonies were different from one another

at their respective "plantings," so also was each colony different from what that colony had been at the time of its founding.

Your tasks in this chapter are to examine and analyze statistical evidence from the Chesapeake Bay (Virginia and Maryland) and Massachusetts Bay colonies so as to answer the following questions:

1. What were the *environmental* and *volitional* differences between the Chesapeake Bay and Massachusetts Bay colonies?
2. What demographic and economic changes took place in the Chesapeake Bay and Massachusetts Bay colonies between 1650 and 1750?
3. How might those changes have affected the respective colonists' thoughts, feelings, and behavior?
4. Were demographic and economic changes moving the Chesapeake Bay and Massachusetts Bay colonies closer together or further apart?

❋ BACKGROUND ❋

In December 1606, the three ships *Susan Constant, Godspeed,* and *Dis-*

---

3. Volitional: of conscious choice; by decision.
4. Seven of the thirteen colonies had been in existence for a century or more when the American Revolution broke out in 1775: Virginia, Massachusetts Bay, Rhode Island, Connecticut, Maryland, New York, and New Jersey. European settlement also existed in the New Hampshire and Delaware areas over a century before the Revolution, although they did not formally become colonies until later.

covery sailed from England bound for the New World. Earlier that year, King James I had granted a charter to the Virginia Company of London (more familiarly known as the London Company to distinguish it from the Virginia Company of Plymouth), a private corporation that hoped to imitate Spain's good fortune by finding gold, silver, and precious gems that would enrich the stockholders. On board the three vessels were 144 pro-

CHAPTER 3

RHYTHMS OF
COLONIAL LIFE:
THE STATISTICS
OF COLONIAL
CHESAPEAKE
BAY AND
MASSACHUSETTS
BAY

spective colonists, the vast majority of them either fortune seekers or salaried company employees (such as goldsmiths, jewelers, and apothecaries[5]). None planned to be permanent settlers.

In spite of meticulous planning by the company, in Virginia things were desperate almost from the start. Only 105 would-be colonists survived the voyage, and a combination of disease, starvation, the eventual hostility of the nearby Native Americans, and conflicts between the settlement's leaders made the situation ever more dire. By the time relief ships sent by the company arrived in January 1608 with provisions and more colonists, only thirty-eight survivors remained at Jamestown.

Nor did the Virginia colony immediately improve. With few colonists skilled in agriculture and clearing land (most colonists had to be taught how to use an axe), the colony depended on food from company relief ships and trading with the Native Americans. Thus in the winter of 1609 to 1610 Jamestown experienced its horrible "starving time," when only sixty of a fall 1609 population of five hundred survived. As one chronicler wrote:

> . . . we were constrained to eat dogs, cats, rats, snakes, toadstools, horsehides, and what not; one man out of the misery endured, killing his wife . . . to eat her, for which he was burned. Many besides fed on the corpses of dead men. . . .[6]

Even after the "starving time," it was by no means clear that Virginia would survive. By 1616, the colony's population hovered at only 380, and a well-coordinated Indian attack in 1622 very nearly wiped out the fledgling settlement.[7] But John Rolfe had experimented with transplanting a variety of West Indian tobacco to the "lusty soyle" of Virginia, where it thrived. In 1614, Virginia shipped four barrels of tobacco to England and by 1617, was exporting 50,000 pounds of tobacco leaves. And in spite of the facts that the London Company initially opposed the cultivation of the "noxious weed" and King James I railed against its importation and use, tobacco ultimately became the colony's salvation.[8]

In the meantime, the company had abandoned its hopes of finding gold and precious gems in Virginia and turned to long-range profits from lumber, hemp, turpentine, and finally tobacco. In order to attract settlers to the colony, in 1618 the company revised its charter to permit individuals to own land—previous to that "greate charter," all land had been owned by the company. Settlers claimed lands touching Chesapeake Bay and the many rivers and streams that fed it (to use the waterways to ship their tobacco). By the time the London Company finally went bankrupt and Vir-

---

5. Apothecary: pharmacist, druggist.
6. Quoted in David Hawke, *The Colonial Experience* (Indianapolis: Bobbs, Merrill Co., 1966), p. 95.

7. The colonists retaliated against the Native Americans by inviting them to a peace conference at which they killed around 250 of them with poisoned wine.
8. A short excerpt from James's *A Counterblast to Tobacco* (1604) may be found in Warren M. Billings, John E. Selby, and Thad W. Tate, *Colonial Virginia: A History* (White Plains, N.Y.: KTO Press, 1986), pp. 40–41n.

ginia became a royal colony (1625), landowners were building homes close to their fields and away from the settlements and stockades. Laborers were found in the form of indentured servants from England who, in exchange for their passage and a land grant after finishing their "indenture" (usually seven years), agreed to work for the landowners.[9] Even so, it was not until around 1675 that Virginia's natural increase and not immigration replenished the colony's population.

Maryland, the other colony on Chesapeake Bay, was created by King Charles I as an immense land grant to George Calvert, a gentleman who had served King James I as secretary of state and in return had been awarded a peerage as Lord Baltimore and promised a land grant in America. James I had died in 1625, before the necessary paperwork had been completed. According to tradition, Calvert himself drew up the document, leaving a blank space where the name of the proposed colony was to go. Charles I filled in the blank with "Terra Mariae" (Mary's Land, or Maryland), named for his wife, Queen Henrietta Maria. According to the terms of the grant, the Calvert family owned all the land, could lease that land to settlers and collect rents, and totally controlled the government. The final charter was issued in 1632, two months after George Calvert's death.

Cecilius Calvert (c. 1605–1675), George Calvert's eldest son, assumed control of the grant (6.8 million acres) and launched the first expedition on November 22, 1633. The first settlers came ashore in Maryland on March 25, 1634. Avoiding many of the errors made by the early settlers of Virginia, Maryland colonists (led by Cecilius's younger brother) purchased land from the Native Americans, planted food crops as well as tobacco, and laid claim to generous land grants on which Calvert charged low rents ("quit rents"). As was the case later in Virginia, the population was dispersed, living on or near their landholdings and thus breaking the English pattern of village life and discouraging the growth of large towns or cities.

As the proprietor, Cecilius Calvert's dream was to reproduce England's manor system in the New World, although it would be several decades before the grand plantations, plantation houses, and planters emerged. Also, since George Calvert had converted to Roman Catholicism, the Calvert family envisioned Maryland as a haven for Catholics in America. Yet the generous land grants and low quit rents attracted people of many religious persuasions, the majority of whom were Protestants. The proprietor wisely allowed religious heterogeneity. Regardless of their faiths, Marylanders worshipped land and tobacco.

Many miles from the Chesapeake settlements an entirely different type of colonization was taking place. Since the 1570s, a growing number of English men and women had called for reforms in the Church of England that would "purify" the lingering traces of Roman Catholicism and embrace many of the ideas of the Protestant denominations founded on the European continent by Martin Luther, John Calvin, and others. Royal and ec-

9. Up to 1675, indentured servants comprised approximately one-half of the colony's total population.

:R 3

MS OF
COLONIAL LIFE:
THE STATISTICS
OF COLONIAL
CHESAPEAKE
BAY AND
MASSACHUSETTS
BAY

clesiastical displeasure coupled with economic hard times in England convinced many of these "Puritans" that they must found a new type of community in the New World. In 1630, a "great fleet" of eleven ships and seven hundred prospective settlers sailed from England, led by John Winthrop, an attorney who would serve as the governor of Massachusetts Bay with few interruptions for the colony's first two decades. In a shipboard sermon, Winthrop challenged his shipmates to build a city upon a hill, because "the eies of all people are uppon us." Thus Puritans believed that a colony built on the word of God and following God's commandments would be an ideal state and would ensure their salvation. As Winthrop explained, "If the Lord seeth it wilbe good for us, he will provide a shelter and a hidinge place for us and ours."[10]

As at Jamestown, the first winter was horrible, as approximately 30 percent of the settlers died and roughly 10 percent more left the settlement, discouraged, in the spring. But fellow Puritans and others escaping economic hard times replenished the population and more, as between 15,000 and 20,000 arrived in the first decade. From then on immigration waned, but Massachusetts Bay grew steadily by natural increase. After the winter of 1630–1631, no "starving time" like that of Virginia took place and from 1640 to 1700, men in the town of Andover in Massachusetts Bay outlived their counterparts in

Middlesex County, Virginia, by an average of sixteen years.[11]

Unlike the Chesapeake colonies, settlers in Massachusetts Bay could not simply travel to an uninhabited area, select a parcel of land, and receive individual title to that land from the colonial governor. Instead, a group of men who wanted to establish a town had to apply to the colonial government (called the General Court) for a land grant for the entire town. Leaders of the prospective new town were then selected, and the single church was organized. Having then received the grant from the General Court, the new town's leaders apportioned the land among the male heads of households who were church members, holding in common some land for grazing and other communal uses (hence the "town common"). In this way, the Puritan leadership retained control of the fast-growing population, ensured Puritan economic and religious domination, and guaranteed that large numbers of dissenters—men and women who might divert the colony from its "holy mission" or its "errand into the wilderness"—would not be attracted to Massachusetts Bay.

Economically, Massachusetts Bay prospered almost from the very beginning. Yet unlike the Chesapeake colonies, Massachusetts Bay did not fit well into England's mercantile system, whereby colonies supplied raw materials to the mother country (in the Chesapeake's case, tobacco) and in turn purchased Great Britain's manu-

10. See Edmund S. Morgan, *The Puritan Dilemma: The Story of John Winthrop* (Boston: Little, Brown & Co., 1958), pp. 36–37, 70.

11. Women in Andover outlived their counterparts in Middlesex County by an average of twenty-two years.

factured products. Because comparatively rocky soil and a short growing season kept crop yields low and agricultural surpluses meager, many people in Massachusetts Bay had to seek other ways of making a living. Many men petitioned the General Court to organize new towns on the frontier; others turned to either the sea as fishermen, traders, shippers, and seamen or native manufacturing enterprises such as iron product manufacturing, rum distilling, shipbuilding, and rope-making. Except for fishing, none of these activities fit into England's mercantile plans for empire, and some undertakings were prohibited outright by the Navigation Acts (1660, 1663, and later, which set up the mercantile system), which most citizens of Massachusetts Bay ignored.

Thus by the mid-eighteenth century, those colonists who once had huddled together for protection and mutual assistance in tiny settlements or fortified stockades in Virginia,

Maryland, and Massachusetts Bay had grown, changed, and matured, as had the colonies they had built. Thus children born on the Chesapeake or in Massachusetts in 1750 lived in significantly different environments than their predecessors who had been born in 1650. Economic, political, social, religious, and cultural channels had been carved, in some cases deeply, in their lands and lives. To what extent were the lives of the colonists of the Chesapeake different from those of their Massachusetts counterparts? In what ways were they similar? What were the environmental and volitional differences between the Chesapeake and Massachusetts Bay colonies? What demographic and economic changes took place in those colonies between 1650 and 1750? How might those changes have affected the respective colonists' thoughts, feelings, and behavior? Were demographic and economic changes moving the colonies closer together or further apart?

❋ THE METHOD ❋

How can we begin to answer such questions? Even the tiny fraction of colonists who left letters, diaries, sermons, or speeches (the John Winthrops, Anne Hutchinsons, Benjamin Franklins, Increase Mathers, William Penns, Thomas Jeffersons, and so forth) rarely if ever addressed these questions or issues. Indeed, in terms of demographic and economic trends and forces, it is not clear that many of

those colonists who left written records *were even aware* of the trends and forces that in part were acting to shape their lives. And, of course, the vast majority of colonists left no written records at all.

Recently, however, historians have become more imaginative in using the comparatively limited material at their disposal. We know, for instance, that almost every person, even the

CHAPTER 3

RHYTHMS OF
COLONIAL LIFE:
THE STATISTICS
OF COLONIAL
CHESAPEAKE
BAY AND
MASSACHUSETTS
BAY

poorest, left some record that he or she existed. That person's name may appear in any number of places, including church records of baptisms, marriages, and deaths; property-holding and tax records; civil or criminal court records; military records; ship manifests; slave auction records; and cemetery records. Thus demographic and economic trends can be reconstructed, in some cases allowing us to understand aspects of these people's lives that they may not have perceived themselves.

How is this done? One important way is to use statistics to help reconstruct the past. Today we are bombarded almost daily with statistics—about the stock market, teen pregnancy, illegal drug use, and Florida voters in the 2000 presidential election, for example. In order to function productively and successfully in today's world, we must use those statistics to aid us in shaping our opinions and making decisions.

Historians have learned to use these same types of statistics and statistical methods and apply them to the past. Working carefully through those materials that still exist, historians begin to reconstruct the demographic and economic trends and forces that affected a past epoch. Were people living longer or shorter? Were people growing richer or poorer? Were women marrying later or earlier? Were women bearing more or fewer children? Were inheritance patterns (the methods of dividing estates among heirs) changing or not changing? To historians, each statistical summary of records (each *set* of statistics or *aggregate* picture) contains important information that increases the understanding of a community or people being studied. Table 1 shows the types of questions historians ask of several different kinds of records.

Having examined each set of statistics, the historian places the sets in some logical order, which may vary de-

Table 1

Type of Record	Questions
Census	Was the population growing, shrinking, or stationary? Was the ratio of males to females roughly equal? Did that ratio change over time?
Marriage	At what age were women marrying? Did that age change over time?
Wills, probate	How were estates divided? Did that method change over time? Based on real estate and personal property listed, was the collective standard of living rising, falling, or stationary? Based on dates of death, was the population living longer?
Land, tax	What percentage of the adult male population owned land? Did that percentage change over time? Was the land evenly distributed among the adult male population?

pending on the available evidence, the central questions the historian is attempting to answer, and the historian's own preferences. Some historians prefer a "birth-to-death" ordering, beginning with age-at-marriage statistics for females and moving chronologically through the collective life of the community's population. Others prefer to isolate the demographic statistical sets (birth, marriage, migration, and death) from the economic sets (such as landholding and division of estates).

Up to this point, the historian has (1) collected the statistics and arranged them into sets, (2) examined each set and measured tendencies or changes over time, and (3) arranged the sets in some logical order. Now the historian must begin asking "why" for each set. For example:

1. Why did the survival rate of children or young people change over time?
2. Why did women marry later?
3. Why did the method of dividing estates change over time?

In many cases, the answer to each question (and other "why" questions) is in one of the other statistical sets. That may cause the historian to alter his or her ordering of the sets to make the story clearer.

The historian is actually linking the sets to one another to form a chain. When two sets have been linked (because one set answers the "why" question of another set), the historian repeats the process until all the sets have been linked to form one chain of evidence. At that point, the historian can summarize the tendencies that have been discovered and, if desired, can connect those trends or tendencies to other events occurring in the period, such as the American Revolution.

One example of how historians link statistical sets together to answer a "why" question is sufficient. Source 15 in the Evidence section shows that the white population growth in Massachusetts Bay was extremely rapid between 1660 and 1700 (the growth rate actually approximates those of many non-Western developing nations today). How can we account for this rapid growth? Look at Source 18, which deals with the survival rate of children born in the town of Andover between 1640 and 1759. Note that between 1640 and 1699, the survival rate was very high (in Sweden between 1751 and 1799, 50 percent of the children born did not reach the age of fifteen). Also examine Source 23, the average number of births per marriage in Andover. Note that between 1655 and 1704, the average number of births per marriage was very high—between 5.3 and 7.6. Thus we can conclude that the population grew so rapidly in Massachusetts Bay between 1660 and 1700 because women gave birth to large numbers of children *and* because a high proportion of those children survived.

Later, however, the growth rate in Massachusetts Bay generally declined.[12] Can you explain this by using other statistical sets?

12. The end of intermittent warfare in England plus crop failures in Northern Ireland accounted for the sharp increase in Massachusetts and Andover growth rates in the 1720s.

CHAPTER 3

RHYTHMS OF
COLONIAL LIFE:
THE STATISTICS
OF COLONIAL
CHESAPEAKE
BAY AND
MASSACHUSETTS
BAY

Begin by examining the statistics from Chesapeake Bay (Sources 1 through 14) and Massachusetts Bay (Sources 15 through 27) separately, linking each statistical set to another to create a "chain of explanation." Having done this for each group, then *compare* the statistics from the Chesapeake Bay and Massachusetts Bay colonies. How do the two areas compare with regard to population or survival rates, landholding, economic systems, inheritance patterns, wealth distribution, and so forth? What were the principal demographic differences and similarities between the two regions? Were the two areas becoming increasingly different or similar?

One thing you will notice is that historical records from which statistics can be derived are far more available for New England than they are for the southern colonies. For one thing, prior to the mid-twentieth century, the lack of air conditioning meant that historical records in the South fell victim to a combination of heat and humidity (in some southern archives, historians could almost smell their evidence decomposing). Also, the primary record-keeping unit in New England was the town, so records from the colonial era were dispersed over many sites. In the South, the county was responsible for keeping records (in Louisiana, the parish), so the destruction of a county courthouse might well destroy all that county's records. Finally, some southern records were destroyed in the American Civil War.

As you will see, many of the statistical sets deal with Middlesex County, Virginia, and the towns of Andover and Concord, Massachusetts. These sites were chosen because historians Darrett and Anita Rutman, Philip Greven, and Robert Gross collected a great deal of statistical information about these places. Middlesex County, Virginia (not to be confused with Middlesex County, Massachusetts), was first settled by European Americans in the late 1640s, where individuals or families immediately began grazing cattle and raising tobacco. Becoming a separate county in 1664, Middlesex by 1700 was one of the wealthiest counties in Virginia.

For its part, Concord, a farm town founded in 1635, was the first town in Massachusetts Bay established away from the Charles River. The area was rich in furs, and settlers initially were able to trap the beaver for income. Andover was organized in 1646, the original settlers coming mainly from other towns in the colony. In Andover, people lived in the village and walked out to farm their land, which was organized in the open-field system (landowners owned several strips of land in large open fields, which they worked in common). In Concord, however, many settlers lived outside the village and near their fields, building clusters of homes along the Concord River (which was spanned by the soon-to-be-famous Old North Bridge).

Working with historical statistics is not so difficult as it may first appear. Often it is helpful to establish a small study group with a few of your classmates, if your instructor permits it. As the study group talks through the problem, each individual can contribute something that possibly the other members of the group did not see, thereby broadening the group's understanding of the problem. Analyzing statistics is a challenging undertaking, but the results can be immensely satisfying, as you come to "see" the *people* the statistics represent.

✳ THE EVIDENCE ✳

CHESAPEAKE BAY

Sources 1 and 2 data U.S. Bureau of the Census, *Historical Statistics of the United States* (Washington, D.C.: U.S. Government Printing Office, 1975), pt. 2, p. 1168.

1. Population Growth, Virginia, 1640–1770.

Year	Whites	Increase (%)	Blacks	Increase (%)
1640	10.292	—	150	—
1650	18,326	78	405	170
1660	26,070	42	950	135
1670	33,309	28	2,000	111
1680	40,596	22	3,000	50
1690	43,701	8	9,345	212
1700	42,170	−4	16,390	75
1710	55,163	31	23,118	41
1720	61,198	11	26,559	15
1730	84,000	37	30,000	13
1740	120,440	43	60,000	100
1750	129,581	8	101,452	69
1760	199,156	35	140,570	39
1770	259,411	30	187,605	33

CHAPTER 3

RHYTHMS OF
COLONIAL LIFE:
THE STATISTICS
OF COLONIAL
CHESAPEAKE
BAY AND
MASSACHUSETTS
BAY

2. Population Growth, Maryland, 1640–1770.

Year	Whites	Increase (%)	Blacks	Increase (%)
1640	563	—	20	—
1650	4,204	647	300	1350
1660	7,668	82	758	153
1670	12,036	57	1,190	57
1680	16,293	35	1,611	35
1690	21,862	34	2,162	34
1700	26,377	21	3,227	49
1710	34,796	32	7,945	146
1720	53,634	54	12,499	57
1730	73,893	38	17,220	38
1740	92,062	25	24,031	40
1750	97,623	6	43,450	81
1760	113,263	16	49,004	13
1770	138,781	23	63,818	30

Sources 3 and 4 data from Darrett B. Rutman and Anita H. Rutman, *A Place in Time: Explicatus* (New York: W. W. Norton, 1984), pp. 28, 64.

3. Population Growth, Middlesex County, Virginia, 1668–1740.

Year	Whites	Increase (%)	Blacks	Increase (%)	Blacks as % of Total
1668	847	—	65	—	7.13
1687	1,337	58	117	80	8.05
1699	1,374	3	397	239	22.42
1704	1,436	5	553	39	27.80
1724	1,423	−1	1,293	134	47.61
1740	1,348	−5	1,596	23	54.21

4. Average Age at First Marriage for White Females, Middlesex County, Virginia, 1670–1749.

Year of Marriage	Average Age at Marriage (years)
1670–1679	18.1
1680–1689	17.5
1690–1699	17.9
1700–1709	19.6
1710–1719	20.1
1720–1729	20.3
1730–1739	20.8
1740–1749	22.0

Source 5 data from Allan Kulikoff, *Tobacco and Slaves: The Development of Southern Cultures in the Chesapeake, 1680–1800* (Chapel Hill: University of North Carolina Press, 1986), p. 60.

5. Age at Marriage, Family Size, and Surviving Children in Tidewater, Maryland, 1650–1800.

	Years		
	1650–1700	1700–1750	1750–1800
Average white female age at first marriage	16.8	18.6	22.2
Average completed family size[13]	9.4	9.0	6.9
Average number of surviving children per couple	3.3	5.0	3.7

Source 6 data from Rutman and Rutman, *A Place in Time*, p. 55.

6. Life Expectancy of Chesapeake-born Males Who Reached the Age of 20, Middlesex County, Virginia, 1670–1729.

Birth Years	Mortality per 100, Ages 20–24[14]	Additional Years Expected to Live from Age 20
1670–1679	9.4	26.4
1680–1689	10.9	24.1
1690–1699	11.4	23.5
1700–1709	11.0	24.1
1710–1719	11.2	23.8
1720–1729	11.3	23.6

13. Completed family size: The average number of children born to women who survived married to age forty-five, hence a "completed" family.
14. The number of males twenty years old who died by the age of twenty-four, per one hundred.

CHAPTER 3

RHYTHMS OF
COLONIAL LIFE:
THE STATISTICS
OF COLONIAL
CHESAPEAKE
BAY AND
MASSACHUSETTS
BAY

Source 7 data from Philip D. Morgan, *Slave Counterpoint: Black Culture in the Eighteenth-Century Chesapeake and Low Country* (Chapel Hill: University of North Carolina Press, 1998), p. 41.

7. Plantation Size in Virginia by Number of Slaves, 1700–1779.

Decade	Number of Slaves on Plantations			
	1–5	6–10	11–20	21+
1700–1709	39%	19%	32%	10%
1710–1719	30	20	27	23
1720–1729	30	29	27	13
1730–1739	28	27	20	25
1740–1749	25	25	32	17
1750–1759	18	22	29	31
1760–1769	15	22	29	33
1770–1779	13	22	35	29

Source 8 data from Social Science Research Council, *The Statistical History of the United States from Colonial Times to the Present* (Stamford, Conn.: Fairfield Publishers, 1965), 765–766; Census Bureau, *Historical Statistics of the United States,* pt. 2, p. 1198.

8. Tobacco Imported by England from Virginia and Maryland (in thousands of pounds) and Maryland Tobacco Prices (in pence sterling/pound), 1620–1770.

Year	Total (in thousands of pounds)	Tobacco Prices (pence sterling/pound
1620	119.0	12.00
1630	458.2	4.00
1640	1,257.0	2.50
1650	–	–
1663	7,371.1	1.55
1672	17,559.0	1.00
1682	21,399.0	0.80
1688	28,385.5	0.75
1700	37,166.0	1.00
1710	23,351.0	0.85
1720	34,138.0	1.19
1730	34,860.0	0.67
1740	35,372.0	0.80
1750	50,785.0	1.16
1670	51,283.0	1.60
1770	38,986.0	2.06

Source 9 data from Census Bureau, *Historical Statistics of the United States,*
pt. 2, pp. 1176–1177.

9. Value of Exports to and Imports from England by Virginia and Maryland, 1700–1770 (in pounds sterling).

Year	Exports (£)	Imports (£)
1700	317,302	173,481
1705	116,768	174,322
1710	188,429	127,639
1715	174,756	199,274
1720	331,482	110,717
1725	214,730	195,884
1730	346,823	150,931
1735	394,995	220,381
1740	341,997	281,428
1745	399,423	197,799
1750	508,939	349,419
1755	489,668	285,157
1760	504,451	605,882
1765	505,671	383,224
1770	435,094	717,782

CHAPTER 3

RHYTHMS OF
COLONIAL LIFE:
THE STATISTICS
OF COLONIAL
CHESAPEAKE
BAY AND
MASSACHUSETTS
BAY

Source 10 data from Rutman and Rutman, *A Place in Time,* p. 129.

10. Wealth Distribution in Middlesex County, Virginia: Personal Property of Deceased Adult Males, 1699–1750.

Through 1699

1. The poorest 31.2% of the male population owned 3.6% of the total wealth.
2. The next poorest 28.6% of the male population owned 12.8% of the total wealth.
3. The next poorest 13.9% of the male population owned 11.1% of the total wealth.
4. The next poorest 20.8% of the male population owned 30.9% of the total wealth.
5. The wealthiest 5.6% of the male population owned 41.6% of the total wealth.

1700–1719

1. The poorest 42.5% of the male population owned 3.4% of the total wealth.
2. The next poorest 26% of the male population owned 7.9% of the total wealth.
3. The next poorest 17.8% of the male population owned 12.6% of the total wealth.
4. The next poorest 7.9% of the male population owned 14.7% of the total wealth.
5. The wealthiest 5.8% of the male population owned 61.5% of the total wealth.

1720–1750

1. The poorest 35.3% of the male population owned 3.1% of the total wealth.
2. The next poorest 30.4% of the male population owned 11.2% of the total wealth.
3. The next poorest 26% of the male population owned 31.3% of the total wealth.
4. The next poorest 5.6% of the male population owned 21.3% of the total wealth.
5. The wealthiest 2.7% of the male population owned 33.2% of the total wealth.

Source 11 data from Rutman and Rutman, *A Place in Time,* p. 238.

11. Division of Estates, Middlesex County, Virginia, 1699–1750.

Time Period	Percentage of All Sons Receiving Land
Through 1699	93
1700–1719	71
1720–1750	62

Sources 12 and 13 from Paul G. E. Clemens, *The Atlantic Economy and Colonial Maryland's Eastern Shore: From Tobacco to Grain* (Ithaca, N.Y.: Cornell University Press, 1980), pp. 194–195.

12. Output of Tobacco and Wheat per Field Hand on Talbot and Kent County (Maryland) Slaveowning Plantations, 1740s and 1760s.

	1740s		1760s	
	Number of farms	Output	Number of farms	Output
Talbot County				
Tobacco (pounds)	59	1,520	22	880
Wheat (bushels)	12	13	18	54
Number of farms in sample	59	—	22	—
Kent County				
Tobacco (pounds)	38	1,540	16	530
Wheat (bushels)	25	40	53	93
Number of farms in sample	40	—	55	—

13. Percentage of Income Earned by Tobacco, Wheat, and Corn on Talbot and Kent County (Maryland) Slaveowning Plantations, 1740s and 1760s.

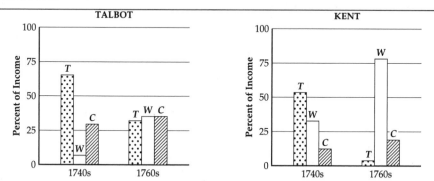

CHAPTER 3

RHYTHMS OF
COLONIAL LIFE:
THE STATISTICS
OF COLONIAL
CHESAPEAKE
BAY AND
MASSACHUSETTS
BAY

Source 14 from Robert D. Mitchell, *Commercialism and Frontier: Perspectives on the Early Shenandoah Valley* (Charlottesville, Va.: University Press of Virginia, 1977), pp. 95–100.

14. Virginia Population West of Blue Ridge Mountains, 1745–1790.

Date	Total Population	Slave Population
1745	c. 10,200	—
1750	c. 17,000	—
1755	c. 20,800	760
1782	—	6,744
1790	74,767	10,715

MASSACHUSETTS BAY

Source 15 data from Census Bureau, *Historical Statistics of the United States*, pt. 2, p. 1168.

15. Growth of White Population, Massachusetts Bay, 1660–1770.

Year	Population	Increase (%)	Average Annual Growth Rate (%)
1660	20,082	—	—
1670	30,000	49.8	4.9
1680	39,752	32.5	3.3
1690	49,504	24.5	2.5
1700	55,941	13.0	1.3
1710	62,390	11.5	1.2
1720	91,008	45.9	4.6
1730	114,116	25.4	2.6
1740	151,613	32.9	3.3
1750	188,000	24.0	2.4
1760	222,600	18.4	1.8
1770	235,308	5.7	.57

Source 16 data from Philip J. Greven Jr., *Four Generations: Population, Land, and Family in Colonial Andover, Massachusetts* (Ithaca, N.Y.: Cornell University Press, 1970), p. 179.

16. Growth of White Population, Town of Andover, 1680–1776.

Year	Population	Increase (%)	Average Annual Growth Rate (%)
1680	435	—	—
1685	600	37.9	7.6
1695	710	18.3	1.8
1705	945	33.1	3.3
1715	1,050	11.1	1.1
1725	1,305	24.3	2.4
1735	1,630	24.9	2.5
1745	1,845	13.2	1.3
1755	2,135	15.7	1.6
1764	2,442	14.4	1.6
1776	2,953	20.9	1.8

Source 17 data from Robert A. Gross, *The Minutemen and Their World* (New York: Hill and Wang, 1976), p. 15.

17. Growth of Population, Town of Concord, 1679–1750.

Year	Population	Increase (%)	Average Annual Growth Rate (%)
1679	480	—	—
1706	920	91.7	3.3
1710	c. 1,000	8.7	2.2
1725	c. 1,500	5.0	3.3
1750	c. 2,000	3.3	1.3

Sources 18 and 19 data from Greven, *Four Generations*, pp. 191, 189, 177. Source 19 data also from Gross, *The Minutemen and Their World*, p. 209.

18. Children Born Between 1640 and 1759 Who Lived to at Least Age 10, Andover.

Years	Rate
1640–1669	917 per 1,000
1670–1699	855 per 1,000
1700–1729	805 per 1,000
1730–1759	695 per 1,000

CHAPTER 3

RHYTHMS OF
COLONIAL LIFE:
THE STATISTICS
OF COLONIAL
CHESAPEAKE
BAY AND
MASSACHUSETTS
BAY

19. Population Density (persons per square mile), Concord and Andover, 1705–1776 (various years).

Year	Concord[15]	Andover
1705	—	16.0
1706	14.7	—
1754	44.2	—
1755	—	36.2
1764	—	41.0
1765	48.0	—
1776	62.7	50.0

Source 20 data from Gross, *The Minutemen and Their World,* pp. 210.

20. Average Landholding, Concord, 1663 and 1749.

Year	Amount of Land
1663	259 acres
1749	56 acres

Source 21 data from James A. Henretta, *The Evolution of American Society, 1700–1815: An Interdisciplinary Approach* (Lexington, Mass.: D. C. Heath, 1973), pp. 29–30.

21. Division of Estates, Andover, Massachusetts.[16]

First generation: 95 percent of all estates divided among all male heirs
Second generation: 75 percent of all estates divided among all male heirs
Third generation: 58 percent of all estates divided among all male heirs
Fourth generation (came to maturity after 1750): under 50 percent of all
    estates divided among all male heirs

15. In 1729, the town of Bedford was formed from lands originally in Concord. Then, in 1735, the town of Acton was created from lands that had been part of Concord. Finally, in 1754, the town of Lincoln was set off from Concord. These losses of lands were taken into account when computing population density for 1754, 1765, and 1776.
16. A widow inherited her late husband's estate only if the couple had no male heirs (sons). Otherwise, the land was passed down to the sons. Daughters received personal property (money, silverware, livestock, and the like).

Sources 22 and 23 data from Greven, *Four Generations,* pp. 33, 105, 183.

22. Average Age at Marriage for Females, Andover, 1650–1724.

Year	Age
1650–1654	18.0
1660–1664	18.8
1670–1674	20.4
1680–1684	21.6
1690–1694	21.6
1700–1704	21.0
1710–1714	24.0
1720–1724	23.9

23. Average Births per Marriage, Andover, 1655–1764.

Year	Births
1655–1664	5.8
1665–1674	5.3
1675–1684	5.7
1685–1694	6.0
1695–1704	7.6
1705–1714	7.5
1715–1724	5.7
1725–1734	4.8
1735–1744	4.1
1745–1754	4.0
1755–1764	3.9

CHAPTER 3

RHYTHMS OF
COLONIAL LIFE:
THE STATISTICS
OF COLONIAL
CHESAPEAKE
BAY AND
MASSACHUSETTS
BAY

Sources 24 and 25 data from Gary B. Nash, "Urban Wealth and Poverty in Pre-Revolutionary America," *Journal of Interdisciplinary History,* 6 (Spring 1976): 545–584.

24. Percentage of Group Migration[17] into Boston, 1747, 1759, and 1771.

Group	1747	1759	1771
Single men	3.0%	8.5%	23.4%
Single women	4.0	16.8	20.0
Widows and widowers	7.9	8.9	4.4
Married couples	33.6	27.4	27.5
Children	51.5	38.4	24.7
	100.0%	100.0%	100.0%

25. Distribution of Wealth by Percentage in Boston, 1687 and 1771.

Wealth Distribution	1687	1771
Wealth possessed by the richest 5% of the people	30.2	48.7
Wealth possessed by the next wealthiest 5% of the people	16.1	14.7
Wealth possessed by the next wealthiest 30% of the people	39.8	27.4
Wealth possessed by the next wealthiest 30% of the people	11.3	9.1
Wealth possessed by the poorest 30% of the people	2.6	0.1

Source 26 from *Historical Statistics of the United States,* p. 1180.

26. Number and Tonnage Capacity of Ships to and from Boston, 1714–1772.

Date	Imports		Exports	
	No. Ships	Tonnage Cap.	No. Ships	Tonnage Cap.
1714–1717	—	—	416	20,927
1754	303	17,575	447	26,669
1768	549	31,983	612	33,695
1770	819	38,360	800	36,965
1772	852	43,633	845	42,506

17. *Migration* refers to internal migration, not emigration from Europe.

Source 27 from Stephen Innes, *Labor in a New Land: Economy and Society in Seventeenth-Century Springfield* (Princeton: Princeton University Press, 1983), p. 465.

27. Population of Springfield, Massachusetts, 1636–1776.

Date	Population	Date	Population
1636	8	1685	540
1640	45	1690	750
1646	100	1738	1,692
1665	288	1765	2,755
1672	304	1776	1,974

❋ QUESTIONS TO CONSIDER ❋

When using statistics, first look at each set individually. For each set, ask the following questions:

1. What does this set of statistics measure?
2. How does what is being measured change over time?
3. Why does that change take place? As noted, the answer to this question can be found in another set or sets. When you connect one set to another, statisticians say that you have made a *linkage*.

Begin by examining Sources 1 through 3, dealing with population growth in Virginia, Maryland, and Middlesex County, Virginia, respectively. How did population growth change over time? How can Sources 4 through 6 help you answer the "why" question for population growth? Are any of the other sources helpful as well?

Although the status of African-Americans in Virginia and Maryland prior to 1650 is not clear, we can be assured that by the latter years of the seventeenth century, almost all blacks living in those colonies were slaves. Since we know that white landowners in the Chesapeake Bay area were raising tobacco as early as the 1620s in Virginia and the 1630s in Maryland, what form of labor was used? How do you account for the increase in black slaves (see Sources 1, 2, 3, 7, and 10)? What was happening to whites who were small farmers? Large farmers?

The prosperity of Virginia and Maryland was linked to the production and price of tobacco. How did those two variables change over time (Source 8)? Can you detect a general trend? As the price of tobacco generally declined, Virginia and Maryland planters increased their production of the crop. How can you prove that they did so (see Source 9)? Also, what was the "balance of trade" (the difference between exports and imports) between the Chesapeake Bay colonies and the mother country? Can you detect any general trends? How might

CHAPTER 3

RHYTHMS OF
COLONIAL LIFE:
THE STATISTICS
OF COLONIAL
CHESAPEAKE
BAY AND
MASSACHUSETTS
BAY

that affect the trends suggested by Source 8?

As you examine and analyze Source 10 (on wealth distribution in Middlesex County, Virginia), be very careful to note that the "wealth clusters" in the three time periods are different. For example, in the wealth distribution through 1699, the poorest group represents 31.2 percent of the male population, whereas in 1700 to 1719 the poorest group is 42.5 percent and in 1720 to 1750 it is 35.3 percent. In spite of this, you nevertheless will be able to see general trends of wealth distribution. What are those trends? Do you think the division of estates (Source 11) had anything to do with the trends you observed in Source 10?

There is little question that by the eighteenth century Chesapeake Bay residents were beginning to face increasingly severe demographic and economic troubles. Can you determine any ways that the people of the Chesapeake Bay were attempting to confront their problems (see Sources 5 and 11)? It also appears that plantation owners were beginning to practice crop diversification instead of relying almost exclusively on tobacco (see Sources 12 and 13). Why do you think they did so (see Source 8)? Finally, Source 14 shows you another potential "safety valve" for Chesapeake Bay residents. What was that option?

Now sum up your work on the Chesapeake Bay colonies. What demographic and economic changes took place in those colonies between 1650 and 1750? Note especially new systems of landholding and labor. How did Chesapeake Bay colonists respond to the demographic and economic

changes? How might those changes have affected people living in the Chesapeake Bay colonies?

Now move on to the statistical sets for Massachusetts Bay (Sources 15 through 27). Repeat the process you used for the Chesapeake Bay colonies. How did population growth (Sources 15 through 17) change over time? What were the long-term trends? How can Sources 18 through 23 help you answer the "why" question?

It is clear from analyzing the statistics (especially Sources 18 through 20) that the Massachusetts Bay colony was experiencing some demographic and economic troubles. What were those difficulties? We also know that child mortality was increasing and crop yield per farm was declining. Can you use the statistics to account for those phenomena as well?

Although no written accounts mention it, we know that the people of Massachusetts Bay (and especially people living in small farming towns such as Andover and Concord) attempted to solve these difficulties by altering certain demographic and economic forces. How did they attempt to do this (see, especially, Sources 21 through 27)? How did they attempt to control population growth? How did they try to arrest the decline in farm size? Can you tell whether or not they were successful? What do Sources 24, 25, and 27 tell you? What does Source 26 tell you about the kinds of employment available to people who migrated to Boston?

Now go back to the central questions you asked of the Chesapeake Bay statistics and ask them about the Massachusetts Bay statistics.

Having analyzed each region of British North America separately, now you should be able to compare the two areas. How would you compare the long-range trends in population growth in the Chesapeake Bay and Massachusetts Bay colonies? Can you explain the differences in the trends? Can you continue the process of comparison to female age at marriage and family size (Sources 4, 5, 22 and 23)? What are the similarities? What are the differences?

Perhaps the most significant differences between the Chesapeake Bay and Massachusetts Bay colonies were in their respective agricultural and labor systems. How can you demonstrate those differences? How would you account for those differences?

Clearly, both the Chesapeake Bay and Massachusetts Bay colonies experienced economic difficulties in the eighteenth century. What was the nature of the economic troubles they faced (see, especially, Sources 7 through 10, 19 and 20)? Were their difficulties similar or different in nature? How did each region respond to its difficulties?

Examine the trends in the Chesapeake Bay and Massachusetts Bay colonies for both the division of estates (Sources 11 and 21) and the distribution of wealth (Sources 10 and 25). What is similar about these trends? What is different?

Finally, from examining and analyzing all of the evidence, determine whether demographic and economic trends were moving the Chesapeake Bay and Massachusetts Bay colonies closer together, farther apart, or (depending on the trend being analyzed) both.

❋ EPILOGUE ❋

By the time that Ralph Waldo Emerson memorialized "the shot heard 'round the world" (1837), Americans had created the myth that all the colonies had rallied to the cause of independence for the same reasons and with similar ardor. Similar in language and customs, overwhelmingly Protestant, and deeply affected both by the Enlightenment and by the Great Awakening, so the argument went, Americans from all the colonies (to return to John Adams's imagery) made their thirteen clocks "strike together—a perfection of mechanism. . . ."

Of course the revolutionists themselves, by then almost all long dead, would have known that this remembered unity was a myth—and perhaps a hope. Washington was chosen to command the Continental Line (as the infant American army was called) and Jefferson was chosen to draft a declaration of independence precisely *because* they were Virginians, their respective selections meant to ensure Virginia's loyalty to a war that had

CHAPTER 3

RHYTHMS OF
COLONIAL LIFE:
THE STATISTICS
OF COLONIAL
CHESAPEAKE
BAY AND
MASSACHUSETTS
BAY

been started by New Englanders and carried on principally by them. And while the British might refer to all colonists as "Yankees," to Americans themselves this title was reserved by southerners for New Englanders— and not in a complimentary fashion.

Indeed, in his still useful and important book *The Birth of the Republic* (revised edition, 1973), historian Edmund S. Morgan has asserted that the colonists first achieved their independence and *then* went about trying to create a sense of unity and nationalism. Their effort was, of course, only partially successful. Even so, when the Frenchman Turgot wrote that Americans were "the hope of the human race," few Americans from any region were eager to disagree.

Although only a few sensed it, the zenith of Virginia already had passed by the outbreak of the American Revolution. Overproduction of tobacco, the resulting soil exhaustion,[18] continued reliance on imported manufactured goods, the opening of new plantation lands to the south and west, the emigration of whites from eastern Virginia, and the overpopulation of slaves acted together to increase Virginia's economic troubles. And by the time of Thomas Jefferson's death in 1826, the leadership of the southern states had passed from the Chesapeake to a more strident South Carolina.

As Virginia had reached its apex before the Revolution, so also had the town of Boston. The largest urban center in British North America in 1740, Boston in turn gave way to Philadelphia, New York, and (by 1800) even Baltimore. Many emigrated from Boston in search of opportunities at other seaports or in the West. Shipping, insurance and banking, wily merchants, and manufacturing eventually saved the city, but Boston would never recapture its position as the center of America.

Thus while the American Revolution obviously brought independence and in the long run became one of the significant events in world history, it failed to alter or reverse the demographic and economic trends and forces that were affecting people in the Chesapeake Bay and Massachusetts Bay colonies. By 1775, those trends and forces were too powerful, their channels too deeply carved, to be erased by even a protracted war. And as for the Chesapeake's economic and labor systems, they would have to be dismantled by force, in part led by those from Massachusetts.

18. See Avery Odelle Craven, *Soil Exhaustion as a Factor in the Agricultural History of Virginia and Maryland, 1606–1860* (Champagne: University of Illinois Press, 1926), esp. pp. 32–35.

CHAPTER

4

What Really Happened in the Boston Massacre? The Trial of Captain Thomas Preston

✳ THE PROBLEM ✳

On the chilly evening of March 5, 1770, a small group of boys began taunting a British sentry (called a "Centinel" or "Sentinel") in front of the Boston Custom House. Pushed to the breaking point by this goading, the soldier struck one of his tormentors with his musket. Soon a crowd of fifty or sixty gathered around the frightened soldier, prompting him to call for help. The officer of the day, Captain Thomas Preston, and seven British soldiers hurried to the Custom House to protect the sentry.

Upon arriving at the Custom House, Captain Preston must have sensed how precarious his position was. The crowd had swelled to more than one hundred, some anxious for a fight, others simply curiosity seekers, and still others called from their homes by the

town's church bells, a traditional signal that a fire had broken out. Efforts by Preston and others to calm the crowd proved useless. And because the crowd had enveloped Preston and his men as it had the lone sentry, escape was nearly impossible.

What happened next is a subject of considerable controversy. One of the soldiers fired his musket into the crowd, and the others followed suit, one by one. The colonists scattered, leaving five dead[1] and six wounded,

1. Those killed were Crispus Attucks (a part African, part Native American seaman in his forties, who also went by the name of Michael Johnson), James Caldwell (a sailor), Patrick Carr (an immigrant from Ireland who worked as a leather-breeches maker), Samuel Gray (a rope-maker), and Samuel Maverick (a seventeen-year-old apprentice).

CHAPTER 4

WHAT REALLY
HAPPENED IN
THE BOSTON
MASSACRE?
THE TRIAL OF
CAPTAIN
THOMAS
PRESTON

some of whom were probably innocent bystanders. Preston and his men quickly returned to their barracks, where they were placed under house arrest. They were later taken to jail and charged with murder.

Preston's trial began on October 24, 1770, delayed by the authorities in an attempt to cool the emotions of the townspeople. Soon after the March 5 event, however, a grand jury had taken sworn depositions from Preston, the soldiers, and more than ninety Bostonians. The depositions leaked out (in a pamphlet, probably published by anti-British extremists), helping to keep emotions at a fever pitch.

John Adams, Josiah Quincy, and Robert Auchmuty had agreed to defend Preston,[2] even though the first two were staunch Patriots. They believed that the captain was entitled to a fair trial and did their best to defend

him. After a difficult jury selection, the trial began, witnesses for the prosecution and the defense being called mostly from those who had given depositions to the grand jury. The trial lasted for four days, an unusually long trial for the times. The case went to the jury at 5:00 P.M. on October 29. Although it took the jury only three hours to reach a verdict, the decision was not announced until the following day.

In this chapter, you will be using portions of the evidence given at the murder trial of Captain Thomas Preston to reconstruct what actually happened on that March 5, 1770, evening in Boston, Massachusetts. Was Preston guilty as charged? Or was he innocent? Only by reconstructing the event that we call the Boston Massacre will you be able to answer these questions.

❉ BACKGROUND ❉

The town of Boston[3] had been uneasy throughout the first weeks of 1770. Tension had been building since the early 1760s because the town was increasingly affected by the forces of migration, change, and maturation. The

2. Adams, Quincy, and Auchmuty (pronounced Aŭk′mŭty) also were engaged to defend the soldiers, a practice that would not be allowed today because of the conflict of interest (defending more than one person charged with the same crime).
3. Although Boston was one of the largest urban centers in the colonies, the town was not incorporated as a city. Several attempts were made, but residents opposed them, fearing they would lose the institution of the town meeting.

protests against the Stamp Act had been particularly bitter there, and men such as Samuel Adams were encouraging their fellow Bostonians to be even bolder in their remonstrances. In response, in 1768 the British government ordered two regiments of soldiers to Boston to restore order and enforce the laws of Parliament. "They will not *find* a rebellion," quipped Benjamin Franklin of the soldiers, "they may indeed *make* one" (italics added).

Instead of bringing calm to Boston, the presence of soldiers only increased tensions. Incidents between Bostonians and redcoats were common on the streets, in taverns, and at the places of employment of British soldiers who sought part-time jobs to supplement their meager salaries. Known British sympathizers and informers were harassed, and Crown officials were openly insulted. Indeed, the town of Boston seemed to be a powder keg just waiting for a spark to set off an explosion.

On February 22, 1770, British sympathizer and informer Ebenezer Richardson tried to tear down an anti-British sign. He was followed to his house by an angry crowd that proceeded to taunt him and break his windows with stones. One of the stones struck Richardson's wife. Enraged, he grabbed a musket and fired almost blindly into the crowd. Eleven-year-old Christopher Seider[4] fell to the ground with eleven pellets of shot in his chest. The boy died eight hours later. The crowd, by now numbering about one thousand, dragged Richardson from his house and through the streets, finally delivering him to the Boston jail. Four days later, the town conducted a huge funeral for Christopher Seider, probably arranged and organized by Samuel Adams. Seider's casket was carried through the streets by children, and approximately two thousand mourners (one-seventh of Boston's total population) took part.

All through the next week Boston was an angry town. Gangs of men and boys roamed the streets at night looking for British soldiers foolish enough to venture out alone. Similarly, off-duty soldiers prowled the same streets looking for someone to challenge

them. A fight broke out at a ropewalk between some soldiers who worked there part time and some unemployed colonists.

With large portions of both the Boston citizenry and the British soldiers inflamed, an incident on March 5 touched off an ugly confrontation that took place in front of the Custom House, a symbol of British authority over the colonies. Both sides sought to use the event to support their respective causes. But Samuel Adams, a struggling attorney with a flair for politics and propaganda, clearly had the upper hand. The burial of the five "martyrs" was attended by almost every resident of Boston, and Adams used the event to push his demands for British troop withdrawal and to heap abuse on the mother country. Therefore, when the murder trial of Captain Thomas Preston finally opened in late October, emotions had hardly diminished.

Crowd disturbances had been an almost regular feature of life in both England and America. Historian John Bohstedt has estimated that England was the scene of at least one thousand crowd disturbances and riots between 1790 and 1810.[5] Colonial American towns were no more placid; demonstrations and riots were almost regular features of the colonists' lives. Destruction of property and burning of effigies were common in these disturbances. In August 1765 in Boston, for example, crowds protesting against the Stamp Act burned effigies and de-

---

4. Christopher Seider is sometimes referred to as Christopher Snider.

5. John Bohstedt, *Riots and Community Politics in England and Wales, 1790–1810* (Cambridge, Mass.: Harvard University Press, 1983), p. 5.

CHAPTER 4

WHAT REALLY
HAPPENED IN
THE BOSTON
MASSACRE?
THE TRIAL OF
CAPTAIN
THOMAS
PRESTON

stroyed the homes of stamp distributor Andrew Oliver and Massachusetts Lieutenant Governor Thomas Hutchinson. Indeed, it was almost as if the entire community was willing to countenance demonstrations and riots as long as they were confined to parades, loud gatherings, and limited destruction of property. In almost no cases were there any deaths, and the authorities seldom fired on the crowds. Yet on March 5, 1770, both the crowd and the soldiers acted uncharacteristically. The result was the tragedy that colonists dubbed the "Boston Massacre." Why did the crowd and the soldiers behave as they did?

To repeat, your task is to reconstruct the so-called Boston Massacre so as to understand what really happened on that fateful evening. Spelling and punctuation in the evidence have been modernized only to clarify the meaning.

✳ THE METHOD ✳

Many students (and some historians) like to think that facts speak for themselves. This is especially tempting when analyzing a single incident like the Boston Massacre, many eyewitnesses of which testified at the trial. However, discovering what really happened, even when there are eyewitnesses, is never quite that easy. Witnesses may be confused at the time, they may see only part of the incident, or they may unconsciously "see" only what they expect to see. Obviously, witnesses also may have some reasons to lie. Thus the testimony of witnesses must be carefully scrutinized, for both what the witnesses *mean* to tell us and other relevant information as well. Therefore, historians approach such testimony with considerable skepticism and are concerned not only with the testimony itself but also with the possible motives of the witnesses.

Neither Preston nor the soldiers testified at the captain's trial because English legal custom prohibited defendants in criminal cases from testifying in their own behalf (the expectation was that they would perjure themselves). One week after the Massacre, however, in a sworn deposition, or statement, Captain Preston gave his side of the story. Although the deposition was not introduced at the trial and therefore the jury was not aware of what Preston himself had said, we have reproduced a portion of Preston's deposition for you to examine. How does Preston's deposition agree or disagree with other eyewitnesses' accounts?

No transcript of Preston's trial survives, if indeed one was ever made. Trial testimony comes from an anonymous person's summary of what each person said, the notes of Robert Treat Paine (one of the lawyers for the prosecution), and one witness's (Richard Palmes's) reconstruction of what his testimony and the cross-examination had been. Although historians would prefer to use the original trial transcript and would do so if one were available, the anonymous summary, Paine's notes, and one witness's recollections are acceptable substitutes because probably all three people were present in the courtroom (Paine and Palmes certainly were) and the accounts tend to corroborate one another.

Almost all the witnesses were at the scene, yet not all their testimony is of equal merit. First try to reconstruct the scene itself: the actual order in which the events occurred and where the various participants were standing. Whenever possible, look for corroborating testimony: two or more reliable witnesses who heard or saw the same things.

Be careful to use all the evidence. You should be able to develop some reasonable explanation for the conflicting testimony and those things that do not fit into your reconstruction very well.

Almost immediately you will discover that some important pieces of evidence are missing. For example, it would be useful to know the individual backgrounds and political views of the witnesses. Unfortunately, we know very little about the witnesses themselves, and we can reconstruct the political ideas of only about one-third of them. Therefore, you will have to rely on the testimonies given, deducing which witnesses were telling the truth, which were lying, and which were simply mistaken.

The fact that significant portions of the evidence are missing is not disastrous. Historians seldom have all the evidence they need when they attempt to tackle a historical problem. Instead, they must be able to do as much as they can with the evidence that is available, using it as completely and imaginatively as they can. They do so by asking questions of the available evidence. Where were the witnesses standing? Which one seems more likely to be telling the truth? Which witnesses were probably lying? When dealing with the testimony of the witnesses, be sure to determine what is factual and what is a witness's opinion. A rough sketch of the scene has been provided. How can it help you?

Also included in the evidence is Paul Revere's famous engraving of the incident, probably plagiarized from a drawing by artist Henry Pelham. It is unlikely that either Pelham or Revere was an eyewitness to the Boston Massacre, yet Revere's engraving gained widespread distribution, and most people—in 1770 and today—tend to recall that engraving when they think of the Boston Massacre. Do not examine the engraving until you have read the trial account closely. Can Revere's engraving help you find out what really happened that night? How does the engraving fit the eyewitnesses' accounts? How do the engraving and the accounts differ? Why?

Keep the central question in mind: What really happened in the Boston Massacre? Throughout this exercise, you will be trying to determine whether an order to fire was actually given. If so, by whom? If not, how can you explain why shots were fired? As commanding officer, Thomas Preston was held responsible and charged with murder. You might want to consider the evidence available to you as either a prosecution or defense attorney. Which side had the stronger case?

CHAPTER 4

WHAT REALLY
HAPPENED IN
THE BOSTON
MASSACRE?
THE TRIAL OF
CAPTAIN
THOMAS
PRESTON

✳ THE EVIDENCE ✳

1. Site of the Boston Massacre, Town House Area, 1770.

Main Street

Shop
Private Dwelling
Office
Private Dwelling

Town House

Private Dwelling

Shops

Court Square

Shops

Quaker Lane

King Street

Private Dwelling

Exchange Tavern

Royal Exchange Lane

Private Dwelling
Private Dwelling
Private Dwelling

Soldiers

Sentry Box

Steps

Custom House

Private Dwelling

Source 2 from *Publications of The Colonial Society of Massachusetts* (Boston: The Colonial Society of Massachusetts, 1905), Vol. VII, pp. 8–9.

2. Deposition of Captain Thomas Preston, March 12, 1770 (Excerpt).

The mob still increased and were outrageous, striking their clubs or bludgeons one against another, and calling out, come on you rascals, you bloody backs, you lobster scoundrels, fire if you dare, G-d damn you, fire and be damned, we know you dare not, and much more such language was used. At this time I was between the soldiers and the mob, parleying with, and endeavoring all in my power to persuade them to retire peaceably, but to no purpose. They advanced to the points of the bayonets, struck some of them and even the muzzles of the pieces, and seemed to be endeavoring to close with the soldiers. On which some well behaved persons asked me if the guns were charged. I replied yes. They then asked me if I intended to order the men to fire. I answered no, by no means, observing to them that I was advanced before the muzzles of the men's pieces, and must fall a sacrifice if they fired; that the soldiers were upon the half cock[6] and charged bayonets, and my giving the word fire under those circumstances would prove me to be no officer. While I was thus speaking, one of the soldiers having received a severe blow with a stick, stepped a little to one side and instantly fired. . . . On this a general attack was made on the men by a great number of heavy clubs and snowballs being thrown at them, by which all our lives were in imminent danger, some persons at the same time from behind calling out, damn your bloods—why don't you fire. Instantly three or four of the soldiers fired. . . . On my asking the soldiers why they fired without orders, they said they heard the word fire and supposed it came from me. This might be the case as many of the mob called out fire, fire, but I assured the men that I gave no such order; that my words were, don't fire, stop your firing. . . .[7]

6. The cock of a musket had to be fully drawn back (cocked) for the musket to fire. In half cock, the cock was drawn only halfway back so that priming powder could be placed in the pan. The musket, however, would not fire at half cock. This is the origin of "Don't go off half cocked." See Source 5.

7. Depositions also were taken from the soldiers, three of whom claimed, "We did our Captain's orders and if we don't obey his commands should have been confined and shot." As with Preston's deposition, the jury was not aware of that statement. In addition, ninety-six depositions were taken from townspeople.

CHAPTER 4

WHAT REALLY
HAPPENED IN
THE BOSTON
MASSACRE?
THE TRIAL OF
CAPTAIN
THOMAS
PRESTON

Source 3 from Hiller B. Zobel, ed., *The Legal Papers of John Adams* (Cambridge, Mass.: Belknap Press of Harvard University Press, 1965), Vol. III, pp. 46–98.

3. The Trial of Captain Thomas Preston (*Rex v. Preston*), October 24–29 (Excerpt).

Witnesses for the King (Prosecution)

Edward Gerrish (or Garrick)

I heard a noise about 8 o'clock and went down to Royal Exchange Lane. Saw some Persons with Sticks coming up Quaker Lane. I said [to the sentry] Capt. Goldsmith owed my fellow Apprentice. He said he was a Gentleman and would pay every body. I said there was none in the Regiment.[8] He asked for me. I went to him, was not ashamed of my face. . . . The Sentinel left his Post and Struck me. I cried. My fellow Apprentice and a young man came up to the Sentinel and called him Bloody back.[9] He called to the Main Guard. . . . There was not a dozen people when the Sentinel called the Guard.

Ebenezer Hinkley

Just after 9 o'clock heard the Cry of Fire. I saw the party come out of the Guard House. A Capt. cried out of the Window "fire upon 'em damn 'em." I followed 'em down before the Custom House door. Capt. Preston was out and commanded 'em. They drew up and charged their Bayonets. Montgomery[10] pushed at the people advancing. In 2 or 3 minutes a Boy threw a small stick over hand and hit Montgomery on Breast. Then I heard the word fire in ¼ minute he fired. I saw some pieces of Snow as big as Egg thrown. 3 or 4 thrown at the same time of pushing on the other End of the file, before 1st gun fired. The body of People about a Rod[11] off. People said Damn 'em they durst not fire don't be afraid. No threats . . . I was a Rod from Capt. Preston. Did not hear him give Order to fire. ½ minute from 1st Gun to 2d. same to 3d. The others quicker. I saw no people striking the Guns or Bayonets nor pelting 'em. I saw Preston between people and Soldiers. I did not see him when 1st firing.

8. To say that there was no gentleman in the regiment was an insult to the sentry's superior officer, Captain Goldsmith.
9. British soldiers' coats were red.
10. Montgomery, one of the soldiers, undoubtedly fired the first shot.
11. A rod equals 16.5 feet.

Peter Cunningham

Upon the cry of fire and Bells ringing went into King Street, heard the Capt. say Turn out the Guard.[12] Saw the Centinel standing on the steps of the Custom house, pushing his Bayonet at the People who were about 30 or 40. Captain came and ordered the Men to prime and load.[13] He came before 'em about 4 or 5 minutes after and put up their Guns with his Arm. They then fired and were priming and loading again. I am pretty positive the Capt. bid 'em Prime and load. I stood about 4 feet off him. Heard no Order given to fire. The Person who gave Orders to Prime and load stood with his back to me, I did not see his face only when he put up their Guns. I stood about 10 or 11 feet from the Soldiers, the Captain about the midway between.

William Wyatt

I heard the bell, . . . saw People running several ways. The largest part went down to the North of the Townhouse. I went the South side, saw an officer leading out 8 or 10 Men. Somebody met the officer and said, Capt. Preston for Gods sake mind what you are about and take care of your Men. He went down to the Centinel, drew up his Men, bid them face about, Prime and load. I saw about 100 People in the Street huzzaing, crying fire, damn you fire. In about 10 minutes I heard the Officer say fire. The Soldiers took no notice. His back was to me. I heard the same voice say fire. The Soldiers did not fire. The Officer then stamped and said Damn your bloods fire be the consequences what it will. Immediately the first Gun was fired. I have no doubt the Officer was the same person the Man spoke to when coming down with the Guard. His back was to me when the last order was given. I was then about 5 or 6 yards off and within 2 yards at the first. He stood in the rear when the Guns were fired. Just before I heard a Stick, which I took to be upon a Gun. I did not see it. The Officer had to the best of my knowledge a cloth coloured Surtout[14] on. After the firing the Captain stepd forward before the Men and struck up their Guns. One was loading again and he damn'd 'em for firing and severely reprimanded 'em. I did not mean the Capt. had the Surtout but the Man who spoke to him when coming with the Guard.

12. To dress and equip so as to be ready for duty.
13. Muskets were loaded from the muzzle with powder, wadding, a ball, and more wadding. The hammer was drawn back halfway, and powder was poured into the small pan under the hammer. There was a small piece of flint attached to the cock (see Source 5) so that when the trigger was pulled, the cock would come down and the flint would spark and ignite the gunpowder in the pan. The fire would then ignite the gunpowder in the breech and fire the gun. If the powder in the pan exploded but did not ignite the powder in the breech, the result was a "flash in the pan" and a musket that did not fire.
14. A type of overcoat.

CHAPTER 4

WHAT REALLY
HAPPENED IN
THE BOSTON
MASSACRE?
THE TRIAL OF
CAPTAIN
THOMAS
PRESTON

Theodore Bliss

At home. I heard the Bells for fire.[15] Went out. Came to the Town House. The People told me there was going to be a Rumpus[16] with the Soldiers. Went to the Custom house. Saw Capt. Preston there with the Soldiers. Asked him if they were loaded. He said yes. If with Ball. He said nothing. I saw the People throw Snow Balls at the Soldiers and saw a Stick about 3 feet long strike a Soldier upon the right. He sallied[17] and then fired. A little time a second. Then the other[s] fast after one another. One or two Snow balls hit the Soldier, the stick struck, before firing. I know not whether he sallied on account of the Stick or step'd back to make ready. I did not hear any Order given by the Capt. to fire. I stood so near him I think I must have heard him if he had given an order to fire before the first firing. I never knew Capt. Preston before. I can't say whether he had a Surtout on, he was dressed in red. I know him to be the Man I took to be the Officer. The Man that fired first stood next to the Exchange lane. I saw none of the People press upon the Soldiers before the first Gun fired. I did after. I aimed a blow at him myself but did not strike him. I am sure the Captain stood before the Men when the first Gun was fired. I had no apprehension[18] the Capt. did give order to fire when the first Gun was fired. I thought, after the first Gun, the Capt. did order the Men to fire but do not certainly know.

Benjamin Burdick

When I came into King Street about 9 o'Clock I saw the Soldiers round the Centinel. I asked one if he was loaded and he said yes. I asked him if he would fire, he said yes by the Eternal God and pushd his Bayonet at me. After the firing the Captain came before the soldiers and put up their Guns with his arm and said stop firing, dont fire no more or dont fire again. I heard the word fire and took it and am certain that it came from behind the Soldiers. I saw a man passing busily behind who I took to be an Officer. The firing was a little time after. I saw some persons fall. Before the firing I saw a stick thrown at the Soldiers. The word fire I took to be a word of Command. I had in my hand a highland broad Sword which I brought from home. Upon my coming out I was told it was a wrangle[19] between the Soldiers and people, upon that I went back and got my Sword. I never used

15. Colonial American towns did not have fire departments. When fires broke out, church bells would be rung, and citizens were expected to come out with buckets to help extinguish the fire.
16. A disturbance.
17. Leaped forward suddenly.
18. Had no doubt.
19. A quarrel.

to go out with a weapon. I had not my Sword drawn till after the Soldier pushed his Bayonet at me. I should have cut his head off if he had stepd out of his Rank to attack me again. At the first firing the People were chiefly in Royal Exchange lane, there being about 50 in the Street. After the firing I went up to the Soldiers and told them I wanted to see some faces that I might swear to them another day. The Centinel in a melancholy tone said perhaps Sir you may.

Diman Morton

Between 9 and 10 I heard in my house the cry of fire but soon understood there was no fire but the Soldiers were fighting with the Inhabitants. I went to King Street. Saw the Centinel over the Gutter, his Bayonet breast high. He retired to the steps—loaded. The Boys dared him to fire. Soon after a Party came down, drew up. The Captain ordered them to load. I went across the Street. Heard one Gun and soon after the other Guns. The Captain when he ordered them to load stood in the front before the Soldiers so that the Guns reached beyond him. The Captain had a Surtout on. I knew him well. The Surtout was not red. I think cloth colour. I stood on the opposite corner of Exchange lane when I heard the Captain order the Men to load. I came by my knowledge of the Captain partly by seeing him lead the Fortification Guard.

Nathaniel Fosdick

Hearing the Bells ring, for fire I supposed I went out and came down by the Main Guard. Saw some Soldiers fixing their Bayonets on. Passed on. Went down to the Centinel. Perceived something pass me behind. Turned round and saw the Soldiers coming down. They bid me stand out of the way and damnd my blood. I told them I should not for any man. The party drew up round the Centinel, faced about and charged their Bayonets. I saw an Officer and said if there was any disturbance between the Soldiers and the People there was the Officer present who could settle it soon. I heard no Orders given to load, but in about two minutes after the Captain step'd across the Gutter. Spoke to two Men—I don't know who—then went back behind his men. Between the 4th and 5th men on the right. I then heard the word fire and the first Gun went off. In about 2 minutes the second and then several others. The Captain had a Sword in his hand. Was dressd in his Regimentals. Had no Surtout on. I saw nothing thrown nor any blows given at all. The first man on the right who fired after attempting to push the People slipped down and drop'd his Gun out of his hand. The Person who stepd in between the 4th and 5th Men I look upon it gave the orders

CHAPTER 4

WHAT REALLY
HAPPENED IN
THE BOSTON
MASSACRE?
THE TRIAL OF
CAPTAIN
THOMAS
PRESTON

to fire. His back was to me. I shall always think it was him. The Officer had a Wig on. I was in such a situation that I am as well satisfied there were no blows given as that the word fire was spoken.

Witnesses for the Prisoner (Preston)

Edward Hill

After all the firing Captain Preston put up the Gun of a Soldier who was going to fire and said fire no more you have done mischief enough.

Richard Palmes

Somebody there said there was a Rumpus in King Street. I went down. When I had got there I saw Capt. Preston at the head of 7 or 8 Soldiers at the Custom house drawn up, their Guns breast high and Bayonets fixed. Found Theodore Bliss talking with the Captain. I heard him say why don't you fire or words to that effect. The Captain answered I know not what and Bliss said God damn you why don't you fire. I was close behind Bliss. They were both in front. Then I step'd immediately between them and put my left hand in a familiar manner on the Captains right shoulder to speak to him. Mr. John Hickling then looking over my shoulder I said to Preston are your Soldiers Guns loaded. He answered with powder and ball. Sir I hope you dont intend the Soldiers shall fire on the Inhabitants. He said by no means. The instant he spoke I saw something resembling Snow or Ice strike the Grenadier[20] on the Captains right hand being the only one then at his right. He instantly stepd one foot back and fired the first Gun. I had then my hand on the Captains shoulder. After the Gun went off I heard the word fire. The Captain and I stood in front about half between the breech and muzzle of the Guns. I dont know who gave the word fire. I was then looking on the Soldier who fired. The word was given loud. The Captain might have given the word and I not distinguish it. After the word fire in about 6 or 7 seconds the Grenadier on the Captains left fired and then the others one after another. . . .

Q. Did you situate yourself before Capt. Preston, in order that you might be out of danger, in case they fired?

A. I did not apprehend myself in any danger.

Q. Did you hear Captain Preston give the word *Fire?*

A. I have told your Honors, that after the first gun was fired, I heard the word, *fire!* but who gave it, I know not.

20. A soldier in the British Grenadier Guards.

Matthew Murray

I heard no order given. I stood within two yards of the Captain. He was in front talking with a Person, I don't know who. I was looking at the Captain when the Gun was fired.

Andrew, a Negro servant to Oliver Wendell[21]

I jump'd back and heard a voice cry fire and immediately the first Gun fired. It seemed to come from the left wing from the second or third man on the left. The Officer was standing before me with his face towards the People. I am certain the voice came from beyond him. The Officer stood before the Soldiers at a sort of a corner. I turned round and saw a Grenadier who stood on the Captain's right swing his Gun and fire. . . .

Jane Whitehouse

A Man came behind the Soldiers walked backwards and forward, encouraging them to fire. The Captain stood on the left about three yards. The man touched one of the Soldiers upon the back and said fire, by God I'll stand by you. He was dressed in dark colored clothes. . . . He did not look like an Officer. The man fired directly on the word and clap on the Shoulder. I am positive the man was not the Captain. . . . I am sure he gave no orders. . . . I saw one man take a chunk of wood from under his Coat throw it at a Soldier and knocked him. He fell on his face. His firelock[22] was out of his hand. . . . This was before any firing.

Newton Prince, a Negro, a member of the South Church

Heard the Bell ring. Ran out. Came to the Chapel. Was told there was no fire but something better, there was going to be a fight. Some had buckets and bags and some Clubs. I went to the west end of the Town House where [there] were a number of people. I saw some Soldiers coming out of the Guard house with their Guns and running down one after another to the Custom house. Some of the people said let's attack the Main Guard, or the Centinel who is gone to King street. Some said for Gods sake don't lets touch the main Guard. I went down. Saw the Soldiers planted by the Custom house two deep. The People were calling them Lobsters, daring 'em to fire saying damn you why don't you fire. I saw Capt. Preston out from behind the Soldiers. In the front at the right. He spoke to some people.

---

21. Andrew was actually Wendell's slave, and Wendell appeared in court to testify that Andrew was honest and truthful.
22. Musket.

CHAPTER 4

WHAT REALLY
HAPPENED IN
THE BOSTON
MASSACRE?
THE TRIAL OF
CAPTAIN
THOMAS
PRESTON

The Capt. stood between the Soldiers and the Gutter about two yards from the Gutter. I saw two or three strike with sticks on the Guns. I was going off to the west of the Soldiers and heard the Guns fire and saw the dead carried off. Soon after the Guard Drums beat to arms.[23] The People whilst striking on the Guns cried fire, damn you fire. I have heard no Orders given to fire, only the people in general cried fire.

James Woodall

I saw one Soldier knocked down. His Gun fell from him. I saw a great many sticks and pieces of sticks and Ice thrown at the Soldiers. The Soldier who was knocked down took up his Gun and fired directly. Soon after the first Gun I saw a Gentleman behind the Soldiers in velvet of blue or black plush trimmed with gold. He put his hand toward their backs. Whether he touched them I know not and said by God I'll stand by you whilst I have a drop of blood and then said fire and two went off and the rest to 7 or 8. . . . The Captain, after, seemed shocked and looked upon the Soldiers. I am very certain he did not give the word fire.

Cross-Examination of Captain James Gifford

Q. Did you ever know an officer order men to fire with their bayonets charged?

A. No, Officers never give order to fire from charged bayonet. They would all have fired together, or most of them.

---

23. A special drumbeat that signaled soldiers to arm themselves.

Source 4 from Anthony D. Darling, *Red Coat and Brown Bess,* Historical Arms Series, No. 12 (Bloomfield, Ontario). Courtesy of Museum Restoration Service, © 1970, 1981.

4. The Position of "Bayonets Charged."

Source 5 from Robert Held, *The Age of Firearms* (N.Y.: Harper, 1957), p. 93. Drawing by Nancy Jenkins. Reprinted by permission of the author.

5. Detail of a Musket.

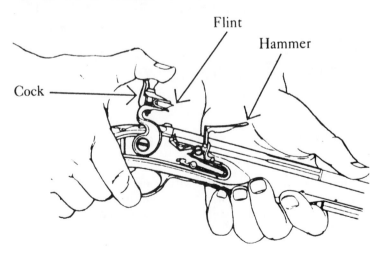

CHAPTER 4

WHAT REALLY
HAPPENED IN
THE BOSTON
MASSACRE?
THE TRIAL OF
CAPTAIN
THOMAS
PRESTON

Source 6: Library of Congress.

6. Paul Revere's Engraving of the Boston Massacre.
[*Notice how he dubbed the Custom House "Butcher's Hall."*]

✳ QUESTIONS TO CONSIDER ✳

In reconstructing the event, begin by imagining the positions of the various soldiers and witnesses. Where were the soldiers standing? Where was Captain Preston standing? Which witnesses were closest to Preston (that is, in the best positions to see and hear what happened)? Where were the other witnesses? Remember that the event took place around 9:00 P.M., when Boston was totally dark.

Next, read closely Preston's deposition and the trial testimony. What major points did Preston make in his own defense? Do you find those points plausible? More important, do the witnesses who were closest to Preston agree or disagree with his recounting, or with each other's? On what points? Be as specific as possible.

Now consider the other witnesses, those who were not so near. What did they hear? What did they see? To what degree do their testimonies agree or disagree, both with each other and with Preston and those closest to him?

Lawyers for both sides spent considerable time trying to ascertain what Captain Preston was wearing on that evening. Why did they consider this important? Based on the evidence, what do you think Preston was wearing on the evening of March 5, 1770? What conclusions could you draw from that?

The attorneys also were particularly interested in the crowd's behavior *prior to* the firing of the first musket. Why did they consider that important? How would you characterize the crowd's behavior? Are you suspicious of testimony that is at direct odds with your conclusion about this point?

Several witnesses (especially Jane Whitehouse) tell a quite different story. To what extent is her recounting of the event plausible? Is it corroborated by other witnesses?

We included Paul Revere's engraving, even though he probably was not an eyewitness, because by the time of Preston's trial, surely all the witnesses would have seen it and, more important, because later Americans have obtained their most lasting visual image of the event from that work. How does the engraving conform to what actually happened? How does it conflict with your determination of what actually took place? If there are major discrepancies, why do you think this is so? (Revere certainly knew a number of the eyewitnesses and could have ascertained the truth from them.)

After you have answered these questions and carefully weighed the eyewitnesses' evidence, answer the central question: What really happened in the Boston Massacre?

✳ EPILOGUE ✳

In his closing arguments in defense of Captain Preston, John Adams noted that the crowd not only had been harassing the soldiers but also had actually threatened to attack them. Yet there was no reliable evidence to prove that Preston had ordered his men to fire into the crowd, Adams insisted. In such doubtful cases, he concluded, the jury must vote for an acquittal. The prosecution's closing summary portrayed Preston as a murderer. The

crowd's actions, the prosecution maintained, were "a few Snow-balls, thrown by a parcel of *Boys*." According to the prosecution, the rest of the people who gathered in the square were peaceful and simply curious about what was happening.

In the trial of Thomas Preston, the jury took only three hours to reach its verdict: not guilty. Some of the jurors were sympathetic to the British, and thus were determined to find

CHAPTER 4

WHAT REALLY
HAPPENED IN
THE BOSTON
MASSACRE?
THE TRIAL OF
CAPTAIN
THOMAS
PRESTON

Preston innocent no matter what evidence was presented. Also, the leaking of the grand jury depositions ultimately helped Preston's defense, since defense attorneys knew in advance what the potentially most damaging witnesses would say in court. Finally, defense attorney John Adams's tactics (to create so much confusion in the minds of the jurors that they could not be certain what actually had taken place) were extremely effective. As it turned out, Preston had the advantage from the very beginning.

As for Thomas Preston himself, the British officer was quickly packed off to England, where he received a pension of £200 per year from the king "to compensate him for his suffering." He did not participate in the American Revolution and died in 1781. Of the eight soldiers (the sentry plus the seven men Preston brought to the Custom House), six were acquitted, and two were convicted of manslaughter and punished by being branded on the thumb. From there they disappeared into the mists of history.

On the road to the American Revolution, many events stand out as important or significant. The Boston Massacre is one such event. However, we must be careful in assessing its importance. After all, the colonists and the mother country did not finally resort to arms until five years after this dramatic event. By that time, most of those killed on King Street on March 5 had been forgotten.

Yet the Boston Massacre and other events have helped shape Americans' attitudes as to what their own Revolution was all about. To most Americans, the British were greedy, heartless tyrants who terrorized a peaceful citizenry. More than one hundred years after the event, the Massachusetts legislature authorized a memorial honoring the martyrs to be placed on the site of the so-called massacre. The Bostonians' convictions were bolstered by Irish immigrants whose ancestors had known British "tyranny" firsthand, and the Bostonians remained convinced that the American Revolution had been caused by Britain's selfishness and oppression. As we can see in the Boston Massacre, the road to the Revolution was considerably more complicated than that.

Today the site of the Boston Massacre is on a traffic island beside the Old State House (formerly called the Town House and seen in the background of Paul Revere's famous engraving) in the midst of Boston's financial district. With the exception of the State House (now a tasteful museum), the site is ringed by skyscrapers that house, among other institutions, BankBoston and Fleet Bank of Massachusetts. Thousands of Bostonians and tourists stand on the Boston Massacre site every day, waiting for the traffic to abate.

Many years ago, John Adams said that "the foundation of American independence was laid" on the evening of March 5, 1770. Although he may have overstated the case, clearly many Americans have come to see the event as a crucial one in the coming of their Revolution against Great Britain.

Now that you have examined the evidence, do you think the Boston Massacre of March 5, 1770, was a justifiable reason for rebellion against the mother country? Could the crowd action on that evening secretly have been directed by the Patriot elite, or was it a spontaneous demonstration of anti-British fury? Why was Paul Revere's engraving at such variance with what actually took place?

Few Americans have stopped to ponder what actually happened on that fateful evening. Like the American Revolution itself, the answer to that question may well be more complex than we think.

CHAPTER

5

The First American Party System: The Philadelphia Congressional Election of 1794

⁕ THE PROBLEM ⁕

For weeks prior to the federal congressional elections of 1794, the city of Philadelphia, the nation's temporary capital, was in a state of extreme political excitement. Not since the battle in Pennsylvania over the ratification of the United States Constitution had the city been the scene of such political tension and argument. The political factions that had appeared like small clouds over the first administration of President George Washington had grown immensely, and by 1794 in Philadelphia, they were on the verge of becoming distinct political parties.

Federalist Thomas Fitzsimons, a congressman since the beginning of the new government, was challenged by wealthy merchant and Democratic-Republican John Swanwick. Friends of the two contestants filled the air with vicious charges and countercharges in hopes of attracting voters to their respective candidates. Fitzsimons's supporters called Swanwick an "unstable, avaricious upstart who was unknown as a public figure until he 'herded with [the people's] enemies [the Democratic-Republicans], and became their tools.'" Swanwick's friends nicknamed Fitzsimons "Billy the Fidler" and portrayed him as a mindless sycophant of Secretary of the Treasury Alexander Hamilton. Meetings were held in various parts of the city to endorse one candidate or the other, and Philadelphia's newspapers were filled with charges and countercharges. Although many people were disturbed by these eruptions in what they considered a still fragile nation, unquestionably the growing factions had broken the political calm. Would political parties shatter the new republic or strengthen it? In Philadelphia in 1794, opinion was divided.

Challenger John Swanwick won a stunning victory over incumbent Thomas Fitzsimons, carrying seven of the city's twelve wards and collecting 56 percent of the votes cast. Federalism in Philadelphia had been dealt a severe blow.

In this chapter, you will be analyzing the evidence to determine why the lesser-known Swanwick won the election. What factors do you think were responsible for his victory? You will not be relying on just one or two types of evidence, as in previous chapters. Instead, you will be examining myriad pieces of evidence to answer that question.

✳ BACKGROUND ✳

The years between 1789 and 1801 were crucial ones for the young nation. To paraphrase a comment by Benjamin Franklin, Americans by 1789 (the first year of the Washington administration) had proved themselves remarkably adept at *destroying* governments: In the American Revolution, they had ended British rule of the thirteen colonies, and in the Constitutional Convention of 1787, they had ultimately destroyed the United States' first attempt at self-government, the Articles of Confederation. But they had yet to prove that they could *build* a central government that could protect their rights and preserve order and independence. For that reason, the period from 1789 to 1801 was important in terms of the survival of the new republic.

Many important questions confronted the nation's citizens during those difficult years. Could the new government create a financial system that would pay off the public debt; encourage commerce, manufacturing,

and investments; and establish a workable federal tax program? Was the central government strong enough to maintain order and protect citizens on the expanding frontier? Could the nation's leaders conceive a foreign policy that would maintain peace, protect international trade, and honor previous treaty commitments? To what extent should national interests overrule the interests and views of the several states?

A much larger question concerned republicanism itself. A republic is a state wherein the supreme power lies with a body of citizens who are qualified to vote. These citizens directly or indirectly chose their representatives. The head of a republic is also chosen directly or indirectly by the voters, unlike hereditary monarchs or other rulers. No republican experiment of this magnitude had ever been tried before, and a number of Americans expressed considerable fears that the experiment might not survive. Some people, such as Rufus

CHAPTER 5

THE FIRST
AMERICAN
PARTY SYSTEM:
THE
PHILADELPHIA
CONGRESSIONAL
ELECTION OF
1794

King of New York,[1] wondered whether the people possessed sufficient intelligence and virtue to be trusted to make wise decisions and choose proper leaders. Others, such as John Adams of Massachusetts, doubted that a government without titles, pomp, and ceremony would command the respect and allegiance of common men and women. Still others, such as William L. Smith of South Carolina,[2] feared that the new government was not strong enough to maintain order and enforce its will throughout the huge expanse of its domain. And finally, men such as Patrick Henry of Virginia and Samuel Adams of Massachusetts were afraid that the national government would abandon republican principles in favor of an aristocratic despotism. Hence, although most Americans were republican in sentiment, they strongly disagreed about the best ways to preserve republicanism and the dangers it faced. Some Americans openly distrusted "the people"—Alexander Hamilton of New York once called them a "headless beast." Others were wary of the government itself, even though George Washington had been chosen as its first president.

Much of the driving force of the new government came from Alexander Hamilton, the first secretary of the treasury. Hamilton used his closeness to Washington and his boldness and imagination to fashion policies that set the new nation on its initial course.

Hamilton's first task was to deal with the massive public debt. The defunct Confederation government had an unpaid debt going back to the War of Independence of more than $54 million. In addition, the various states had amassed $21.5 million of their own debts. In a bold move in 1790, the secretary of the treasury proposed that the new federal government assume the debts of both its predecessor and the states, thus binding creditors to the central government. After considerable debate and some compromising, Congress passed Hamilton's plan virtually intact. At one stroke, the "credit rating" of the new government became among the best in the world.

To pay for this ambitious proposal, as well as to give the federal government operating capital, Hamilton recommended a system of taxation that rested primarily on taxes on foreign imports (tariffs) and an excise tax on selected products manufactured in the United States (tobacco products such as snuff and pipe tobacco, sugar products, and whiskey). The excise tax, however, raised considerable protest, especially in western Pennsylvania, where whiskey was an important commodity. In that area, farmers tried to prevent the collection of the tax, a protest that eventually grew into the Whiskey Rebellion of 1794. Prompted by Hamilton, President Washington called out fifteen thousand troops and dispatched them to western Pennsylvania, but the rebellion had fizzled out by the time the troops arrived.

1. Rufus King (1755–1827) was a native of Massachusetts who moved to New York in 1786. He was a U.S. senator from 1789 to 1796 and minister to Great Britain from 1796 to 1803. He supported Alexander Hamilton's financial plans. In 1816, he was the Federalist candidate for president, losing in a landslide to James Monroe.

2. William L. Smith (1758–1812) was a Federalist congressman from South Carolina and later U.S. minister to Portugal. He was a staunch supporter of Alexander Hamilton.

Thus by 1794, when he announced that he was leaving office, Hamilton had put his "system" in place. Revenue was coming into the government coffers; the debt was being serviced; and the semipublic Bank of the United States had been created in 1791 to handle government funds, make available investment capital, and expand the nation's currency in the form of bank notes. The collapse of the Whiskey Rebellion had proved that the new federal government could enforce its laws throughout the nation. Finally, by meddling in the business of Secretary of State Thomas Jefferson, Hamilton had been able to redirect American foreign policy to a more pro-British orientation. This was because Hamilton believed the new, weak republic needed British protection of its commerce, British revenue (in the form of tariffs), and a friendly neighbor to the north (Canada, a British possession). Using the popular Washington as a shield, Hamilton became the most powerful figure in the new government and the one most responsible for making that new government work.

It is not surprising, however, that these issues and policies provoked sharp disagreements that eventually created two rival political factions: the Federalists, led by Hamilton, and the Democratic-Republicans, led by James Madison and Thomas Jefferson. Federalists generally advocated a strong central government, a broad interpretation of the Constitution, full payment of national and state debts, the establishment of the Bank of the United States, encouragement of commerce, and a pro-British foreign policy. Democratic-Republicans generally favored a central government with limited powers, a strict interpretation of the Constitution, and a pro-French foreign policy; they opposed the bank.[3]

First appearing in Congress in the early 1790s, these two relatively stable factions gradually began taking their ideas to the voters, creating the seeds of what would become by the 1830s America's first political party system. Although unanticipated by the men who drafted the Constitution, this party system became a central feature of American political life, so much so that today it would probably be impossible to conduct the affairs of government or hold elections without it.

Yet Americans of the 1790s did not foresee this evolution. Many feared the rise of these political factions, believing that the new government was not strong enough to withstand their increasingly vicious battles. Most people did not consider themselves members of either political faction, and there were no highly organized campaigns or platforms to bind voters to one faction or another. It was considered bad form for candidates openly to seek office (one *stood* for office but never *ran* for office), and appeals to voters were usually made by friends or political allies of the candidates. Different property qualifications for voting in each state and the exclusion of women limited the size of the electorate; in the 1790s, most states did not let the voters select presidential electors. All these factors impeded the

3. These are general tendencies. Some Federalists and Democratic-Republicans did not stand with their respective factions on all these issues.

CHAPTER 5

THE FIRST
AMERICAN
PARTY SYSTEM:
THE
PHILADELPHIA
CONGRESSIONAL
ELECTION OF
1794

rapid growth of the modern political party system.

Still, political battles during the 1790s grew more intense and ferocious. As Hamilton's economic plans and Federalism's pro-British foreign policy (the climax of which was the Jay Treaty of 1795) became clearer, Democratic-Republican opposition grew more bitter. Initially, the Federalists had the upper hand, perhaps because of that group's identification with President Washington. But gradually, the Democratic-Republicans gained strength, so much so that by 1800 their titular leader, Thomas Jefferson, was able to win the presidential election and put an end to Federalist control of the national government.

How can we explain the success of the Democratic-Republicans over their Federalist opponents? To answer this question, it is necessary to study in depth several key elections of the 1790s. Although many such contests are important for understanding the eventual Democratic-Republican victory in 1800, we have selected for further examination the 1794 race for the federal congressional seat from the city of Philadelphia. Because that seat had been held by a Federalist since the formation of the new government, this election was both an important test of strength of the rival Democratic-Republicans and representative of similar important contests being held in that same year in New York, Massachusetts, Maryland, and elsewhere. Because Philadelphia was the nation's capital in 1794, political party development was more advanced there than in other towns and cities of the young republic, thus offering us a harbinger of things to come nationwide.

❋ THE METHOD ❋

Observers of modern elections use a variety of methods to analyze political contests and determine why particular candidates won or lost. Some of the more important methods are as follows:

1. *Study the candidates.* How a candidate projects himself or herself may be crucial to the election's outcome. Candidates have backgrounds, voting records, personalities, and idiosyncrasies voters can assess. Candidates travel extensively, are seen by voters either in person or on television, and have several opportunities to appeal to the electorate. Postelection polls have shown that many voters respond as much to the candidates as people (a strong leader, a warm person, a confident leader, and so forth) as they do to the candidates' ideas. For example, in 1952, voters responded positively to Dwight Eisenhower, even though many were not sure of his positions on a number of important issues. Similarly, in 1980, Ronald Reagan proved to be an extremely attractive presidential candidate, as much for his personal style as for his ideas and policies.

2. *Study the issues.* Elections often give citizens a chance to clarify their thinking on leading questions of the day. To make matters more compli-

cated, certain groups (economic, ethnic, and interest groups, for example) respond to issues in different ways. The extent to which candidates can identify the issues that concern voters and can speak to these issues in an acceptable way can well mean the difference between victory and defeat. For example, in 1976, candidate Jimmy Carter was able to tap voters' post-Watergate disgust with corruption in the federal government and defeat incumbent Gerald Ford by speaking to that issue.

3. *Study the campaigns.* Success in devising and implementing a campaign strategy in modern times has been a crucial factor in the outcomes of elections. How does the candidate propose to deal with the issues? How are various interest groups to be lured under the party banner? How will money be raised, and how will it be spent? Will the candidate debate her or his opponent? Will the candidate make many personal appearances, or will she or he conduct a "front-porch" campaign? How will the candidate's family, friends, and political allies be used? Which areas (neighborhoods, regions, states, sections) will be targeted for special attention? To many political analysts, it is obvious that a number of superior candidates have been unsuccessful because of poorly run campaigns. By the same token, many less-than-superior candidates have won elections because of effectively conducted campaigns.

4. *Study the voters.* Recently, the study of elections has become more sophisticated. Polling techniques have revealed that people similar in demographic variables such as age, sex, race, income, marital status, ethnic group, and religion tend to vote in similar fashions. For example, urban blacks voted overwhelmingly for Jimmy Carter in 1976 and Al Gore in 2000.

These sophisticated polling techniques, also used for Gallup polls, Nielsen television ratings, and predicting responses to new consumer products, rest on important assumptions about human behavior. One assumption is that human responses tend to be strongly influenced (some say *determined*) by demographic variables; similar people tend to respond similarly to certain stimuli, such as candidates and campaigns. Another assumption is that these demographic patterns are constant and do not change rapidly. Finally, it is assumed that if we know how some of the people responded to certain stimuli, we can calculate how others possessing the same demographic variables will respond to those same stimuli.

Although there are many such patterns of voting behavior, they are easily observable. After the demographic variables that influence these patterns have been identified, a demographic sample of the population is created. Thus fifty white, male, middle-aged, married, Protestant, middle-income voters included in a sample might represent perhaps 100,000 people who possess these same variables. The fifty in the sample would then be polled to determine how they voted, and from this information we could infer how the 100,000 voted. Each population group in the sample would be polled in a similar fashion. By doing this, we can speculate with a fair amount of precision who voted for whom, thereby understanding which groups

CHAPTER 5

THE FIRST
AMERICAN
PARTY SYSTEM:
THE
PHILADELPHIA
CONGRESSIONAL
ELECTION OF
1794

within the voting population were attracted to which candidate. Of course, the answer to why they were attracted still must be sought with one of the other methods: studying the candidates, studying the issues, and studying the campaigns.

These four approaches are methods for analyzing modern electoral contests. In fact, most political analysts use a combination of these approaches. But can these methods be used to analyze the 1794 congressional election in Philadelphia? Neither candidate openly sought the office, and neither made appearances in his own behalf. Although there certainly were important issues, neither political faction drew up a platform to explain to voters where its candidate stood on those issues. Neither political faction conducted an organized campaign. No polls were taken to determine voter concerns. At first glance, then, it appears that most if not all of these approaches to analyzing modern elections are useless in any attempt to analyze the 1794 Fitzsimons-Swanwick congressional contest.

These approaches, however, are not as useless as they initially appear. Philadelphia in 1794 was not a large city—it contained only about 45,000 people—and many voters knew the candidates personally because both were prominent figures in the community. Their respective backgrounds were generally well known. Moreover, Fitzsimons, as the incumbent, had a voting record in Congress, and most voters would have known how Swanwick stood on the issues, either

through Swanwick's friends or through the positions he took as a member of the Democratic Society. Furthermore, the Federalists and Democratic-Republicans had taken general positions on some of the important issues. In addition, we are able to establish with a fair amount of certainty which voters cast ballots for Fitzsimons and which supported Swanwick. Finally, it is possible to identify important trends and events occurring in Philadelphia. In sum, although we might not have all the evidence we would like to have (historians almost never do), intelligent use of the evidence at our disposal enables us to analyze the 1794 election with all or most of the approaches used in analyzing modern political contests.

As you examine the various types of evidence, divide it into four groups, one group for each general approach used in analyzing elections (candidates, issues, campaigns, voters). For example, there are two excerpts from Philadelphia newspapers (one Federalist and one Democratic-Republican) dealing with the excise tax and the Whiskey Rebellion in western Pennsylvania. In what group would you put this evidence? Follow this procedure for all the evidence, noting that occasionally a piece of evidence could fit into more than one group. Such an arrangement of the evidence will give you four ways to analyze why the 1794 congressional election in Philadelphia turned out the way it did. Then, having examined and analyzed the evidence by groups, you will have to assess what principal factors explain Swanwick's upset victory.

✳ THE EVIDENCE ✳

1. The Candidates.

Thomas Fitzsimons (1741–1811) was born in Ireland and migrated to the colonies sometime before the Revolution, probably in 1765. He entered commerce as a clerk, worked his way up in his firm, and secured his position by marrying into the principal merchant's family. Fitzsimons served as a captain of the Pennsylvania militia during the Revolution, was a member of the Continental Congress in 1782 and 1783, and was elected to the Pennsylvania House of Representatives in 1786 and 1787. He was a delegate to the Constitutional Convention in 1787, was a signer of the Constitution, and was elected to the federal House of Representatives in 1788. He was a member of the Federalist inner circle in Philadelphia and a firm supporter of Alexander Hamilton's policies. He was a strong supporter of the excise tax (see approach 2 in the Questions to Consider section), was an instrumental figure in the compromise that brought the national capital to Philadelphia for ten years (1790–1800), and helped draft the legislation chartering the Bank of the United States in 1791. He was one of the original founders and directors of the Bank of North America, the director and president of the Insurance Company of North America, and a key figure in dispensing federal patronage in Philadelphia. He was a Roman Catholic.

John Swanwick (1740–1798) was born in England. He and his family arrived in the colonies in the early 1770s. His father was a wagon master and minor British government official. During the Revolution, his father became a Tory and was exiled, but John Swanwick embraced the Patriot cause. In 1777, he was hired as a clerk in the merchant firm of Robert Morris. His fluency in both French and German made him invaluable to the firm, and he quickly rose to full partnership in 1783, the firm then being known as Willing, Morris & Swanwick. In 1794, he bought out Morris's share in the company. He was one of Philadelphia's leading export merchants, was a stockholder in the Bank of North America, and held a number of minor offices (under Morris) in the Confederation government. He supported the federal Constitution and Hamilton's early financial policies. Swanwick was elected to the state legislature in 1792. By 1793, he had drifted away from Federalism and had become a Democratic-Republican. In 1794, he joined the Pennsylvania Democratic Society[4] and was soon

---

4. Democratic Societies were organizations composed principally of artisans and laborers and founded by Democratic-Republican leaders as political pressure groups against the Washington

CHAPTER 5

THE FIRST
AMERICAN
PARTY SYSTEM:
THE
PHILADELPHIA
CONGRESSIONAL
ELECTION OF
1794

made an officer. Swanwick also was an officer in a society that aided immigrants. He opposed the excise tax but thought the Whiskey Rebellion (see approach 2 in the Questions to Consider section) in western Pennsylvania was the wrong method of protest. He wrote poetry and was never admitted to Philadelphia's social elite. He owned a two-hundred-acre country estate. He was a member of the Protestant Episcopal church.

Source 2 from *Gazette of the United States* (a pro-Federalist Philadelphia newspaper), August 10, 1794.

2. A Pro-Federalist View of the Excise Tax and the Whiskey Rebellion.

. . . These Societies [the Democratic Societies], strange as it may seem, have been formed in a free elective government for the sake of *preserving liberty.* And what is the liberty they are striving to introduce? It is the liberty of reviling the rulers who are chosen by the people and the government under which they live. It is the liberty of bringing the laws into contempt and persuading people to resist them [a reference to the Whiskey Rebellion]. It is the liberty of condemning every system of Taxation because they have resolved that they will not be subject to laws—that they will not pay any taxes. To suppose that societies were formed with the purpose of opposing and with the hope of destroying government, might appear illiberal provided they had not already excited resistance to the laws and provided some of them had not publicly avowed their opinions that they *ought not to pay any taxes.* . . .

Source 3 from *General Advertiser* (a pro–Democratic-Republican Philadelphia newspaper), August 20, 1794.

3. A Pro–Democratic-Republican View of the Excise Tax and the Whiskey Rebellion.

As violent means appear the desire of high toned government men, it is to be hoped that those who derive the most benefit from our revenue laws

---

administration. Many Federalists believed that some Democratic Society members had been behind the Whiskey Rebellion. President Washington condemned the societies in 1794.

will be the foremost to march against the Western insurgents. Let stock-holders, bank directors, speculators and revenue officers arrange themselves immediately under the banner of the treasury, and try their prowess in arms as they have done in calculation. The prompt recourse to hostilities which two certain great characters [Hamilton and Washington?] are so anxious for, will, no doubt, operate upon the knights of our country to appear in military array, and then the poor but industrious citizen will not be obliged to spill the blood of his fellow citizen before conciliatory means are tried. . . .

Source 4 from Harold C. Syrett, ed., *The Papers of Alexander Hamilton* (New York: Columbia University Press, 1972), Vol. XVII, pp. 15–19.

4. Alexander Hamilton to President Washington, August 2, 1794.

If the Judge shall pronounce that the case described in the second section of that Act exists, it will follow that a competent force of Militia should be called forth and employed to suppress the insurrection and support the Civil Authority in effectuating Obedience to the laws and punishment of Offenders.

It appears to me that the very existence of Government demands this course and that a duty of the highest nature urges the Chief Magistrate to pursue it.[5]

Source 5 from Paul L. Ford, ed., *Writings of Thomas Jefferson* (New York: G. P. Putnam's Sons, 1895), Vol. VI, pp. 516–519.

5. Thomas Jefferson to James Madison, December 28, 1794.

And with respect to the transactions against the excise law [the Whiskey Rebellion], it appears to me that you are all swept away in the torrent of governmental opinion, or that we do not know what these transactions

5. The Militia Act ("that Act") of 1792 required that a Supreme Court justice ("the Judge," in this case Justice James Wilson) certify that the disturbance could not be controlled by civil authorities (as defined in the "second section" of the Act) before the president could order out the state militia. The "Chief Magistrate" referred to is President Washington. The majority of the United States Army was in the Northwest Territory, about to engage the Native Americans in the Battle of Fallen Timbers (August 20, 1794). Justice Wilson released his opinion that Washington could call out the troops on August 4, two days after Hamilton wrote to Washington.

CHAPTER 5

THE FIRST
AMERICAN
PARTY SYSTEM:
THE
PHILADELPHIA
CONGRESSIONAL
ELECTION OF
1794

have been. We know of none which, according to the definitions of the law, have been anything more than riotous. . . . The excise law is an infernal one. . . . The information of our militia, returned from the Westward, is uniform, that the people there let them pass quietly; they were objects of their laughter, not of their fear.

Sources 6 through 8 from Ronald M. Baumann, "Philadelphia's Manufacturers and the Excise Tax of 1794: The Forging of the Jeffersonian Coalition," *Pennsylvania Magazine of History and Biography* 106 (January 1982): 26, 28–30.

6. Excise Tax Statistics.

There were 23 tobacconists and snuffmakers in Philadelphia in 1794 who owned real property from £26 to over £2501 and who employed over 400 workers. In addition, there were sugar refiners in the city, and Philadelphia also had 21 brewers and distillers.

7. Swanwick and the Democratic Society.

Swanwick was a member of the Democratic Society of Pennsylvania. The society passed a resolution opposing the excise tax. President Washington condemned the society in 1794, saying that he believed that it and other similar societies were responsible for the Whiskey Rebellion. The society endorsed Swanwick in 1794 and worked actively in his behalf.

8. Philadelphia Wards, 1794.

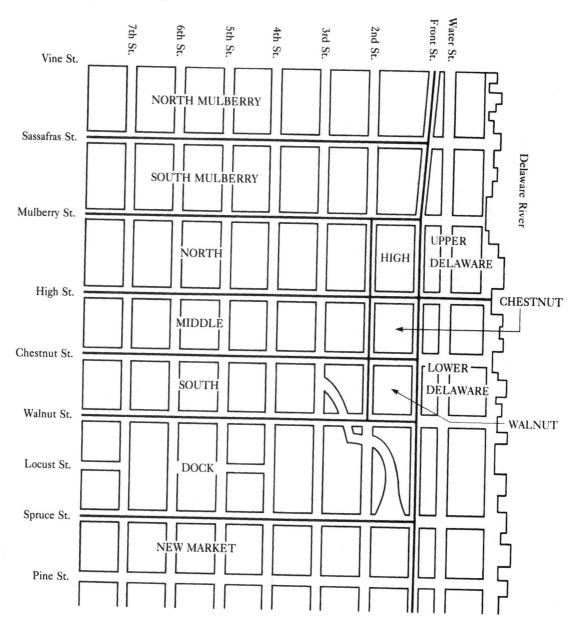

CHAPTER 5

THE FIRST
AMERICAN
PARTY SYSTEM:
THE
PHILADELPHIA
CONGRESSIONAL
ELECTION OF
1794

Source 9 from James Hardie, *The Philadelphia Directory and Register* (Philadelphia, 1794).

9. A Sample of Occupations by Ward (Males Only), Philadelphia, 1794.[6]

	Upper Delaware	North Mulberry	South Mulberry	High	North	Chestnut	Middle	Walnut	South	Dock	New Market	Lower Delaware	Occupation Totals
Gentleman	3	22	31	7	21	1	15	2	8	17	25	5	157
Merchant	76	47	65	47	90	38	63	20	26	101	83	43	699
Artisan	95	353	338	333	183	46	164	48	73	131	222	71	1,757
Laborer	18	93	103	10	70	7	27	8	12	38	56	1	443
Shopkeeper	13	24	39	24	44	9	23	4	6	7	35	8	236
Inn and tavern keeper	8	17	12	3	13	5	22	3	4	12	11	6	116
Captain	6	17	14	0	3	0	1	4	1	7	37	0	90
Government employee	2	12	13	0	16	2	13	1	7	14	18	0	98
Seaman	7	15	5	1	3	1	2	2	2	9	21	2	70
Teacher	1	5	12	0	6	0	2	0	3	5	6	0	40
Doctor	1	3	10	3	5	3	2	3	6	10	9	0	55
Grocer	10	22	20	3	37	2	20	0	5	25	34	6	184
Clergy	0	5	8	0	0	0	3	0	3	4	4	0	27
Lawyer	0	3	11	2	1	0	4	1	13	12	5	1	53
Clerk	5	16	18	3	7	1	12	1	4	10	12	1	90
Broker	0	1	2	0	3	2	4	4	3	2	1	0	22
Other	1	5	0	1	3	1	0	0	1	1	2	0	15
Unknown	1	7	14	1	1	0	2	0	1	2	8	0	37
Ward totals	247	667	715	138	506	118	379	101	178	407	589	144	

6. Poor people were notoriously undercounted in city directories, as were nonpermanent residents, such as seamen.

Sources 10 and 11 from Billy G. Smith, *The "Lower Sort": Philadelphia's Laboring People, 1750–1800* (Ithaca, N.Y.: Cornell University Press, 1990), pp. 101, 110, 114, 116, 121, 232. For household budgets, Smith calculated the costs of food, rent, fuel, and clothing and then established how much of these items were consumed.

10. Cost of Living Index,[7] Philadelphia (Base Year 1762 = 100).

Year	Food	Rent	Firewood	Clothing	Household Budget
1788	99		74	139	123
1789	107	165[8]	76	82	115
1790	134		79	92	131
1791	130		97	92	131
1792	131		106	110	136
1793	143		111	119	144
1794	161		130	137	158

11. Index of Real Wages,[9] Philadelphia (Base Year 1762 = 100).

Year	Laborers	Sailors	Tailors	Shoemakers
1788	95	—	68	63
1789	77	—	69	63
1790	66	59	76	44
1791	74	59	63	48
1792	88	70	80	55
1793	81	84	57	143
1794	90	161	78	·77

7. An index number is a statistical measure designed to show changes in a variable (such as wages or prices) over time. A base year is selected and given the value of 100. The index for subsequent years is then expressed as a percentage of the base year.
8. No other rent index is available for 1788 through 1794. The rent index in 1798, however, was 184.
9. Real wages are wages that are actually paid, adjusted for the cost of living. To find a person's real wage, one would take the index of that person's actual wage divided by the index of household budget and multiply that figure by 100. Real wages allow us to see whether a person's wages are exceeding or falling behind the cost of living.

CHAPTER 5

THE FIRST
AMERICAN
PARTY SYSTEM:
THE
PHILADELPHIA
CONGRESSIONAL
ELECTION OF
1794

Source 12 from James Hardie, *The Philadelphia Directory and Register* (Philadelphia, 1794).

12. First-Person Account of the Yellow Fever.

Having mentioned this disorder to have occasioned great devastation in the year 1793, a short account of it may be acceptable to several of our readers. . . .

This disorder made its first appearance toward the latter end of July, in a lodging house in North Water Street,[10] and for a few weeks seemed entirely confined to that vicinity. Hence it was generally supposed to have been imported and not generated in the city. This was the opinion of Doctors Currie, Cathrall and many others. It was however combated by Dr. Benjamin Rush, who asserts that the contagion was generated from the stench of a cargo of damaged coffee. . . .

But from whatever fountain we trace this poisoned stream, it has destroyed the lives of many thousands—and many of those of the most distinguished worth. . . . During the month of August the funerals amounted to upwards of three hundred. The disease had then reached the central streets of the city and began to spread on all sides with the greatest rapidity. In September its malignance increased amazingly. Fear pervaded the stoutest heart, flight became general, and terror was depicted on every countenance. In this month 1,400 more were added to the list of mortality. The contagion was still progressive and towards the end of the month 90 & 100 died daily. Until the middle of October the mighty destroyer went on with increasing havoc. From the 1st to the 17th upwards of 1,400 fell victims to the tremendous malady. From the 17th to the 30th the mortality gradually decreased. In the whole month, however, the dead amounted to upwards of 2,000—a dreadful number, if we consider that at this time near one half of the inhabitants had fled. Before the disorder became so terrible, the appearance of Philadelphia must to a stranger have seemed very extraordinary. The garlic, which chewed as a preventative[,] could be smelled at several yards distance, whilst other[s] hoped to avoid infection by a recourse to smelling bottles, handkerchiefs dipped in vinegar, camphor bags, &c. . . .

During this melancholy period the city lost ten of her most valuable physicians, and most of the others were sick at different times. The number of deaths in all amounted to 4041.[11]

10. See Source 8. Working-class areas were particularly hard hit. On Fetter Lane (near North Water Street), 50 percent of the residents died. See Smith, *The "Lower Sort,"* pp. 25–26.
11. The population of Philadelphia (including its suburbs) was 42,444 in 1790.

Sources 13 and 14 from L. H. Butterfield, ed., *Letters of Benjamin Rush*[12] (Princeton, N.J.: Published for the American Philosophical Society, 1951), Vol. II, pp. 644–645, 657–658.

13. Benjamin Rush to Mrs. Rush, August 29, 1793, on the Yellow Fever.

Be assured that I will send for you if I should be seized with the disorder, for I conceive that it would be as much your duty not to desert me in that situation as it is now mine not to desert my patients. . . .

Its symptoms are very different in different people. Sometimes it comes on with a chilly fit and a high fever, but more frequently it steals on with headache, languor, and sick stomach. These symptoms are followed by stupor, delirium, vomiting, a dry skin, cool or cold hands and feet, a feeble slow pulse, sometimes below in frequency the pulse of health. The eyes are at first suffused with blood, they afterwards become yellow, and in most cases a yellowness covers the whole skin on the 3rd or 4th day. Few survive the 5th day, but more die on the 2 and 3rd days. In some cases the patients possess their reason to the last and discover much less weakness than in the last stage of common fevers. One of my patients stood up and shaved himself on the morning of the day he died. Livid spots on the body, a bleeding at the nose, from the gums, and from the bowels, and a vomiting of black matter in some instances close the scenes of life. The common remedies for malignant fevers have all failed. Bark, wine, and blisters make no impression upon it. Baths of hot vinegar applied by means of blankets, and the cold bath have relieved and saved some. . . .

This day I have given mercury, and I think with some advantage. . . .

12. Dr. Benjamin Rush (1745–1813) was a Pennsylvanian who was graduated from the College of New Jersey (Princeton, 1760) and studied medicine at the College of Philadelphia and the University of Edinburgh. Practicing medicine in Philadelphia, he was elected to the Continental Congress in 1776 and was a signer of the Declaration of Independence. He supported the ratification of the Constitution. By 1794, he had changed allegiances and was considered a Democratic-Republican. He participated in many reform movements, including the abolition of slavery, the end to capital punishment, temperance, an improved educational system, and prison reform. His protégé, Dr. Michael Leib, was extremely active in Democratic-Republican politics. Most physicians in Philadelphia in 1794 were Federalists. The majority fled the city when the fever broke out. Of the doctors who stayed, Rush was one of the most prominent.

CHAPTER 5

THE FIRST
AMERICAN
PARTY SYSTEM:
THE
PHILADELPHIA
CONGRESSIONAL
ELECTION OF
1794

14. Benjamin Rush to Mrs. Rush, September 10, 1793, on the Yellow Fever.

My dear Julia,

Hereafter my name should be Shadrach, Meshach, or Abednego, for I am sure the preservation of those men from death by fire was not a greater miracle than my preservation from the infection of the prevailing disorder. I have lived to see the close of another day, more awful than any I have yet seen. Forty persons it is said have been buried this day, and I have visited and prescribed for more than 100 patients. Mr. Willing is better, and Jno. Barclay is out of danger. Amidst my numerous calls to the wealthy and powerful, *I do not forget the poor,* . . .[13]

15. Yellow Fever Committee.

Of the eighteen people cited for contributions to the Citizens' Committee on the Fever, nine were definitely Democratic-Republicans. Of the remaining nine, only one was an avowed Federalist.

Source 16 from J. H. Powell, *Bring Out Your Dead: The Great Plague of Yellow Fever in Philadelphia in 1793* (Philadelphia: University of Pennsylvania Press, 1949), p. 123.

16. Federalist Comment on Rush.

Rush "is become the darling of the common people and his humane fortitude and exertions will render him deservedly dear."

13. Italics added.

17. Sampling of Deaths from Yellow Fever, Philadelphia, 1793 Epidemic.[14]

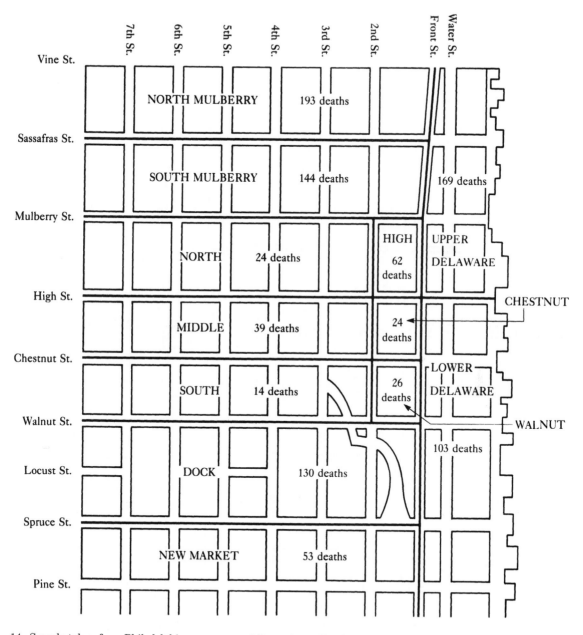

14. Sample taken from Philadelphia newspapers. After a time, officials simply stopped recording the names of those who died, except for prominent citizens. Therefore, although James Hardie reported that 4,041 people had died, one scholar has estimated the death toll at as high as 6,000, roughly one out of every seven Philadelphians.

CHAPTER 5

THE FIRST
AMERICAN
PARTY SYSTEM:
THE
PHILADELPHIA
CONGRESSIONAL
ELECTION OF
1794

Source 18 from Baumann, "Philadelphia's Manufacturers and the Excise Tax of 1794," p. 27.

18. Congressional Election, Philadelphia, 1794.[15]

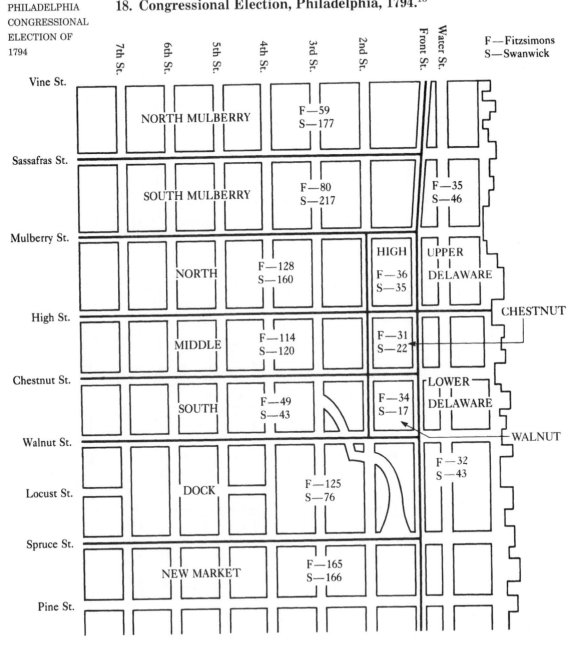

15. Total votes: Swanwick, 1,122; Fitzsimons, 888.

✳ QUESTIONS TO CONSIDER ✳

Philadelphia in 1794 was a prosperous, bustling city filled with small shops, market halls, inns, and merchants' warehouses. Houses ranged from imposing two-story brick and stone edifices to cramped wood-frame buildings containing one or two families and frequently boarders as well. The population was both ethnically and racially diverse; in the 1790s, one in ten residents was a free black. Laid out in a grid pattern of square blocks and straight streets along the Delaware River, Philadelphia was a "walking city" where most people lived within a six-to-ten-block area from the docks. Uncontrolled business cycles, high infant and child mortality rates, and recurring epidemics such as yellow fever made life unstable and uncertain for most residents.

No single method of analyzing elections will give you the answer to the central question of why John Swanwick was able to defeat Thomas Fitzsimons. Instead, you must use all four approaches, grouping the evidence by approach and determining what each approach tells you about why the election turned out as it did.

Before examining each group of evidence, however, try to discover who tended to vote for each candidate. Source 9 shows occupations by ward. Although there are exceptions, occupations can often be used to establish a person's wealth and status. Today many people introduce themselves by telling their name, occupation, and address. What are these people really saying? Examine carefully the occupational makeup of each ward. This can

be done by matching the figures in Source 9 to the map in Source 8. For example, look at the artisan (skilled labor) population. Only a very few lived in High, Chestnut, and Walnut wards, areas that tended to be more upper-class neighborhoods. Instead, most artisans lived on the city's fringes, in North Mulberry, South Mulberry, North, Middle, Dock, and New Market wards. Follow the same procedure for merchants, laborers, shopkeepers, and so on. Although early American cities were not as residentially segregated by socioeconomic class as today's cities, you will be able to see general tendencies that will allow you to characterize each of Philadelphia's wards in 1794.

Keeping those characterizations in mind (or by using notes), turn to Source 18, the election results. How could you use these three sources (8, 9, and 18) to determine who tended to support Fitzsimons and Swanwick? Historians call this process *overlaying evidence* because they are overlaying one source on another.

Pennsylvania had one of the most liberal suffrage laws in the nation. All adult white males who had lived in the state for two years preceding an election *and* had paid any state or county taxes could vote. Of the occupational groups listed in Source 9, only laborers and seamen contained large percentages of men who could not vote. Keep this in mind as you overlay the evidence.

Having established who tended to vote for Fitzsimons and who tended to vote for Swanwick, you are ready to

CHAPTER 5

THE FIRST
AMERICAN
PARTY SYSTEM:
THE
PHILADELPHIA
CONGRESSIONAL
ELECTION OF
1794

answer the question of why one of the candidates was more appealing to the majority of Philadelphia voters. Here is where the four major approaches explained earlier can be brought into play.

1. *Candidates.* Source 1 supplies biographical information about the two candidates. Do not neglect to study the additional material on Swanwick (Source 7); this is material that voters not personally acquainted with the candidates still would have known. What are the significant points of comparison and contrast between the candidates?

One significant point of difference is religion. Fitzsimons was a Roman Catholic, and Swanwick belonged to the Protestant Episcopal church. Most of Philadelphia's voters were Protestant, the two largest denominations being Lutheran and Quaker. Very few voters belonged to either the Roman Catholic or the Episcopal church. Was religion a factor in this election? How can you prove that it was or was not?

One interesting point in Swanwick's biographical sketch is that, although wealthy, he was never admitted to Philadelphia's social elite circles, a fact that some of the voters probably knew. Do you think this was an important consideration in the voters' minds? How would you prove your point?

2. *Issues.* There were a number of issues in this election, and it was fairly clear how each faction stood on those issues. Two of the most important issues were the excise tax (Sources 2, 3, 6, and 7) and the Whiskey Rebellion (Sources 4 and 5).

As noted above, to raise money, Hamilton proposed, Congress passed, and President Washington signed a bill placing an excise tax on selected domestic manufactured products, an act that eventually touched off the Whiskey Rebellion of 1794. Indeed, there is some evidence that Hamilton actually anticipated such a reaction to the excise tax when he proposed it, convinced that the crushing of such an uprising would prove that the new government had the power to enforce its laws. When examining the impact of the excise tax and the Whiskey Rebellion on the election, use the sources to answer the following questions:

a. Which groups in Philadelphia did the excise tax affect most? How? Remember to think of people as both workers and consumers.

b. How did the candidates stand on the excise tax?

c. Which groups of Philadelphians would have been likely to favor their respective positions?

d. How did each faction stand on the Whiskey Rebellion? (See Sources 2 through 5.)

e. How did the candidates stand on this issue?

f. Which groups of Philadelphians would have been likely to favor their respective positions?

3. *Campaign.* Although there were a few mass meetings and some distribution of literature, there was no real campaign in the modern sense. In the absence of an organized campaign, how did voters make up their minds?

4. *Voters.* At the time of the election, other important trends in Philadel-

phia might have influenced voters. For example, review the evidence on the cost of living and on real wages compiled by Billy G. Smith (Sources 10 and 11). On cost of living, if the cost of living index in 1762 was 100, were the indexes for food, firewood, and clothing rising or falling? Using household budget indexes, how much more expensive was it to live in Philadelphia in 1794 than it was in 1788 (158 minus 123 equals 35, divided by 123 equals 28.5 percent)?

Remember that real wages are actual wages adjusted for the cost of living. As you can see in Source 11, tailors and shoemakers (called "cordwainers" at this time) experienced modest gains in real wages from 1788 to 1794. Note, however, that real wages were extremely volatile and could fluctuate wildly. For example, real wages for shoemakers fell 30.2 percent between 1788 and 1790, then began a gradual recovery, due in part to a protective tariff on shoes passed by Congress in 1790. In 1793, the retail prices for shoes jumped 64.8 percent, largely because war in Europe created a great international demand for American shoes. As a result, real wages for shoemakers spiraled from 55 to 143, a gain of 160 percent. But in 1794, real wages dropped 46.2 percent. As for sailors, their wages skyrocketed from 1793 to 1794 (almost 80 percent). Keep in mind, however, that the war between Great Britain and France that broke out in 1793 made that occupation an extremely dangerous one. In sum, can the cost of living and real wage indexes give you any clues to how these occupational groups might have voted?

The pieces of evidence that appear at first glance to have nothing to do with the Fitzsimons-Swanwick contest are Sources 12 through 17, on the 1793 yellow fever epidemic that virtually paralyzed the city. After all, the fever broke out more than a year prior to the election and was over by the end of October 1793. Most of those who had fled the city had returned and were in Philadelphia during the "campaign" and voting.

Yet a closer analysis of Sources 12 through 17 offers some fascinating insights, although you will have to use some historical imagination to relate them to the election. To begin with, James Hardie (Source 12) reported that the fever initially appeared "in a lodging house in North Water Street; and for a few weeks seemed entirely confined to that vicinity." Where was North Water Street (Source 8)? Who would have lived there (Sources 8 and 9)? So long as the fever was confined to that area, Hardie does not appear to have been overly concerned. What does that tell you? Hardie further reported that almost half the total population had fled the city. Which groups would have been most likely to flee (approximately 20,000 of Philadelphia's 45,000 fled)? Who could not leave? If businessmen closed their businesses when they fled, what was the situation of workers who could not afford to leave? What impact might this have had on the election a year later?

Although perhaps a bit too graphic, Dr. Benjamin Rush's August 29, 1793, letter to his wife (Source 13) is valuable because it establishes the fact that Rush, although he could have abandoned the sick, refused to do so

CHAPTER 5

THE FIRST
AMERICAN
PARTY SYSTEM:
THE
PHILADELPHIA
CONGRESSIONAL
ELECTION OF
1794

and stayed in Philadelphia. This was an act of remarkable courage, for no one knew what caused yellow fever and people believed that it struck its victims almost completely at random. Consider, however, not what Rush *says* in Source 13 but rather *who he was*. Refer again to footnote 12. Also examine Rush's letter of September 10, 1793 (Source 14), especially the last sentence. Do you think Rush might have been a factor in the Fitzsimons-Swanwick election? In what way?

Sources 15 and 16 attempt to tie the fever epidemic to party politics in Philadelphia. How might Philadelphia voters have reacted to the two parties (the Federalists and the Democratic-Republicans) after the fever? How might the voters have reacted to Dr. Rush?

Finally, examine Source 17 with some care. Where did the fever victims tend to reside? What types of people lived in those wards?

Now you are ready to answer the question of why the 1794 congressional election in Philadelphia turned out the way it did (Source 18). Make sure, however, that your opinion is solidly supported by evidence.

❋ EPILOGUE ❋

As the temporary national capital in 1794, Philadelphia was probably somewhat more advanced than the rest of the nation in the growth of political factions. However, by the presidential election of 1800, most of the country had become involved in the gradual process of party building. By that time, the Democratic-Republicans were the dominant political force, aided by more aggressive campaign techniques, their espousal of a limited national government (which most Americans preferred), their less elitist attitudes, and their ability to brand their Federalist opponents as aristocrats and pro-British monocrats.[16] Although Federalism retained considerable strength in New England and the Middle States, by 1800 it no longer was a serious challenge to the Democratic-Republicans on the national level.

For his part, John Swanwick never saw the ultimate triumph of Democratic-Republicanism because he died in the 1798 yellow fever epidemic in Philadelphia. Fitzsimons never again sought political office, preferring to concentrate his energies on his already successful mercantile and banking career. Hamilton died in a duel with Aaron Burr in 1804. After he left the presidency in 1809, Jefferson retired to his estate, Monticello, to bask in the glories of being an aging founding father. He died in 1826 at the age of eighty-three.

By 1826, many of the concerns of the Federalist era had been resolved. The War of 1812 had further secured

16. A monocrat is a person who favors a monarchy. It was considered a disparaging term in the United States during the period.

American independence, and the death of the Federalist faction had put an end to the notion of government by an entrenched (established) and favored elite. At the same time, however, new issues had arisen to test the durability of the republic and the collective wisdom of its people. After a brief political calm, party battles once again were growing fiercer, as the rise of Andrew Jackson threatened to split the brittle Jeffersonian coalition. Westward expansion was carrying Americans into territories owned by other nations, and few doubted that an almost inevitable conflict lay ahead. American cities, such as Philadelphia, were growing in both population and socioeconomic problems. The twin specters of slavery and sectional conflict were claiming increasing national attention. Whether the political system fashioned in the 1790s could address these crucial issues and trends and at the same time maintain its republican principles was a question that would soon have to be addressed.

Land, Growth, and Justice:
The Removal
of the Cherokees

✳ THE PROBLEM ✳

In the spring of 1838, General Winfield Scott and several units of the U.S. Army (including artillery regiments) were deployed to the Southeast to collect Native Americans known as Cherokees[1] and remove them to lands west of the Mississippi River. Employing bilingual Cherokees to serve as interpreters at $2.50 per day, Scott constructed eleven makeshift stockades and on May 23 began rounding up Native Americans and herding them into these temporary prisons. According to John G. Burnett, a soldier who participated in the removal,

> Men working in the fields were arrested and driven to the stockades. Women were dragged from their homes by soldiers whose language they could not understand. Children were often separated from their parents and driven into the stockades with the sky for a blanket and the earth for a pillow. And often the old and infirm were prodded with bayonets to hasten them to the stockades.[2]

Just behind the soldiers came whites, eager to claim homesteads, search for gold, or pick over the belongings that

1. The Cherokees referred to themselves as Ani'Yun'wiya ("principal people"). The origin of the term *Cherokee* is unknown, but the name almost certainly was given to them by Native American neighbors. See Russell Thornton, *The Cherokees: A Population History* (Lincoln: University of Nebraska Press, 1990), pp. 7–8.

2. See John G. Burnett, "The Cherokee Removal Through the Eyes of a Private Soldier," *Journal of Cherokee Studies* 3 (1978): 180–185.

the Cherokees did not have time to carry away.

On August 23, 1838, the first of thirteen parties of Cherokees began their forced march to the West, arriving in what had been designated as Indian Territory (later Oklahoma) on January 17, 1839. With some traveling by boat while others journeyed overland, a total of approximately thirteen thousand Cherokees participated in what became known as the Trail of Tears. (See Map 1.) It has been estimated that over four thousand died in the squalid stockades or along the way.[3] But recent research has determined that the figure may have been higher than that, in part because of shoddy record keeping and in part because numerous Cherokees died in an epidemic almost immediately on reaching their destination. In addition, conflict broke out between new arrivals and those Cherokees (around six thousand) who had earlier moved. And, once in the West, those who opposed removal took out their vengeance on the leaders of the Cherokee removal faction. Cherokee advocates of removal (including leaders Major Ridge, John Ridge, Elias Boudinot, and Thomas Watie) were murdered.[4]

The forced removal of the Cherokees marked the end of a debate that was older than the United States itself. As white populations mushroomed and settlements moved ever westward, the question of how to deal with Native Americans came up again and again, especially when Native American peoples refused to sell or give their lands to whites by treaty.

In 1829, Andrew Jackson became president. In his view, Native Americans should be removed from their lands in order to make way for expanding white settlements. And although he was not known as an accomplished speaker or writer (his spelling was nearly as poor as that of George Washington), in his First Annual Message to Congress (see Source 1 in the Evidence section) Jackson almost surely was the most articulate voice in favor of removal.[5] On the other hand, throughout the history of this debate, other voices from both white and Native American people were raised in opposition to removal.

Your tasks in this chapter are to examine and analyze the principal arguments both in favor of and opposed to the removal of the Cherokees. What were the strengths and weaknesses of each position?

3. The official U.S. Army count of those removed to Indian Territory totaled 13,149, of whom 11,504 actually arrived in the West. Based on the tribal census of 1835, at least 2,000 died in the stockades.

4. See Russell Thornton, "The Demography of the Trail of Tears Period: A New Estimate of Cherokee Population Losses," in William L. Anderson, ed., *Cherokee Removal: Before and After* (Athens, Ga.: University of Georgia Press, 1991), pp. 75–95.

5. From George Washington to Woodrow Wilson, no president of the United States appeared in person before Congress. All communications between the president and Congress were conducted in writing.

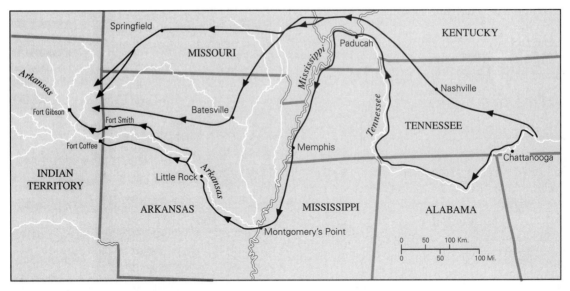

Map 1. The Trail of Tears, 1838–1839.
Adapted from Grace Steele Woodward, *The Cherokees* (Norman: University of
Oklahoma Press, 1963), pp. 206–207.

✳ BACKGROUND ✳

The origins of the Cherokees are clouded in mystery. Linguistically related to the Iroquois of New England and northern New York, it is thought that the Cherokees migrated south into present-day Georgia, Tennessee (itself a derivation of the name of a Cherokee town, Tanasi), South Carolina, and North Carolina and settled the area somewhere between the years 600 and 1000, centuries before the first regular contact with white people, in the late 1600s. Spread across much of the Southeast, the Cherokees were divided into three main groups: the Lower Towns, along the upper Savannah River in South Carolina; the Middle Towns, along the Little Tennessee River and its tributaries in western North Carolina; and the

Overhill Towns, in eastern Tennessee and extreme western North Carolina. (See Map 2.)

Sometime before their regular contact with Europeans, the Cherokees became sedentary. Women performed most of the farm duties, raising corn and beans, while men hunted deer and turkey and caught fish to complete their diet. The Cherokees built towns organized around extended families. Society was *matrilineal*, meaning that property and position passed from generation to generation through the mother's side of the family. Each town theoretically was autonomous, and there were no leaders (or chiefs, in European parlance) who ruled over all the towns. Local leaders led by persuasion and example, and all adults, in-

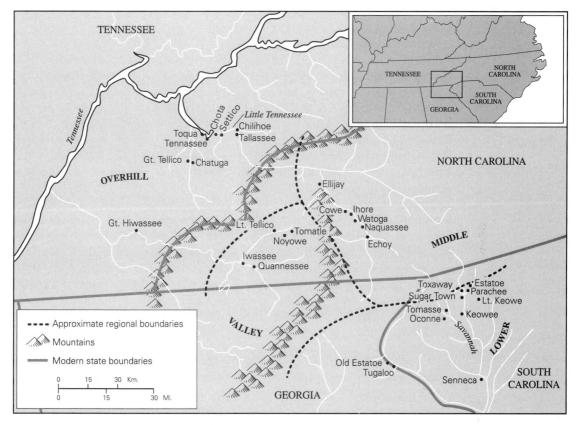

Map 2. Cherokee Settlements, 1775.

From Duane H. King, ed., *The Cherokee Nation: A Troubled History* (Knoxville: University of Tennessee Press, 1979), p. 50.

cluding women, could speak in town councils. Indeed, Cherokee governing practices were considerably more democratic and consensual than the Europeans' hierarchical ways.

Initial contacts with Europeans were devastating. Europeans brought with them measles and smallpox, against which Native Americans were not immune. Also, Cherokees were attracted to European goods such as fabrics, metal hoes and hatchets, firearms, and (tragically) alcohol. In order to acquire these goods, Cherokees traded deerskins for them. By the early 1700s, Cherokees were killing an average of fifty thousand deer each year to secure their hides for barter, and estimates are that by 1735 over 1 million deer had been killed, almost certainly depleting the herds. Gradually, the Cherokees were losing their self-sufficiency and becoming increasingly dependent on European goods.

With European colonization and expansion in North America, the Chero-

CHAPTER 6

LAND, GROWTH,
AND JUSTICE:
THE REMOVAL
OF THE
CHEROKEES

kees inevitably became swept up into European peoples' wars. Initially siding with the British against the French, the Cherokees turned against the British when the colonial governor of South Carolina called thirty-two chieftains to a conference and then killed twenty-nine of them. The British retaliated against a Cherokee outburst by destroying the Lower Towns, killing over one hundred Cherokee warriors, and driving the survivors into the mountains. In the American Revolution, the Cherokees, hoping to stem white western expansion, again sided with the British. American patriots destroyed over fifty Cherokee towns, scalping men and women indiscriminately.

After the American Revolution, the new U.S. government pursued a policy of attempting to "civilize" the Cherokees. Aided by government Indian agent Return J. Meigs (who lived with the Cherokees from 1801 to 1823) and a number of missionaries, the Cherokee Nation was able to adapt to many of the "white man's ways." Anglo-European gender roles were adopted, as men gave up hunting and took over agriculture from women. Plows, spinning wheels, and looms were introduced, and Cherokee women took up the making of cloth and clothing. As it did with white settlers, landownership and agriculture produced a class system. By 1824, the most affluent Cherokees owned 1,277 African American slaves, and most Cherokees were living in log homes similar to those of their white neighbors.

Cherokees were becoming "civilized" culturally as well. Mission boarding schools, supported by white contributions, dotted the landscape, and Cherokee children learned to read, write, and compute and also learned Anglo-European gender roles. Around 1809, the Native American Sequoyah began devising a Cherokee alphabet (he called it a syllabary) of eighty-five phonetic symbols that allowed Cherokees to become literate in their own language. In 1828, the first edition of the newspaper the *Cherokee Phoenix* appeared, edited by Cherokee Elias Boudinot.

Governmental and political forms also were modeled after Anglo-European institutions. A Native American police force was instituted in 1808, and in the following year a detailed census was taken. In 1827, a formal constitution was adopted, modeled on the United States Constitution, setting up a representative government and courts for the Cherokee Nation. Women, who were more nearly equal to men in traditional Cherokee society, saw their position deteriorate, as they were prohibited from voting or serving as representatives by the new constitution. In many ways, then, Cherokees had remade their economy, society, culture, and government. And although some people clung stubbornly to the old ways, Cherokee adaptation was generally widespread.

As it turned out, adaptation to the white persons' ways would not save the Cherokees. In 1802, the U.S. government and the state of Georgia reached an agreement whereby the federal government promised to "extinguish, for the use of Georgia, as early as the same can be peaceably obtained upon reasonable terms . . . the Indian titles to all lands lying within the limits of the state."[6] The Louisiana Purchase (1804) acquired territory in the West that theoretically could be used for the relocation of the eastern Native Americans. Slowly the federal government began purchasing Cherokee lands in Tennessee, southern Kentucky, northern Alabama, South Carolina, and northeastern Georgia. In 1818, a trickle of Cherokees began to migrate to lands west of the Mississippi River.

The vast majority of Cherokees, however, refused to move. They had built farms, sawmills, tanneries, ferries, stores, and towns. The Treaty of Hopewell (1785) had promised that they would be able to hold onto their land "forever." In addition, Christian missionaries who lived among the Cherokees strengthened their resolve to resist removal, believing that the Cherokees were making great strides at becoming "civilized" where they were.

Yet one Cherokee chieftain's 1775 statement turned out to be prophetic: "Indian Nations before the Whites are like balls of snow before the sun."[7] In 1828, three events took place that would change the Cherokee Nation forever. First, gold was discovered in Cherokee lands in Georgia, setting off a rush of around four thousand whites into Cherokee territory.[8] Cherokees

fought back by attacking and burning the houses of the white prospectors, and federal troops had to be dispatched to restore order. Then, in November 1828, Tennessean Andrew Jackson was elected president. Although Cherokees had been his allies in the earlier war against the Creeks, Jackson had made no secret of the fact that he strongly favored the removal of all Native Americans to lands west of the Mississippi River. As a person who had made a great deal of money in land speculation, it is possible that Jackson recognized the potential profits that could be made by acquiring Cherokee lands and was interested in helping other land speculators.

With Jackson as president, the state of Georgia realized that it could now move with impunity. In December 1828, over three months before Jackson's inauguration, the Georgia legislature passed a bill declaring that as of June 1, 1830, all Cherokee territory would be subject to Georgia laws, and Cherokee laws (including their constitution) would be null and void. The Georgia legislature also made provisions for a lottery to distribute Cherokee lands to whites. In 1829, the Georgia legislature passed an act requiring all whites living in Cherokee territory to secure licenses, an obvious attempt to expel white missionaries who, many Georgians believed, were urging the Native Americans to resist white encroachment.

In his First Annual Message to Congress of December 8, 1829 (see

6. Quoted in Samuel Carter III, *Cherokee Sunset, A Nation Betrayed: A Narrative of Travail and Triumph, Persecution and Exile* (Garden City, N.Y.: Doubleday, 1976), p. 28.

7. J. G. M. Ramsey, *Annals of Tennessee* (Charleston, S.C.: Walker and James, 1853), pp. 117–118.

8. Some of those who made a great deal of money from the Georgia gold rush included the South Carolina political leader John C. Calhoun, his son-in-law Thomas G. Clemson

(who used some of the profits to found Clemson College in South Carolina), and future governor of New York and Democratic presidential candidate Samuel J. Tilden.

CHAPTER 6

LAND, GROWTH,
AND JUSTICE:
THE REMOVAL
OF THE
CHEROKEES

Source 1), President Jackson made his case for the "voluntary" removal of all Native Americans east of the Mississippi River.[9] Responding to the president's message, in February 1830 the House of Representatives took up the Indian Removal Bill. The bill, however, reignited a furious debate both in Congress and among the general public. Hundreds of petitions were sent to Congress, the majority from religious groups and benevolent societies opposed to removal. Many congressional opponents of the bill were genuinely concerned with the welfare of Native Americans, but at least an equal number were Jackson's political opponents who sought to embarrass the president. On April 23, 1830, the Senate approved the Indian Removal Bill by a vote of 28–19, the House following suit on May 24 by the close margin of 102–97. Jackson signed the bill on May 28, 1830.[10] The act empowered the president to trade land in the West for lands on which Native Americans east of the Mississippi then resided, to pay Native Americans for improvements they had made to lands they were giving up, to assist and protect Native Americans during their migration, and to superintend and care for them once they had reached their destinations.

Cherokees were divided over how to respond to the imminent loss of their lands. Believing the fight was over, about two thousand voluntarily moved west to join some Cherokees who had moved even earlier. But the majority resisted removal, appealing twice to the U.S. Supreme Court. In *Cherokee Nation v. Georgia* (1831), Chief Justice John Marshall dismissed the Cherokees' suit on technical grounds.[11] In his written opinion, however, he hinted that he might be sympathetic to the Cherokees' cause if they could bring a case to the Supreme Court in another way, and the next year, in *Worcester v. Georgia* (1832), Marshall declared that Georgia's laws did not extend to the Cherokees.[12] But President Jackson refused to enforce the Court's decision, and many Cherokees came to realize that their cause was lost.

In 1835, a minority of Cherokees signed the Treaty of New Echota whereby the Cherokees promised that, in return for $5 million and land in the West, they would give up all claims to lands they occupied in Georgia, North Carolina, Tennessee, and Alabama.[13]

9. Approximately sixty Native American nations still resided east of the Mississippi, the largest among them being the Choctaws, Creeks, Chickasaws, and Seminoles, all in the southeastern United States.

10. For the text of the Removal Act, see Wilcomb E. Washburn, ed., *The American Indian and the United States: A Documentary History* (New York: Random House, 1973), Vol. III, pp. 2169–2171.

11. Marshall ruled that the Supreme Court could not be the court of original jurisdiction, since the Cherokee Nation was not a sovereign nation such as France or Great Britain, within the meaning of Article III, Section 2, of the Constitution, and therefore the case had to originate in a lower court.

12. Samuel Worcester was a white missionary who refused to secure a Georgia license to live among the Cherokees. He and a fellow missionary were thrown into jail and appealed their case to the Supreme Court.

13. The Cherokee census of 1835 reported 8,946 living in Georgia, 3,644 in North Carolina, 2,528 in Tennessee, and 1,424 in Alabama, for a total of 16,542.

Outraged over actions of this minority (who were derisively labeled the "Treaty Party"), 15,665 Cherokees purportedly signed a petition to the U.S. Congress protesting their removal. The Senate, which earlier had ratified the Treaty of New Echota by a single vote, tabled the petition on April 9, 1838, and General Winfield Scott was given his orders.

About 1,100 Cherokees were permitted to remain in North Carolina, principally because a white merchant named William Holland Thomas had used money from the Treaty of New Echota to purchase thousands of acres in western North Carolina on which he encouraged Cherokees to settle (he kept the land title in his own name). In 1837, the North Carolina General Assembly acknowledged the Cherokees' right to remain in North Carolina. The fact that the land Thomas purchased for the Cherokees was land that virtually no one else wanted probably was a factor in the legislature's decision. In addition to the 1,100 Cherokees who were allowed to stay in North Carolina, an additional 300 remained scattered throughout Georgia, Alabama, and Tennessee. Some had hidden themselves from Scott's soldiers, while others were related by blood and marriage to their white neighbors.

Eyewitness accounts of the Trail of Tears, by both Native Americans and U.S. Army escorts, make for grim reading. As many as 2,500 or more died in the makeshift stockades prior to the journey. And of the 13,149 (cited by army records) who began the trip, only 11,504 arrived in Indian Territory. In addition, several hundred died soon after their arrival, by either disease or violence between the new arrivals and earlier migrants or between the "accommodationists" and the last-ditch resisters.

What were the principal arguments both in favor of and opposed to "voluntary" removal of the Cherokees? What were the strengths and weaknesses of each position?

✳ THE METHOD ✳

As you examine and analyze the principal arguments both in favor of and opposed to Cherokee removal, almost immediately you will see that some of the speakers and writers chose to *rephrase* the question. For example, instead of listing the reasons the Cherokees should be removed (Source 1), President Jackson preferred to discuss *why the Cherokees could not remain where they were.* By carefully reading his answers (there were several) to that question, you will be able to infer what his answers would have been to the question of *why the Cherokees ought to be removed.*

The same holds true for speakers and writers opposed to Cherokee removal. In some cases, they offered

[125]

CHAPTER 6

LAND, GROWTH,
AND JUSTICE:
THE REMOVAL
OF THE
CHEROKEES

what they thought were alternatives that would bave been superior to that of removal. As in the case of Jackson's message, you will have to infer from what opponents said or wrote what they *would have* said or written regarding why the Cherokees ought *not to have been* removed.

As with Jackson, many other speakers and writers offered more than one answer to the question. Therefore, as you examine and analyze the evidence, be sure to take notes carefully.

The second central question in this chapter asks you to assess the strengths and weaknesses of the principal points both in favor of and opposed to Cherokee removal. This is not nearly so easy as it may first appear. For one thing, you may not be able to uncover the real reasons a speaker or writer took a particular position. For example, almost no one in favor of removal said that Cherokees should be removed because whites wanted their lands. Indeed, Jackson himself may have come as close as any proponent of removal when he wrote that Cherokees "have neither the intelligence, the industry, the moral habits, nor the desire of improvement . . . in their condition."[14] Similarly, no opponent of removal would have been crass enough to say that the opponent's true motive was to embarrass President Jackson politically. Without considerably more information than is available here, you will have to take the speaker's or writer's comments at face

value. Jackson, for example, always claimed that removal was the most humane policy for the Cherokees themselves. Is there any evidence to the contrary?

Moreover, as you assess the strengths and weaknesses of each speaker's or writer's position, you will almost inevitably be drawn into the interesting but highly dangerous process of evaluating the alternatives to removal. Typically, historians concern themselves with what *actually did* happen rather than what *might have* happened. To be sure, some of the opponents of removal did advocate alternatives to removal, and in some cases you may have to deal with such alternatives as you determine the strengths and weaknesses of a particular position. If you plan to do this, however, use the actual facts at your disposal to assess a particular alternative. Do not *create* facts to fit your hypothesis—perhaps the worst charge that can be made against a historian. Also remember that you are dealing with people from the early 1800s, *not* the twenty-first century. Avoid putting ideas and thought processes contemporary to you into their minds.

Let us offer a final note of caution. As you examine each piece of evidence, avoid the temptation to "take sides" in the debate or to make the historical individuals into one-dimensional heroes or villains. Analyze the logic of each of the arguments, even when you find the conclusions of a speaker or speakers reprehensible.

Now proceed to the Evidence section of the chapter. Take notes as you read each selection.

14. Fifth Annual Message to Congress, December 3, 1833, in James D. Richardson, *A Compilation of the Messages and Papers of the Presidents* (New York: Bureau of National Literature, 1897), Vol. III, p. 1252.

✳ THE EVIDENCE ✳

Source 1 from James D. Richardson, *A Compilation of the Messages and Papers of the Presidents* (New York: Bureau of National Literature, 1897), Vol. III, pp. 1019–1022.

1. Excerpt from President Andrew Jackson's First Annual Message to Congress, December 8, 1829.

The condition and ulterior destiny of the Indian Tribes within the limits of some of our States, have become objects of much interest and importance. It has long been the policy of Government to introduce among them the arts of civilization, in the hope of gradually reclaiming them from a wandering life. This policy has, however, been coupled with another, wholly incompatible with its success. Professing a desire to civilize and settle them, we have, at the same time, lost no opportunity to purchase their lands, and thrust them further into the wilderness. By this means they have not only been kept in a wandering state, but been led to look upon us as unjust and indifferent to their fate. Thus, though lavish in its expenditures upon the subject, Government has constantly defeated its own policy; and the Indians, in general, receding further and further to the West, have retained their savage habits. A portion, however, of the Southern tribes, having mingled much with the whites, and made some progress in the arts of civilized life, have lately attempted to erect an independent government, within the limits of Georgia and Alabama. These States, claiming to be the only Sovereigns within their territories, extended their laws over the Indians; which induced the latter to call upon the United States for protection.

Under these circumstances, the question presented was, whether the General Government had a right to sustain those people in their pretensions? The Constitution declares, that "no new State shall be formed or erected within the jurisdiction of any other State," without the consent of its legislature.[15] If the General Government is not permitted to tolerate the erection of a confederate State within the territory of one of the members of this Union, against her consent; much less could it allow a foreign and independent government to establish itself there. Georgia became a member of the Confederacy which eventuated in our Federal Union, as a sovereign State, always asserting her claim to certain limits; which having been originally defined in her colonial charter, and subsequently recognised in

15. See U.S. Constitution, Article IV, Section 3.

CHAPTER 6

LAND, GROWTH,
AND JUSTICE:
THE REMOVAL
OF THE
CHEROKEES

the treaty of peace, she has ever since continued to enjoy, except as they have been circumscribed by her own voluntary transfer of a portion of her territory to the United States, in the articles of cession of 1802. Alabama was admitted into the Union on the same footing with the original States, with boundaries which were prescribed by Congress. There is no constitutional, conventional, or legal provision, which allows them less power over the Indians within their borders, than is possessed by Maine or New York. Would the People of Maine permit the Penobscot tribe to erect an Independent Government within their State? and unless they did, would it not be the duty of the General Government to support them in resisting such a measure? Would the People of New York permit each remnant of the Six Nations within her borders, to declare itself an independent people under the protection of the United States? Could the Indians establish a separate republic on each of their reservations in Ohio? and if they were so disposed, would it be the duty of this Government to protect them in the attempt? If the principle involved in the obvious answer to these questions be abandoned, it will follow that the objects of this Government are reversed; and that it has become a part of its duty to aid in destroying the States which it was established to protect.

Actuated by this view of the subject, I informed the Indians inhabiting parts of Georgia and Alabama, that their attempt to establish an independent government would not be countenanced by the Executive of the United States; and advised them to emigrate beyond the Mississippi, or submit to the laws of those States.

Our conduct towards these people is deeply interesting to our national character. Their present condition, contrasted with what they once were, makes a most powerful appeal to our sympathies. Our ancestors found them the uncontrolled possessors of these vast regions. By persuasion and force, they have been made to retire from river to river, and from mountain to mountain; until some of the tribes have become extinct, and others have left but remnants, to preserve, for a while, their once terrible names. Surrounded by the whites, with their arts of civilization, which, by destroying the resources of the savage, doom him to weakness and decay; the fate of the Mohegan, the Narragansett, and the Delaware, is fast overtaking the Choctaw, the Cherokee, and the Creek. That this fate surely awaits them, if they remain within the limits of the States, does not admit of a doubt. Humanity and national honor demand that every effort should be made to avert so great a calamity. It is too late to inquire whether it was just in the United States to include them and their territory within the bounds of new States whose limits they could control. That step cannot be retraced. A State cannot be dismembered by Congress, or restricted in the exercise of her constitutional power. But the people of those States, and of every State, actuated by feelings of justice and a regard for our national honor, submit to you the interesting question, whether something cannot be done, consistently with the rights of the States, to preserve this much injured race?

As a means of effecting this end, I suggest, for your consideration, the propriety of setting apart an ample district West of the Mississippi, and without the limits of any State or Territory, now formed, to be guarantied to the Indian tribes, as long as they shall occupy it: each tribe having a distinct control over the portion designated for its use. There they may be secured in the enjoyment of governments of their own choice, subject to no other control from the United States than such as may be necessary to preserve peace on the frontier, and between the several tribes. There the benevolent may endeavor to teach them the arts of civilization; and, by promoting union and harmony among them, to raise up an interesting commonwealth, destined to perpetuate the race, and to attest the humanity and justice of this Government.

This emigration should be voluntary: for it would be as cruel as unjust to compel the aborigines to abandon the graves of their fathers, and seek a home in a distant land.[16] But they should be distinctly informed that, if they remain within the limits of the States, they must be subject to their laws. In return for their obedience, as individuals, they will, without doubt, be protected in the enjoyment of those possessions which they have improved by their industry. But it seems to me visionary to suppose, that, in this state of things, claims can be allowed on tracts of country on which they have neither dwelt nor made improvements, merely because they have seen them from the mountain, or passed them in the chace [*sic*]. Submitting to the laws of the States, and receiving, like other citizens, protection in their persons and property, they will, ere long, become merged in the mass of our population.

Source 2 from Andrew A. Lipscomb and Albert Ellergy Bergh, eds., *The Writings of Thomas Jefferson* (Washington, D.C.: Thomas Jefferson Memorial Association, 1903), Vol. XVI, pp. 450–454.

2. President Thomas Jefferson to Captain Hendrick, the Delawares, Mohicans, and Munries, December 21, 1808.

. . . The picture which you have drawn, my son, of the increase of our numbers and the decrease of yours is just, the causes are very plain, and

16. Jackson believed, perhaps naively, that a majority of Cherokees would move to the West voluntarily. See his Third Annual Message to Congress, December 6, 1831, in Richardson, *Messages and Papers of the Presidents*, Vol. III, p. 1117.

CHAPTER 6

LAND, GROWTH,
AND JUSTICE:
THE REMOVAL
OF THE
CHEROKEES

the remedy depends on yourselves alone. You have lived by hunting the deer and buffalo—all these have been driven westward; you have sold out on the sea-board and moved westwardly in pursuit of them. As they became scarce there, your food has failed you; you have been a part of every year without food, except the roots and other unwholesome things you could find in the forest. Scanty and unwholesome food produce diseases and death among your children, and hence you have raised few and your numbers have decreased. Frequent wars, too, and the abuse of spirituous liquors, have assisted in lessening your numbers. The whites, on the other hand, are in the habit of cultivating the earth, of raising stocks of cattle, hogs, and other domestic animals, in much greater numbers than they could kill of deer and buffalo. Having always a plenty of food and clothing they raise abundance of children, they double their numbers every twenty years, the new swarms are continually advancing upon the country like flocks of pigeons, and so they will continue to do. Now, my children, if we wanted to diminish our numbers, we would give up the culture of the earth, pursue the deer and buffalo, and be always at war; this would soon reduce us to be as few as you are, and if you wish to increase your numbers you must give up the deer and buffalo, live in peace and cultivate the earth. You see then, my children, that it depends on yourselves alone to become a numerous and great people. Let me entreat you, therefore, on the lands now given you to begin to give every man a farm; let him enclose it, cultivate it, build a warm house on it, and when he dies, let it belong to his wife and children after him. Nothing is so easy as to learn to cultivate the earth; all your women understand it, and to make it easier, we are always ready to teach you how to make ploughs, hoes, and necessary utensils. If the men will take the labor of the earth from the women they will learn to spin and weave and to clothe their families. In this way you will also raise many children, you will double your numbers every twenty years, and soon fill the land your friends have given you, and your children will never be tempted to sell the spot on which they have been born, raised, have labored and called their own. When once you have property, you will want laws and magistrates to protect your property and persons, and to punish those among you who commit crimes. You will find that our laws are good for this purpose; you will wish to live under them, you will unite yourselves with us, join in our Great Councils and form one people with us, and we shall all be Americans; you will mix with us by marriage, your blood will run in our veins, and will spread with us over this great island. Instead, then, my children, of the gloomy prospect you have drawn of your total disappearance from the face of the earth, which is true, if you continue to hunt the deer and buffalo and go to war, you see what a brilliant aspect is offered to your future history, if you give up war and hunting. Adopt the culture of the earth and raise domestic animals; you see how from a small family you may become a great nation by adopting the course which from the small beginning you describe has made us a great nation. . . .

Sources 3 through 5 from Theda Perdue and Michael D. Green, eds., *The Cherokee Removal: A Brief History with Documents* (Boston: Bedford Books, 1995), pp. 124, 35, 38–41, 98–102.

3. Petition of Cherokee Women, May 2, 1817.

The Cherokee ladys now being present at the meeting of the chiefs and warriors in council have thought it their duty as mothers to address their beloved chiefs and warriors now assembled.

Our beloved children and head men of the Cherokee Nation, we address you warriors in council. We have raised all of you on the land which we now have, which God gave us to inhabit and raise provisions. We know that our country has once been extensive, but by repeated sales has become circumscribed to a small track [*sic*], and [we] never have thought it our duty to interfere in the disposition of it till now. If a father or mother was to sell all their lands which they had to depend on, which their children had to raise their living on, which would be indeed bad & to be removed to another country. We do not wish to go to an unknown country [to] which we have understood some of our children wish to go over the Mississippi, but this act of our children would be like destroying your mothers.

Your mothers, your sisters ask and beg of you not to part with any more of our land. We say ours. You are our descendants; take pity on our request. But keep it for our growing children, for it was the good will of our creator to place us here, and you know our father, the great president,[17] will not allow his white children to take our country away. Only keep your hands off of paper talks for its our own country. For [if] it was not, they would not ask you to put your hands to paper, for it would be impossible to remove us all. For as soon as one child is raised, we have others in our arms, for such is our situation & will consider our circumstance.

Therefore, children, don't part with any more of our lands but continue on it & enlarge your farms. Cultivate and raise corn & cotton and your mothers and sisters will make clothing for you which our father the president has recommended to us all. We don't charge any body for selling any

17. President James Monroe.

CHAPTER 6

LAND, GROWTH,
AND JUSTICE:
THE REMOVAL
OF THE
CHEROKEES

lands, but we have heard such intentions of our children. But your talks become true at last; it was our desire to forwarn you all not to part with our lands. . . .

4. John Ridge (a Cherokee leader) to Albert Gallatin,[18] February 27, 1826.

. . . Their principal dependence for subsidence is on the production of their own farms. Indian corn is a staple production and is the most essential article of food in use. Wheat, rye & oats grow very well & some families have commenced to introduce them on their farms. Cotton is generally raised for domestic consumption and a few have grown it for market & have realized very good profits. I take pleasure to state, tho' cautiously, that there is not to my knowledge a solitary Cherokee to be found that depends upon the chase for subsistence and every head of a family has his house & farm. The hardest portion of manual labor is performed by the men, & the women occasionally lend a hand to the field, more by choice and necessity than any thing else. This is applicable to the poorer class, and I can do them the justice to say, they very contentedly perform the duties of the kitchen and that they are the most valuable portion of our Citizens. They sew, they weave, they spin, they cook our meals and act well the duties assigned them by Nature as mothers as far as they are able & improved. The African slaves are generally mostly held by Half breeds and full Indians of distinguished talents. In this class the principal value of property is retained and their farms are conducted in the same style with the southern white farmers of equal ability in point of property. Their houses are usually of hewed logs, with brick chimneys & shingled roofs, there are also a few excellent Brick houses & frames. Their furniture is better than the exterior appearance of their houses would incline a stranger to suppose. They have their regular meals as the whites, Servants to attend them in their repasts, and the tables are usually covered with a clean cloth & furnished with the usual plates, knives & forks &c. Every family more or less possess hogs, Cattle & horses and a number have commenced to pay attention to the introduction of sheep, which are increasing very fast. The horse is in general use for purposes of riding, drawing the plough or wagon. . . .

18. Albert Gallatin (1761–1849) was a congressman, secretary of the treasury, and diplomat. When Ridge wrote to Gallatin, Gallatin had just been nominated as U.S. minister to Great Britain.

Superstition is the portion of all uncivilized Nations and Idolatry is only engendered in the Brain of rudeness. The Cherokees in their most savage state, never worshipped the work of their own hands—neither fire or water nor any one or portion of splendid fires that adorn heaven's Canopy above. They believed in a great first cause or Spirit of all Good & in a great being the author of all evil. These [were] at variance and at war with each other, but the good Spirit was supposed to be superior to the bad one. These immortal beings had on both sides numerous intelligent beings of analogous dispositions to their chieftains. They had a heaven, which consisted of a visible world to those who had undergone a change by death. This heaven was adorned with all the beauties which a savage imagination could conceive: An open forest, yet various, giving shade & fruit of every kind; Flowers of various hues & pleasant to the Smell; Game of all kinds in great abundance, enough of feasts & plenty of dances, & to crown the whole, the most beautiful women, prepared & adorned by the great Spirit, for every individual Indian that by wisdom, hospitality & Bravery was introduced to this happy & immortal region. The Bad place was the reverse of this & in the vicinity of the good place, where the wretched, compelled to live in hunger, hostility & darkness, could hear the rejoicings of the happy, without the possibility of reaching its shores.

Witches or wizards were in existence and pretended to possess Supernatural powers & intercourse with the Devil or bad Spirit. They were supposed capable of transforming themselves into the beasts of the forest & fowls of the air & take their nocturnal excursions in pursuit of human victims, particularly those suffering from disease, & it was often necessary for their friends to employ witch shooters to protect the sick from such visitors. Such characters were the dread of the Country, & many a time have I trembled at the croaking of a frog, hooting of an owl or guttural hoarseness of a Raven by night in my younger days. After the people began to be a little more courageous, these witches had a bad time of it. They were often on suspicion butchered or tomahawked by the enraged parents, relatives or friends of the deceased, particularly if the sickness was of short duration. The severity of revenge fell most principally on the grey hairs of aged persons of both sexes. To stop this evil, it was necessary to pass a law considering all slaughters of this kind in the light of murder, which has effected the desired remedy. There [are] yet among us who pretend to possess powers of milder character, Such as making rain, allaying a storm or whirlwinds, playing with thunder & foretelling future events with many other trifling conjurations not worth mentioning, but they are generally living monuments of fun to the young and grave Ridicule for those in maturer years. There [are] about 8 churches, where the gospel is preached

CHAPTER 6

LAND, GROWTH,
AND JUSTICE:
THE REMOVAL
OF THE
CHEROKEES

on sabbath days with in the Nation. They are missionary stations supported by moravians, Presbyterians, Baptists and methodists and each of these churches have a goodly number of pious & exemplary members and others, not professors, attend to preaching with respectable deportment. I am not able to say the precise number of actual christians, but they are respectable in point of number & character. And many a drunken, idle & good for nothing Indian has been converted from error & have become useful Citizens: Portions of Scripture & sacred hymns are translated and I have frequently heard with astonishment a Cherokee, unacquainted with the English take his text & preach, read his hymn & sing it, Joined by his audience, and pray to his heavenly father with great propriety & devotion. The influence of Religion on the life of the Indians is powerful & lasting. I have an uncle, who was given to all the vices of savagism in drunkenness, fornication and roguery & he is now tho' poorer in this world's goods but rich in goodness & makes his living by hard labor & is in every respect an honest praying christian.

In respect to marriage, we have no law regulating it & polygamy is still allowed to Native Cherokees. Increase of morality among the men, the same among the women & a respect for their characters & matrimonial happiness is fast consuming this last vestige of our ignorance. We attempted to pass a law regulating marriage, but as nearly all the members of our Legislature, tho' convinced of the propriety, had been married under the old existing ceremony, [and] were afraid it would reflect dishonor on them, it failed. Time will effect the desired change in this system & it is worthy of mention, even now, that the most respectable portion of our females prefer, tho' not required by law to be united in marriage attended by the solemnities of the Christian mode. Indians, tho' naturally highminded, are not addicted to as much revenge as they have been represented, and I can say this, much it is paid for them to endure an intended Insult but they are ready to forgive if they discover marks of repentance in the countenance of an enemy. In regard to Intemperance, we are still as a nation grossly degraded. We are however on the improve. Five years ago our best chiefs during their official labors would get drunk & continue so for two or three days. It is now not the case & any member who should thus depart from duty would now be expelled from the Council. Among the younger class, a large number are of fine habits, temperate & genteel in their deportment. The females aspire to gain the affection of such men & to the females we may always ascribe the honor of effecting the civilization of man. There are about 13 Schools established by missionaries in the Nation and may contain 250 students. They are entirely supported by the humane Societies in different parts of the U. States. The Nation has not as yet contributed to the support of these Schools. Besides this, some of our most respectable people have their children educated at the academies in the adjoining states. Two cherokee females have recently completed their Education, at the expense of their father, at a celebrated female Academy in Salem, North Carolina. They are highly accomplished & in point of appearance & deportment; they would pass for the genteel & wellbred ladies in any Country.

I know of some others who are preparing for an admission in the same institution. I suppose that there are one third of our Citizens, that can read & write in the English Language. George Guess[19] a Cherokee who is unacquainted with the English has invented 86 characters, in which the cherokees read & write in their own Language and regularly correspond with their Arkansas friends. This mode of writing is most extensively adopted by our people particularly by those who are ignorant of the English Language. A National Academy of a high order is to be soon established by law at our seat of Government. The edifice will be of Brick & will be supported by the Nation. It is also in contemplation to establish an English & Cherokee printing press & a paper edited in both languages at our seat of Government. In our last Session, $1500 was appropriated to purchase the press and regulations adopted to carry the object into effect. We have also a Society organized called the "Moral & Literary Society of the Cherokee Nation." A library is attached to this Institution. . . .

5. Excerpt from William Penn (pseudonym for Jeremiah Evarts of the American Board of Commissioners for Foreign Missions), "A Brief View of the Present Relations Between the Government and People of the United States and the Indians Within Our National Limits," November 1829.

. . . The positions here recited are deemed to be incontrovertible. It follows, therefore,

That the removal of any nation of Indians from their country by force would be an instance of gross and cruel oppression:

That all attempts to accomplish this removal of the Indians by bribery or fraud, by intimidation and threats, by withholding from them a knowledge of the strength of their cause, by practising upon their ignorance, and their

19. George Guess: Sequoyah.

CHAPTER 6

LAND, GROWTH,
AND JUSTICE:
THE REMOVAL
OF THE
CHEROKEES

fears, or by vexatious opportunities, interpreted by them to mean nearly the same thing as a command;—all such attempts are acts of oppression, and therefore entirely unjustifiable:

That the United States are firmly bound by treaty to protect the Indians from force and encroachments on the part of a State; and a refusal thus to protect them would be equally an act of bad faith as a refusal to protect them against individuals: and

That the Cherokees have therefore the guaranty of the United States, solemnly and repeatedly given, as a security against encroachments from Georgia and the neighboring States. By virtue of this guaranty the Cherokees may rightfully demand, that the United States shall keep all intruders at a distance, from whatever quarter, or in whatever character, they may come. Thus secured and defended in the possession of their country, the Cherokees have a perfect right to retain that possession as long as they please. Such a retention of their country is no just cause of complaint or offence to any State, or to any individual. It is merely an exercise of natural rights, which rights have been not only acknowledged but repeatedly and solemnly confirmed by the United States.

Although these principles are clear and incontrovertible, yet many persons feel an embarrassment from considering the Cherokees *as living in the State of Georgia*. All this embarrassment may be removed at once by bearing in mind, that the Cherokee country is not in Georgia. . . .

[*Here Penn argued that the Cherokees owned their land by treaty with the U.S. government, that in 1825 the state of Georgia made a treaty with the Creek Nation to acquire their land, and hence would have to do so with the Cherokees as well.*]

If the separate existence of the Indian tribes *were* an inconvenience to their neighbours, this would be but a slender reason for breaking down all the barriers of justice and good faith. Many a rich man has thought it very inconvenient, that he could not add the farm of a poor neighbour to his possessions. Many a powerful nation has felt it to be inconvenient to have a weak and dependent state in its neighbourhood, and has therefore forcibly joined the territory of such state to its own extensive domains. But this is done at the expense of honour and character, and is visited by the historian with his severest reprobation.

In the case before us the inconvenience is altogether imaginary. If the United States were examined, with a view to find a place where Indians could have a residence assigned them, so that they might be as little as possible in the way of the whites, not a single tract, capable of sustaining inhabitants, could be found more secluded than the present country of the

Cherokees. It is in the mountains, among the head waters of rivers diverging in all directions; and some parts of it are almost inaccessible. The Cherokees have ceded to the United States all their best land. Not a twentieth part of what remains is of a very good quality. More than half is utterly worthless. Perhaps three tenths may produce moderate crops. The people of the United States have a free passage through the country, secured by treaty. What do they want more? If the Cherokee country were added to Georgia, the accession would be but a fraction joined to the remotest corner of that great State;—a State now scarcely inferior in size to any State in the Union except Virginia; a State having but six or seven souls to a square mile, counting whites and blacks, and with a soil and climate capable of sustaining a hundred to the square mile with the greatest of ease. There is no mighty inconvenience, therefore, in the arrangement of Providence, by which the Cherokee claim a resting place on the land which God gave to their fathers. . . .

There is one remaining topic, on which the minds of many benevolent men are hesitating; and that is, *whether the welfare of the Indians would not be promoted by a removal.* Though they have a right to remain where they are; though the whole power of the United States is pledged to defend them in their possessions; yet it is supposed by some, that they would act wisely, if they would yield to the pressure, quietly surrender their territory to the United States, and accept a new country beyond the Mississippi, with a new guaranty.

In support of this supposition, it is argued, that they can never remain quiet where they are; that they will always be infested by troublesome whites; and that the states, which lay claim to their territory, will persevere in measures to vex and annoy them.

Let us look a moment at this statement. Is it indeed true, that, in the very prime and vigour of our republican government, and with all our boasted reliance upon constitutions and laws, we cannot enforce as plain an act of Congress as is to be found in our national statute-book? Is it true, that while treaties are declared in the constitution to be the supreme law of the land, a whole volume of these supreme laws is to be at once avowedly and utterly disregarded? Is the Senate of the United States, that august body, as our newspapers have called it a thousand times, to march in solemn procession, and burn a volume of treaties? Are the archives of state to be searched, and a hundred and fifty rolls, containing treaties with the Indians, to be brought forth and consigned to the flames on Capitol Hill, in the presence of the representatives of the people, and all the dignitaries of our national government? When ambassadors from foreign nations inquire, *What is the cause of all this burning?* are we to say, "Forty years ago

CHAPTER 6

LAND, GROWTH,
AND JUSTICE:
THE REMOVAL
OF THE
CHEROKEES

President Washington and the Senate made treaties with the Indians, which have been repeated and confirmed by successive administrations. The treaties are plain, and the terms reasonable. But the Indians are weak, and their white neighbors will be lawless. The way to please these white neighbours is, therefore, to burn the treaties, and then call the Indians our dear children, and deal with them precisely as if no treaties had ever been made." Is this answer to be given to the honest inquires of intelligent foreigners? Are we to declare to mankind, that in our country law is totally inadequate to answer the great end for which human laws are made, that is, the protection of the weak against the strong? And is this confession to be made without feeling and without shame? It cannot be. The people of the United States will never subject themselves to so foul a reproach. They will not knowingly affix to the character of a republican government so indelible a stigma. Let it not be said, then, that the laws of the country cannot be executed. Let it never be admitted, that the faith of the nation must be violated, lest the government should come into collision with white intruders upon Indian lands:—with intruders, whose character is admitted to be lawless; and who can be invested with power, in no other way than by tamely yielding to their acts of encroachment and aggression.

The laws can be executed with perfect ease. The Indians can be defended. The faith of the nation can be preserved. Let the President of the United States, whenever the Indians shall be threatened, issue his proclamation, describing the danger and asserting the majesty of the laws. Let him refer to the treaties and the acts of Congress, which his oath of office obliges him to enforce; let him recite the principal provisions of these treaties and acts, and declare, in the face of the world, that he shall execute the laws, and that he shall confidently rely upon the aid and co-operation of all good citizens:—let him do this, and neither he, nor the country, will be disappointed. Law will triumph, and oppression will hide its head.

Source 6 from *Speeches on the Passage of the Bill for the Removal of the Indians, Delivered in the Congress of the United States, April and May, 1830* (Boston: Perkins and Marvin, 1830), pp. 25–28.

6. Excerpt from Speech of Senator Theodore Frelinghuysen of New Jersey.

. . . It is alleged, that the Indians cannot flourish in the neighborhood of a white population—that whole tribes have disappeared under the influence of this propinquity. As an abstract proposition, it implies reproach somewhere. Our virtues certainly have not such deadly and depopulating power. It must, then, be our vices that possess these destructive energies—and shall we commit injustice, and put in, as our plea for it, that our intercourse with the Indians has been so demoralizing that we must drive them from it, to save them? True, Sir, many tribes have melted away—they have sunk lower and lower—and what people could rise from a condition to which policy, selfishness, and cupidity, conspired to depress them?

Sir, had we devoted the same care to elevate their moral condition, that we have to degrade them, the removal of the Indians would not now seek for an apology in the suggestions of humanity. But I ask, as to the matter of fact, how stands the account? Wherever a fair experiment has been made, the Indians have readily yielded to the influences of moral cultivation. Yes, Sir, they flourish under this culture, and rise in the scale of being. They have shown themselves to be highly susceptible of improvement, and the ferocious feelings and habits of the savage are soothed and reformed by the mild charities of religion. They can very soon be taught to understand and appreciate the blessings of civilization and regular government. And I have the opinions of some of our most enlightened statesmen to sustain me. . . .

[*Here Frelinghuysen quoted from the messages to Congress of Presidents Jefferson (1801, 1803, 1806, 1808), Madison (1809), and Monroe (1824), all of whom reported on the rapid adaptation by Native Americans of Anglo-European "civilization."*]

Now, Sir, when we consider the large space which these illustrious men have filled in our councils, and the perfect confidence that is due to their official statements, is it not astonishing to hear it gravely maintained that the Indians are retrograding in their condition and character; that all our public anxieties and cares bestowed upon them have been utterly fruitless; and that, for very pity's sake, we must get rid of them, or they will perish on our hands? Sir, I believe that the confidence of the Senate has been abused by some of the letter-writers, who give us such sad accounts of Indian wretchedness. I rejoice that we may safely repose upon the statements contained in the letters of Messrs. J. L. Allen, R. M. Livingston, Rev. Cyrus Kingsbury, and the Rev. Samuel A. Worcester.[20] The character of these witnesses is without reproach; and their satisfactory certificates of the improvement of the tribes continue and confirm the history furnished to us in the several messages from which I have just read extracts.

It is further maintained, "that one of the greatest evils to which the Indians are exposed, is that incessant pressure of population, that forces them from seat to seat, without allowing time for moral and intellectual

---

20. Friends of the Cherokees and missionaries who worked with them. Samuel A. Worcester was the principal figure in *Worcester v. Georgia* (1832).

CHAPTER 6

LAND, GROWTH,
AND JUSTICE:
THE REMOVAL
OF THE
CHEROKEES

improvement." Sir, this is the very reason—the deep, cogent reason—which I present to the Senate, now to raise the barrier against the pressure of population, and, with all the authority of this nation, say to the urging tide, "Thus far, and no farther." Let us save them now, or we never shall. For is it not clear as the sunbeam, Sir, that a removal will aggravate their woes? If the tide is nearly irresistible at this time; when a few more years shall fill the regions beyond the Arkansas with many more millions of enterprising white men, will not an increased impulse be given, that shall sweep the red men away into the barren prairies, or the Pacific of the west?

If these constant removals are so afflictive, and allow no time for moral improvement; if this be the cause why the attempts at Indian reformation are alleged to have been so unavailing; do not the dictates of experience, then, plead most powerfully with us, to drive them no farther?—to grant them an abiding place, where these moral causes may have a fair and uninterrupted operation in moulding and refining the Indian character? And, Sir, weigh a moment the considerations that address us on behalf of the Cherokees especially. Prompted and encouraged by our counsels, they have in good earnest resolved to become men, rational, educated, Christian men; and they have succeeded beyond our most sanguine hopes. They have established a regular constitution of civil government, republican in its principles. Wise and beneficent laws are enacted. The people acknowledge their authority, and feel their obligation. A printing press, conducted by one of the nation, circulates a weekly newspaper, printed partly in English, and partly in the Cherokee language. Schools flourish in many of their settlements. Christian temples, to the God of the Bible, are frequented by respectful, devout, and many sincere worshippers. God, as we believe, has many people among them, whom he regards as the "apple of his eye." They have become better neighbors to Georgia. She made no complaints during the lapse of fifty years, when the tribes were a horde of ruthless, licentious and drunken savages; when no law controlled them; when the only judge was their will, and their avenger the tomahawk.

Then Georgia could make treaties with them, and acknowledge them as nations; and in conventions trace boundary lines, and respect the landmarks of her neighbor: and now, when they begin to reap the fruits of all the paternal instructions, so repeatedly and earnestly delivered to them by the Presidents; when the Cherokee has learned to respect the rights of the white man, and sacredly to regard the obligations of truth and conscience; is this the time, Sir, to break up a peaceful community, to put out its council fires, to annul its laws and customs, to crush the rising hopes of its youth, and to drive the desponding and discouraged Indian to despair? Although it be called a sickly humanity to sympathize with Indians—every freeman in the land, that has one spark of the spirit of his fathers, will denounce the proposed measure as an unparalleled stretch of cruel injustice—unparalleled certainly in our history. And if the deed be done, Sir, how it is regarded in heaven will, sooner or later, be known on earth; for this is the judgment place of public sins. And all these ties are to be broken asunder, for a State that was silent, and acquiesced in the relations of the Indians to our present government; that pretended to no right of direct interference, whilst these tribes were really dangerous; when their ferocious incursions justly disturbed the tranquillity of the fireside, and waked the "sleep of the cradle;"—for a State that seeks it now against an unoffending neighbor, which implores, by all that is dear in the graves of her fathers, in the traditions of by-gone ages; that beseeches by the ties of nature, of home, and of country, to let her live unmolested, and die near the dust of her kindred!

Our fears have been addressed in behalf of those States, whose legislation we resist: and it is inquired with solicitude, Would you urge us to arms with Georgia? No, Sir. This tremendous alternative will not be necessary. Let the general government come out, as it should, with decided and temperate firmness, and officially announce to Georgia, and the other States, that if the Indian tribes choose to remain, they will be protected against all interference and encroachment; and such is my confidence in the sense of justice, in the respect for law, prevailing in the great body of this portion of our fellow-citizens, that I believe they would submit to the authority of the nation. I can expect no other issue. . . .

❋ QUESTIONS TO CONSIDER ❋

Remember that your task in this chapter is to use the evidence to answer the following two questions: (1) What were the principal arguments for and against the removal of the Cherokees? (2) What, in your opinion, were the strengths and weaknesses of each position?

President Andrew Jackson gave four principal reasons why, in his opinion, the Cherokees should not remain where they were as a political entity separate from the state of Georgia (Source 1). What were those four reasons? How important was it, in Jackson's opinion, that the Cherokees become "civilized"? In his view, what would be the results of permitting the Cherokees to remain in the East? Finally, Jackson strongly maintained that any such emigration "should be voluntary" but, in his view, what would happen to the Cherokees who refused to leave? Why couldn't the

CHAPTER 6

LAND, GROWTH,
AND JUSTICE:
THE REMOVAL
OF THE
CHEROKEES

president of the United States intervene to help the Cherokees remain where they were?

President Thomas Jefferson's letter of December 21, 1808 (Source 2), while not specifically referring to the Cherokees, accurately summarized his general policy with regard to Native Americans living within the boundaries of the United States. What did Jefferson believe were the causes of population decline among Native American people (note that Jackson also dealt with this problem, and in a way not terribly different from that of Jefferson)? How, in Jefferson's view, could that situation be reversed? In return for staying on their lands, what would Native Americans have had to give up? What was Jackson's opinion on this topic? In your view, which president was more eager to eliminate Native American cultures: Jackson or Jefferson? Also note that Jefferson realized that Native Americans were not simply wandering hunters, but that they already cultivated the earth ("all your women understand it"). What stereotype did Jefferson seem to believe? See Source 4 for a refutation of that stereotype. What do you make of the phrase, "you will unite yourselves with us, join in our Great Councils and form one people with us"? What was Jefferson proposing? How did Jackson treat the same subject?

John Ridge (Source 4) was a Cherokee leader who eventually joined the "Treaty Party" and moved west, where he was murdered by Cherokees who thought he had betrayed them. In 1826, however, Ridge still was looking for a way for Cherokees to remain in the East and, therefore, he opposed

removal. Why did Ridge think that Cherokees could remain successfully on their lands? If many whites defended the Cherokees' right to stay because they became "civilized" and others believed they could remain and simultaneously retain their traditional culture, what was Ridge's position? Can you infer what the Cherokee women petitioners (Source 3) might have thought of that?

Jeremiah Evarts (Source 5) also opposed removal. How did Evarts contest President Jackson's opinion that the Cherokees' position was unconstitutional, according to Article IV, Section 3 of the Constitution? (Remember that even though Evarts wrote months before Jackson's message, the president's position was well known.) What was Evarts's opinion of the much-circulated notion in Georgia that Cherokees were inhabiting some of the best land in the state? What was his position on the inability of the government to protect the Cherokees where they were from intruding whites?

Senator Theodore Frelinghuysen was deeply and genuinely concerned about the fate of Native Americans. The speech excerpted here (Source 6) took approximately six hours to deliver, so it is not possible to include all of the points he made in opposition to removal. Frelinghuysen began his speech by admitting that many Native Americans living in close proximity to whites had experienced great difficulties. Yet why does he say this has happened? Why does he believe that removal will *not* work, and moreover, is *not* necessary? What alternative (by inference) might Frelinghuysen have supported? How important was it to Frelinghuysen that the Cherokees become "civilized"? Did he seem less concerned than Andrew Jackson about making the Cherokees more like their white neighbors?

Having extracted from the evidence the principal arguments for and against removal, now use your text, the Background section of this chapter, and the help of your instructor to explain the strengths and weaknesses of each principal argument. In order to do so, take each argument for or against removal and use historical facts to determine its strengths and weaknesses. In some cases, another piece of evidence will assist you. For example, President Jackson claimed that the Cherokees' position was unconstitutional. Jeremiah Evarts, however, attempted (with some success) to challenge Jackson's position.

One more example will suffice. In his essay opposing removal, Evarts maintained that the Cherokees already had given up their best lands and what remained in their hands were lands that were "utterly worthless." What fact, however, did Evarts omit? In what way might that fact weaken his position?

Always keep in mind that a statement of opinion (a hypothesis) must be proved by using *facts,* and *not* by using other statements of opinion. What is the matter with the following two statements? (1) The Cherokees should be removed because they lack the industry to make their lands produce. (2) The Cherokees ought not to be removed because their lifestyle is superior to that of whites.

✳ EPILOGUE ✳

The war between the older immigrants and the newer arrivals to Indian territory went on for seven years, until peace between the two factions of Cherokees finally was made in 1846. During that period, some Cherokees reversed their trek and returned to North Carolina. When the Civil War broke out in 1861, factionalism once again emerged, with some Cherokees supporting the Confederacy and others backing the Union. Fighting between these factions (a "mini–Civil War") claimed the lives of as many as 25 percent of the Cherokee population.

In 1868, Congress recognized the obvious fact that the Cherokees who remained in the East had become a distinct group, named the Eastern Band of the Cherokees (as opposed to the migrating group, which was called the Cherokee Nation). In 1875, the federal government began to acquire land in North Carolina for a reservation, named the Qualla Boundary, which ultimately contained around 56,000 acres. In 1889, the Eastern Band received a charter from North Carolina granting the Cherokees what amounted to home rule in the Qualla Boundary. Then the federal govern-

CHAPTER 6

LAND, GROWTH,
AND JUSTICE:
THE REMOVAL
OF THE
CHEROKEES

ment began an intensive program to "civilize" the eastern Cherokees, an effort that was ultimately unsuccessful. Cherokees clung stubbornly to their own language and traditions, and by 1900, fewer than one-fourth of the population could speak English—approximately half of them young people in white-administered boarding schools. Because they consistently voted Republican, after 1900 the Democratic majority in North Carolina disfranchised the Cherokees by passing a law requiring literacy tests prior to voting.

Meanwhile the Cherokee Nation (in the West) was experiencing its own difficulties. In spite of the fact that the 1830 Indian Removal Act guaranteed that Native Americans would always hold the land onto which they were placed, land grants to railroad companies and a territorial land rush stripped a good deal of land away from the Cherokees. In 1891, the Cherokee Nation owned 19.5 million acres. By 1971, it owned but 146,598.

In North Carolina, the creation of the Great Smoky Mountains National Park in 1934 offered the Eastern Band a way out of its economic quagmire. In November 1934, the council appropriated $50,000 for tourist facilities, and in 1937 the first Cherokee-owned motel (Newfound Lodge) was open for business. In 1939, an estimated 169,000 people visited the national park and purchased around $30,000 worth of Cherokee crafts.

The development of tourism undoubtedly helped alleviate a severe economic crisis for the Eastern Band. In 1932, at the low point of the Great Depression, it was estimated that 200 of the 496 Cherokee families in North Carolina needed public assistance. The New Deal did provide some jobs, through the Indian Emergency Conservation Work Program, a separate version of the Civilian Conservation Corps. But tourism also presented the Eastern Band with the problem of whether Cherokees could retain their cultural identity while at the same time catering to the desires of visitors with money.[21] In the 1990s, the Eastern Band turned to casino gambling to increase their revenues, although income from tourism and gambling is not evenly dispersed and many Cherokees still live extremely modestly.

By then, of course, the principal voices on both sides of the issue had long been stilled. In 1837 (one year before the beginning of the Trail of Tears), Andrew Jackson left the presidency to his hand-picked successor, Martin Van Buren, and retired to his plantation, the Hermitage, near Nashville, Tennessee. He died in 1845, still convinced that his advocacy of Cherokee removal was the most humane alternative for the Native Americans themselves.

For his part, however, before his death in 1826, Thomas Jefferson had changed his position to one of supporting removal. Frustrated over what he considered to be the slow progress Native Americans were making in adopting "civilization," the principal author of the Declaration of Independence

21. Because tourists expected to see Native Americans with ornate feathered headdresses (typical of Plains Indians but never worn by Cherokees), Cherokees accommodatingly wore them.

came to believe that Native American people and white people could not live side by side unless the Native Americans abandoned their own culture in favor of that of the whites.[22]

The removal of most of the Cherokees in 1838–1839 (and in a second forced migration in 1841 to 1844) is a chapter in the history of the United States that is important to know. It is also important to undertand that there were many voices on both sides of the removal issue, thus making the subject of Cherokee removal not only a tragic one but an exceedingly complex one as well.

22. See Bernard W. Sheehan, *Seeds of Extinction: Jeffersonian Philanthropy and the American Indian* (Chapel Hill: University of North Carolina Press, 1973).

7

Away from Home:
The Working Girls
of Lowell

❉ THE PROBLEM ❉

Just before the War of 1812, the successful New England merchant Francis Cabot Lowell toured Great Britain. Among other things, Lowell was very interested in the English textile industry. The invention of the power loom enabled spinning and weaving operations to be combined within one factory, but the factory system had spawned mill towns with overcrowded slums, horrible living conditions, and high death rates. The potential profits that the new technology offered were great, yet Lowell knew that Americans already feared the Old World evils that appeared to accompany the factory system.

Back in Boston once again, Lowell and his brother-in-law built a power loom, patented it, raised money, formed a company, and built a textile factory. Realizing that their best source of available labor would be young women from the surrounding New England rural areas and that farm families would have to be persuaded to let their daughters work far from home in the new factories, the company managers developed what eventually came to be known as the Lowell system.

In this chapter, you will be looking at what happened when people's ideas about women's "proper place" conflicted with the labor needs of the new factory system. What did the general public fear? How did the working girls react?

✤ BACKGROUND ✤

By the end of the eighteenth century, the American economy began undergoing a process that historians call modernization. This process involves a number of changes, including the rapid expansion of markets, commercial specialization, improved transportation networks, the growth of credit transactions, the proliferation of towns and cities, and the rise of manufacturing and the factory system. Quite obviously, all these factors are interrelated. Furthermore, such changes always have profound effects on people's lifestyles as well as on the pace of life itself.

While the frontier moved steadily westward, the South was primarily agrarian—tied to cash crops such as cotton and tobacco. New England's economy, however, quickly became modernized. Although agriculture was never completely abandoned in New England, by the early 1800s it was increasingly difficult to obtain land, and many small New England farms suffered from soil exhaustion. Young men, of course, could go west—in fact, so many of them left New England that soon there was a "surplus" of young women in the area. In addition, the transformation of New England agriculture and the demise of much of the "putting-out" system of the first local textile manufacturing left many single female workers underemployed or unemployed. What were these farmers' daughters supposed to do? What were their options?

At the same time that these economic developments were occurring, ideas about white middle-class women and their place in society also were changing. Even before the American Revolution, sharp distinctions between the "better sort" and the "poorer sort" were noticeable, especially in cities like Boston. The Revolution itself, with its emphasis on "republican virtues," drew many women away from their purely domestic duties and into patriotic work for the cause. The uncertainties of the early national period, which followed the Revolution, only intensified the concern about the new republic: How could such a daring experiment in representative government succeed? An essential part of the answer to this question was the concept of "republican motherhood": Women would take on the important task of raising children to be responsible citizens who possessed the virtues (and value system) necessary for the success of the newly independent nation.

Those who study women's history disagree on the question of whether women's status improved or declined as a result of the emphasis on republican motherhood. Nevertheless, it was clear that the new focus on motherhood and child rearing would not only reduce the variety of roles women could play but also limit women's proper place to their own homes.

As historian Alice Kessler-Harris notes in her study of wage-earning women in the United States, there was a direct conflict for poorer or unmarried women between their need to earn money and the ideology that home and family should be central to *all* women's lives.[1] This emphasis on domestic ideology, Kessler-Harris concludes, sharpened class divisions and eroded any possibility of real independence for women. Historian Christine Stansell reaches many of the same conclusions in her study of gender and class in New York City.[2] In addition, according to Stansell, young unmarried working women often dressed and behaved in ways that directly challenged domestic ideology and women's place within the home. Such alternative ways of living, especially on the part of young, white, native-born, Protestant women, were deeply disturbing to many Americans, both male and female.

In periods of rapid change, people often try to cling to absolute beliefs and even create stereotypes that implicitly punish those who do not conform. Such a stereotype began to emerge after the American Revolution. According to this stereotype, every "true" woman was a "lady" who behaved in certain ways because of her female nature. Historian Barbara Welter has called this phenomenon the "cult of true womanhood."[3] True women possessed four virtues: piety, purity, submissiveness, and domesticity. These characteristics, it was thought, were not so much learned as

they were biologically natural, simply an inherent part of being born female. Women's magazines, etiquette books for young ladies, sermons and religious tracts, and popular short stories and novels all told women what they were like and how they should feel about themselves. Such sources are called "prescriptive literature" because they literally prescribe how people should—and should not—behave.

Of course, historians of women do not argue that there was a direct correlation between how people were *supposed* to behave and how they actually *did* behave. The doctrine of separate spheres could also be both restrictive for women and beneficial for women. At best, it was a complex metaphor for the negotiation and renegotiation of gender relations. But it is clear that in the nineteenth century, the cult of domesticity (the doctrine of separate spheres) established a very powerful and long-lasting set of gender expectations that influenced law and public policy decisions as well as interpersonal relationships.[4]

What, then, was expected of New England farmers' daughters and other respectable (white) women? They were supposed to be pious, more naturally religious than men (real men might occasionally swear, but real women never did). Because they were naturally logical and rational, men

1. Alice Kessler-Harris, *Out to Work: A History of America's Wage-Earning Women* (New York: Oxford, 1982).

2. Christine Stansell, *City of Women: Sex and Class in New York, 1789–1860* (New York: Knopf, 1986).

3. Barbara Welter, "The Cult of True Womanhood, 1820–1860," *American Quarterly* 18 (Summer 1966): 151–174.

4. Linda Kerber, "Separate Spheres, Female Worlds, and Women's Place: The Rhetoric of Women's History," *Journal of American History* 75 (1988): 9–39; Nancy Cott, review of *A Shared Experience: Men, Women, and the History of Gender,* edited by Laura McCall and Donald Yacovne, *American Historical Review* 105 (2000): 170–171.

might pursue education, but true women should not because they might be led into error if they strayed from the Bible. As daughters, wives, or even sisters, women had the important responsibility of being the spiritual uplifters to whom men could turn when necessary.

Just as important as piety was the true woman's purity. This purity was absolute because whereas a man might "sow his wild oats" and then be saved by the love of a good woman, a "fallen woman" could never be saved. In the popular fiction of the period, a woman who had been seduced usually became insane, died, or did both. If she had a baby, it also came to a bad end. Only on her wedding night did a true woman surrender her virginity, and then out of duty rather than passion, because it was widely believed that pure women were not sexually responsive. In fact, many young women of this era knew nothing at all about their own bodies or the nature of sexual intercourse until they married.

Submission and domesticity were perhaps not as vital as piety and purity. Although women who did not submit to men's leadership were destined to be unhappy (according to the thought of the day), they could correct their mistaken behavior. Men were, after all, stronger and more intelligent, the natural protectors of women. A true woman, wrote then-popular author Grace Greenwood, should be like a "perpetual child," who is always "timid, doubtful, and clingingly dependent." Such pious, pure, submissive women were particularly well suited to the important task of creating a pleasant, cheerful home—a place

where men could escape from their worldly struggles and be fed, clothed, comforted, and nursed if they were ill. Even a woman who did not have very much money could create such a haven, people believed, simply by using her natural talents of sewing, cooking, cleaning, and flower arranging.

Simultaneously, then, two important trends were occurring in the early 1800s: the northern economy was modernizing, and sexual stereotypes that assigned very different roles to men and women were developing. Whereas a man should be out in the world of education, work, and politics, a woman's place was in the home, a sphere where she could be sheltered.

But what would happen if the economic need for an increased supply of labor clashed with the new ideas about women's place in society? If a young unmarried woman went to work in a factory far away from her parents' farm, would she still be respectable? Where would she live? Who would protect her? Perhaps the experience of factory work itself would destroy those special feminine characteristics all true women possessed. All these fears and more would have to be confronted in the course of the development of the New England textile industry during the 1830s and 1840s.

Although the first American textile mill using water-powered spinning machines was built in 1790, it and the countless other mills that sprang up throughout New England during the next thirty years depended heavily on the putting-out system. The mills made only the yarn, which was then distributed ("put out") to women who wove the cloth in their own homes and returned the finished products to the mills. In 1820, two-thirds of all American cloth was still being produced by women working at home. But the pace of modernization accelerated sharply with the formation of the Boston Manufacturing Company, a heavily capitalized firm that purchased a large tract of rural land in the Merrimack River valley. The Boston Associates adopted the latest technology and, more important, concentrated all aspects of cloth production inside their factories. Because they no longer put out work, they had to attract large numbers of workers, especially young women from New England farms, to their mills. Lowell, Massachusetts (the "City of Spindles"), and the Lowell mills became a kind of model, an experiment that received a good deal of attention in both Europe and America. As historian Thomas Dublin has shown, most of the young women at the Lowell mills were fifteen to thirty years old, unmarried, and from farm families that were neither the richest nor the poorest in their area. Although some of the Lowell girls occasionally sent small amounts of money back to their families, most used their wages for new clothes, education, and dowries.[5] These wages were significantly higher than those for teaching, farm labor, or domestic services, the three other major occupations open to women.

The factory girls were required to live and eat in boardinghouses run according to company rules and supervised by respectable landladies. The company partially subsidized the cost of room and board and also encouraged the numerous lecture series, evening schools, and church-related activities in Lowell. Girls worked together in the mills, filling the unskilled and semiskilled positions, and men (about one-fourth of the work force) performed the skilled jobs and served as overseers (foremen). Work in the mills also was characterized by strict regulations and an elaborate system of bells that signaled mealtimes and work times.

During the 1840s, factory girls occasionally published their own magazines, the most famous of which was the *Lowell Offering*. This journal grew out of a working women's self-improvement society and was sponsored by a local Lowell minister. When the minister was transferred, the mill owners partially subsidized the magazine. The female editors, who were former mill workers, insisted that the magazine was for "literary" work rather than for labor reform. The Evidence section presents a description of Lowell mills and boardinghouses and several selections from the *Lowell Offering* and other sources.

The conflict between economic modernization and the cult of true womanhood was indirectly recognized by many New Englanders and directly experienced by the Lowell mill girls. What forms did this conflict take? What fears and anxieties did it reveal? How did the mill girls attempt to cope with this tension?

5. A dowry is the money, goods, or property that a woman brings into her marriage.

❋ THE METHOD ❋

When historians use prescriptive literature as evidence, they ask (1) what message is being conveyed, (2) who is sending the message, (3) why it is being sent, and (4) for whom it is intended. Most of the evidence you are using in this chapter is in some ways prescriptive—that is, it tells people how women *should* behave.

An early major criticism of the effects of factory work on young women was written by Orestes Brownson, a well-known New England editor and reformer. A sharply contrasting view appears in the excerpts from a brief, popular book about Lowell written by Reverend Henry Mills in 1845. Reverend Mills was a local Protestant minister who was asked by the textile company owners to conduct surveys into the workers' habits, health, and moral character. Depending heavily on information provided by company officials, overseers, and landladies, Reverend Mills published *Lowell, As It Was, and As It Is.*

Yet the controversy continued, because only one year later, the journal owned by the Lowell Female Labor Reform Association, *Voice of Industry,* painted a much darker picture of the factory girls' "slavery." Although purchased by a militant group of women factory workers, the *Voice* had originated as a labor reform paper. Its editorial policy always addressed larger, worker-oriented issues such as a shorter workday and dedicated a special column to women workers' concerns.

The young women who worked in the textile mills also actively partici-pated in the debate. The evidence in the selections from the *Lowell Offering* was written by factory girls during the years 1840 to 1843. Also presented is an excerpt from a book written by Lucy Larcom, one of the few children (under age fifteen) employed in the Lowell mills in the late 1830s. She was a factory girl for more than ten years, after which she went west and obtained a college education. She became a well-known teacher and author when she returned to New England. Larcom published a book about her New England girlhood when she was sixty-five years old. The final set of evidence includes two pictures of "typical" mill girls in 1860 and letters written by mill girls and their families. Although the letters were *descriptive,* the girls were also presenting an image of themselves as they wished to be seen. Thus, in that sense, the letters were also *prescriptive.*

First read through the evidence, looking for elements of the cult of true womanhood in the factory girls' writings and in the Lowell system itself. Be sure to consider all four questions: What message is being conveyed? Who is sending the message? Why is it being sent? For whom is it intended? This will tell you a great deal not only about the social standards for respectable young white women but also about the fears and anxieties aroused by a factory system that employed women away from their homes.

Reading about how people *should* behave, however, does not tell us how people actually behaved. Remember that the central question of this problem involves a clash: a conflict be-tween ideas (the cult) and reality (the factory system). Go through the evidence again, this time trying to reconstruct what it was really like for the young women who lived and worked in Lowell. Ask yourself to what degree and in what ways they might have deviated from the ideal of "true" women.

Also ask whether they could have achieved this ideal goal—and whether they really wanted to—while working and living in Lowell. In other words, try to clarify in your own mind the forms of the conflict and the reactions (of both society and the young women) to that conflict.

❄ THE EVIDENCE ❄

Source 1 from Orestes A. Brownson, *Boston Quarterly Review* 3 (July 1840): 368–370.

1. Slave Labor Versus Free Labor, 1840.

In regard to labor, two systems obtain: one that of slave labor, the other that of free labor. Of the two, the first is, in our judgment, except so far as the feelings are concerned, decidedly the least oppressive. If the slave has never been a free man, we think, as a general rule, his sufferings are less than those of the free laborer at wages. As to actual freedom, one has just about as much as the other. The laborer at wages has all the disadvantages of freedom and none of its blessings, while the slave, if denied the blessings, is freed from the disadvantages. . . .

It is said there is no want in this country. There may be less in some other countries. But death by actual starvation in this country is, we apprehend, no uncommon occurrence. The sufferings of a quiet, unassuming but useful class of females in our cities, in general seamstresses, too proud to beg or to apply to the almshouse, are not easily told. They are industrious; they do all that they can find to do. But yet the little there is for them to do, and the miserable pittance they receive for it, is hardly sufficient to keep soul and body together. . . .

The average life—working life, we mean—of the girls that come to Lowell, for instance, from Maine, New Hampshire, and Vermont, we have been assured, is only about three years. What becomes of them then? Few of them ever marry[6]; fewer still ever return to their native places with repu-

---

6. According to historian Thomas Dublin in *Women at Work* (New York: Columbia University Press, 1979), the working women of Lowell tended to marry in about the same proportion as

tations unimpaired. "She has worked in a factory" is almost enough to damn to infamy the most worthy and virtuous girl. . . .

Source 2 from Reverend Henry A. Mills, *Lowell, As It Was, and As It Is* (Lowell, Mass.: Powers, Bagley, and Dayton, 1845).

2. A Lowell Boardinghouse, 1845.

[*Reverend Mills began by describing the long blocks of boardinghouses, each three stories high, which were built in a style reminiscent of country farmhouses. Clean, well painted, and neat, these houses contained common eating rooms, parlors, and sleeping rooms for two to six boarders. The boarders, Reverend Mills observed, were sometimes a bit crowded but actually lived under better conditions than seamstresses and milliners in other towns. Men and women lived in separate houses with strict rules.*]

. . . *Regulations to be observed by persons occupying the Boarding-houses belonging to the Merrimack Manufacturing company.*

They must not board any persons not employed by the company, unless by special permission.

No disorderly or improper conduct must be allowed in the houses.

The doors must be closed at 10 o'clock in the evening; and no person admitted after that time, unless a sufficient excuse can be given.

Those who keep the houses, when required, must give an account of the number, names, and employment of their boarders; also with regard to their general conduct and whether they are in the habit of attending public worship.

The buildings, both inside and out, and the yards about them, must be kept clean and in good order. If the buildings or fences are injured, they will be repaired and charged to the occupant.

No one will be allowed to keep swine.

[*The meals might seem rushed, Mills noted, but that was common among all Americans, particularly businesspeople. Working girls could choose whichever boardinghouses they preferred, rents were very low, and their living arrangements were very respectable.*]

---

nonworking New England women, although the Lowell women married three to five years later in life and had a distinct tendency to marry men who were tradesmen or skilled workers rather than farmers.

No tenant is admitted who has not hitherto borne a good character, and who does not continue to sustain it. In many cases the tenant has long been keeper of the house, for six, eight, or twelve years, and is well known to hundreds of her girls as their adviser and friend and second mother. . . .

. . . Employing chiefly those who have no permanent residence in Lowell, but are only temporary boarders, upon any embarrassment of affairs they return to their country homes, and do not sink down here a helpless caste, clamouring for work, starving unless employed, and hence ready for a riot, for the destruction of property, and repeating here the scenes enacted in the manufacturing villages of England. . . .

To obtain this constant importation of female hands from the country, it is necessary to secure *the moral protection of their characters while they are resident in Lowell.* This, therefore, is the chief object of that moral police referred to, some details of which will now be given.

It should be stated, in the outset, that no persons are employed on the Corporations who are addicted to intemperance, or who are known to be guilty of any immoralities of conduct. As the parent of all other vices, intemperance is most carefully excluded. Absolute freedom from intoxicating liquors is understood, throughout the city, to be a prerequisite to obtaining employment in the mills, and any person known to be addicted to their use is at once dismissed. . . . In relation to other immoralities, it may be stated, that the suspicion of criminal conduct, association with suspected persons, and general and habitual light behavior and conversation, are regarded as sufficient reasons for dismissions, and for which delinquent operatives are discharged.

[*Reverend Mills also described the discharge system at the factories. For those girls whose conduct was satisfactory and who had worked at least a year, honorable discharges were issued. Discharge letters could be used as recommendations for other jobs. Those who received dishonorable discharges for infractions such as stealing, lying, leaving the job without permission, or other "improper conduct" would have difficulty finding other employment.*]

This system, which has been in operation in Lowell from the beginning, is of great and important effect in driving unworthy persons from our city, and in preserving the high character of our operatives.

[*Male overseers, or foremen, also were closely screened and had to possess good moral character. In response to Reverend Mills's questions about the male overseers, one factory owner responded as follows.*]

Lowell, May 10, 1841

Dear Sir:—

I employ in our mills, and in the various departments connected with them, thirty overseers, and as many second overseers. My overseers are married men, with families, with a single exception, and even he has engaged a tenement, and is to be married soon. Our second overseers are younger men, but upwards of twenty of them are married, and several others are soon to be married. Sixteen of our overseers are members of some regular church, and four of them are deacons. Ten of our second overseers are also members of the church, and one of them is the Superintendent of a Sunday School. I have no hesitation in saying that in all the sterling requisites of character, in native intelligence, and practical good sense, in sound morality, and as active, useful, and exemplary citizens, they may, as a class, safely challenge comparison with any class in our community. I know not, among them all, an intemperate man, nor, at this time, even what is called a moderate drinker.

[Furthermore, the girls were expected to obey numerous rules.]

Still another source of trust which a Corporation has, for the good character of its operatives, is the moral control which they have over one another. Of course this control would be nothing among a generally corrupt and degraded class. But among virtuous and high-minded young women, who feel that they have the keeping of their characters, and that any stain upon their associates brings reproach upon themselves, the power of opinion becomes an ever-present, and ever-active restraint. A girl, *suspected* of immoralities, or serious improprieties of conduct, at once loses caste. Her fellow-boarders will at once leave the house, if the keeper does not dismiss the offender. In self-protection, therefore, the matron is obliged to put the offender away. Nor will her former companions walk with, or work with her; till at length, finding herself everywhere talked about, and pointed at, and shunned, she is obliged to relieve her fellow-operatives of a presence which they feel brings disgrace. From this power of opinion, there is no appeal; and as long as it is exerted in favor of propriety of behavior and purity of life, it is one of the most active and effectual safeguards of character. . . .

[Punctuality was required of both overseers and workers.]

All persons are required to observe the regulations of the room in which they are employed. They are not allowed to be absent from their work without the consent of their overseer, except in case of sickness, and then they are required to send him word of the cause of their absence.

All persons are required to board in one of the boarding-houses belonging to the company, and conform to the regulations of the house in which they board.

All persons are required to be constant in attendance on public worship, at one of the regular places of worship in this place.

Persons who do not comply with the above regulations will not be employed by the company.

Persons entering the employment of the company are considered as engaging to work one year.

All persons intending to leave the employment of the company, are required to give notice of the same to their overseer, at least two weeks previous to the time of leaving.

Any one who shall take from the mills, or the yard, any yarn, cloth, or other article belonging to the company, will be considered guilty of STEAL-ING—and prosecuted accordingly.

. . . All persons who shall have complied with [the rules], on leaving the employment of the company, shall be entitled to an honorable discharge, which will serve as a recommendation to any of the factories in Lowell. No one who shall not have complied with them will be entitled to such a discharge.

Source 3 courtesy of the American Textile History Museum.

3. Timetable of the Lowell Mills, 1853.

TIME TABLE OF THE LOWELL MILLS,

Arranged to make the working time throughout the year average 11 hours per day.

TO TAKE EFFECT SEPTEMBER 21st., 1853.

The Standard time being that of the meridian of Lowell, as shown by the Regulator Clock of AMOS SANBORN, Post Office Corner, Central Street.

From March 20th to September 19th, inclusive.

COMMENCE WORK, at 6.30 A. M. LEAVE OFF WORK, at 6.30 P. M., except on Saturday Evenings.
BREAKFAST at 6 A. M. DINNER, at 12 M. Commence Work, after dinner, 12.45 P. M.

From September 20th to March 19th, inclusive.

COMMENCE WORK at 7.00 A. M. LEAVE OFF WORK, at 7.00 P. M., except on Saturday Evenings.
BREAKFAST at 6.30 A. M. DINNER, at 12.30 P.M. Commence Work, after dinner, 1.15 P. M.

BELLS.

From March 20th to September 19th, inclusive.

Morning Bells.	Dinner Bells.	Evening Bells.
First bell,..........4.30 A. M.	Ring out,..............12.00 M.	Ring out,...........6.30 P. M.
Second, 5.30 A. M.; Third, 6.20.	Ring in,...........12.35 P. M.	Except on Saturday Evenings.

From September 20th to March 19th, inclusive.

Morning Bells.	Dinner Bells.	Evening Bells.
First bell,..........5.00 A. M.	Ring out,..........12.30 P. M.	Ring out at..........7.00 P. M.
Second, 6.00 A. M.; Third, 6.50.	Ring in,.............1.05 P. M.	Except on Saturday Evenings.

SATURDAY EVENING BELLS.

During APRIL, MAY, JUNE, JULY, and AUGUST, Ring Out, at 6.00 P. M.
The remaining Saturday Evenings in the year, ring out as follows :

SEPTEMBER.	NOVEMBER.	JANUARY.
First Saturday, ring out 6.00 P. M.	Third Saturday ring out 4.00 P. M.	Third Saturday, ring out 4.25 P. M.
Second " " 5.45 "	Fourth " " 3.55 "	Fourth " " 4.35 "
Third " " 5.30 "		
Fourth " " 5.20 "	DECEMBER.	FEBRUARY.
OCTOBER.	First Saturday, ring out 3.50 P. M.	First Saturday, ring out 4.45 P. M.
First Saturday, ring out 5.05 P. M.	Second " " 3.55 "	Second " " 4.55 "
Second " " 4.55 "	Third " " 3.55 "	Third " " 5.00 "
Third " " 4.45 "	Fourth " " 4.00 "	Fourth " " 5.10 "
Fourth " " 4.35 "	Fifth " " 4.00 "	MARCH.
Fifth " " 4.25 "	JANUARY.	First Saturday, ring out 5.25 P. M.
NOVEMBER.	First Saturday, ring out 4.10 P. M.	Second " " 5.30 "
First Saturday, ring out 4.15 P. M.	Second " " 4.15 "	Third " " 5.35 "
Second ". " 4.05 "		Fourth " " 5.45 "

YARD GATES will be opened at the first stroke of the bells for entering or leaving the Mills.

.*.   *SPEED GATES commence hoisting three minutes before commencing work.*

Penhallow, Printer, Wyman's Exchange, 28 Merrimack St.

Source 4 from *Voice of Industry,* January 2, 1846, in H. R. Warfel et al., eds., *The American Mind* (New York: American Book Company, 1937), p. 392.

4. "Slaver" Wagons, 1846.

We were not aware, until within a few days, of the *modus operandi* of the factory powers in this village of forcing poor girls from their quiet homes to become their tools and, like the Southern slaves, to give up their life and liberty to the heartless tyrants and taskmasters.

Observing a singular-looking "long, low, black" wagon passing along the street, we made inquiries respecting it, and were informed that it was what we term a "slaver." She makes regular trips to the north of the state [Massachusetts], cruising around in Vermont and New Hampshire, with a "commander" whose heart must be as black as his craft, who is paid a dollar a head for all he brings to the market, and more in proportion to the distance—if they bring them from such a distance that they cannot easily get back.

This is done by "hoisting false colors," and representing to the girls that they can tend more machinery than is possible, and that the work is so very neat, and the wages such that they can dress in silks and spend half their time in reading. Now, is this true? Let those girls who have been thus deceived, answer.

Let us say a word in regard to the manner in which they are stowed in the wagon, which may find a similarity only in the manner in which slaves are fastened in the hold of a vessel. It is long, and the seats so close that it must be very inconvenient.

Is there any humanity in this? Philanthropists may talk of Negro slavery, but it would be well first to endeavor to emancipate the slaves at home. Let us not stretch our ears to catch the sound of the lash on the flesh of the oppressed black while the oppressed in our very midst are crying out in thunder tones, and calling upon us for assistance.

Source 5 from *Lowell Offering,* Series I, Issue 1 (1840). Courtesy of the American Textile History Museum.

5. Title Page of *Lowell Offering.*

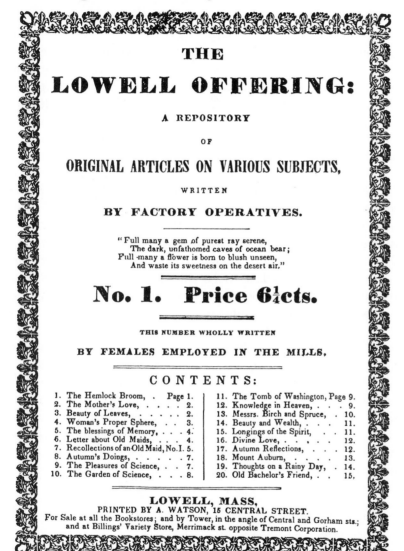

THE
LOWELL OFFERING:

A REPOSITORY

OF

ORIGINAL ARTICLES ON VARIOUS SUBJECTS,

WRITTEN

BY FACTORY OPERATIVES.

"Full many a gem of purest ray serene,
The dark, unfathomed caves of ocean bear;
Full many a flower is born to blush unseen,
And waste its sweetness on the desert air."

No. 1.   Price 6¼cts.

THIS NUMBER WHOLLY WRITTEN

BY FEMALES EMPLOYED IN THE MILLS.

CONTENTS:

LOWELL, MASS,
PRINTED BY A. WATSON, 15 CENTRAL STREET.
For Sale at all the Bookstores; and by Tower, in the angle of Central and Gorham sts.;
and at Billings' Variety Store, Merrimack st. opposite Tremont Corporation.

Source 6 from *Lowell Offering,* Series I, Issue 1 (1840), p. 16.

6. Editorial Corner.

The Lowell Offering is strictly what it purports to be, a "Repository of original articles on various subjects, written by Factory Operatives."—The objects of the publication are, to encourage the cultivation of talent; to preserve such articles as are deemed most worthy of preservation; and to correct an erroneous idea which generally prevails in relation to the intelligence of persons employed in the Mills. This number is wholly the offering of Females. . . .

We are persuaded that the citizens generally, and those engaged in the Mills particularly, will feel and manifest a lively interest in the prosperity of the Lowell Offering. That it is faultless—that the severe and captious critic will find no room for his vocation, is not to be expected. Nevertheless, while the work makes no noisy pretensions to superior excellency, it would claim no unusual indulgences. It asks only that, all the circumstances incident to its peculiar character being duly weighed, it shall be fairly and candidly judged. The Editors do not hesitate to say, that they anticipate for a favorable reception at the hands of those who have at heart the interests of that important and interesting portion of our population, whose intellectual elevation and moral welfare it aims to promote. . . .

An opinion extensively prevails, not merely beyond the limits of Massachusetts, that the Manufacturing city of Lowell is a nucleus of depravity and ignorance.

Confessedly, wherever there exists *any* depravity or ignorance, there is *too much* of it. We have this to testify however, that they who know least of the people of Lowell, including the Factory Operatives, entertain the most unworthy and unjust opinions of them. Close personal observation has satisfied us, that in respect of morality and intelligence, they will not suffer in comparison with the inhabitants of any part of moral and enlightened New England. . . .

Sources 7 and 8 from *Lowell Offering,* Series II, Vol. II (1842), p. 192; Series II, Vol. III (1842), pp. 69–70.

7. Dignity of Labor.

From whence originated the idea, that it was derogatory to a lady's dignity, or a blot upon the female character, to labor? and who was the first to say, sneeringly, "Oh, she *works* for a living"? Surely, such ideas and expressions ought not to grow on republican soil. The time has been, when ladies of the first rank were accustomed to busy themselves in domestic employment.

Homer tells us of princesses who used to draw water from the springs, and wash with their own hands the finest of the linen of their respective families. The famous Lucretia used to spin in the midst of her attendants; and the wife of Ulysses, after the siege of Troy, employed herself in weaving, until her husband returned to Ithaca. And in later times, the wife of George the Third of England, has been represented as spending a whole evening in hemming pocket-handkerchiefs, while her daughter Mary sat in the corner, darning stockings.

Few American fortunes will support a woman who is above the calls of her family; and a man of sense, in choosing a companion to jog with him through all the up-hills and down-hills of life, would sooner choose one who *had* to work for a living, than one who thought it beneath her to soil her pretty hands with manual labor, although she possessed her thousands. To be able to earn one's own living by laboring with the hands, should be reckoned among female accomplishments; and I hope the time is not far distant when none of my countrywomen will be ashamed to have it known that they are better versed in useful, than they are in ornamental accomplishments.

C.B.

8. Editorial: Home in a Boardinghouse.

[*Factory boardinghouses were not really like homes, the editor pointed out. A place to eat and lodge, the boardinghouses often seemed crowded and impersonal.*]

But these are all trifles, compared with the perplexities to which we are subjected in other ways; and some of these things might be remedied by the girls themselves. We now allude to the importunities of evening visitors, such as peddlers, candy and newspaper boys, shoe-dealers, book-sellers, &c., &c., breaking in upon the only hours of leisure we can call our own, and proffering their articles with a pertinacity which will admit of no denial. . . . And then they often forget, if they ever knew, the rules of politeness which should regulate all transient visitors. . . .

The remedy is entirely with the girls. Treat all of these comers with a politeness truly lady-like, when they appear as gentlemen, but let your manners change to stern formality when they forget that they are in the company of respectable females. . . .

C.B.

Sources 9 through 11 from *Lowell Offering,* Series I, Issue 1 (1840), pp. 17–19, 61, 44–46.

9. Factory Girls.

"She has worked in a factory, *is sufficient to damn to infamy the most worthy and virtuous girl.*"

So says Mr. Orestes A. Brownson; and either this horrible assertion is true, or Mr. Brownson is a slanderer. I assert that it is *not* true, and Mr. B. may consider himself called upon to prove his words, if he can.

This gentleman has read of an Israelitish boy who, with nothing but a stone and sling, once entered into a contest with a Philistine giant, arrayed in brass, whose spear was like a weaver's beam; and he may now see what will probably appear to him quite as marvellous; and that is, that a *factory girl* is not afraid to oppose herself to the *Editor of the Boston Quarterly Review.* True, he has upon his side fame, learning, and great talent; but I have what is better than either of these, or all combined, and that is *truth.* Mr. Brownson has not said that this thing should be so; or that he is glad it is so; or that he deeply regrets such a state of affairs; but he has said it *is* so; and *I* affirm that it is *not.*

And whom has Mr. Brownson slandered? A class of girls who in this city alone are numbered by thousands, and who collect in many of our smaller towns by hundreds; girls who generally come from quiet country homes, where their minds and manners have been formed under the eyes of the worthy sons of the Pilgrims, and their virtuous partners, and who return again to become the wives of the free intelligent yeomanry of New England and the mothers of quite a portion of our future republicans. Think, for a moment, how many of the next generation are to spring from mothers doomed to infamy! "Ah," it may be replied, "Mr. Brownson acknowledges that you may still be worthy and virtuous." Then we must be a set of worthy and virtuous idiots, for no virtuous girl of common sense would choose for an occupation one that would consign her to infamy. . . .

That there has been prejudice against us, we know; but it is wearing away, and has never been so deep nor universal as Mr. B's statement will lead many to believe. Even now it may be that "the mushroom aristocracy" and "would-be fashionables" of Boston, turn up their eyes in horror at the sound of those vulgar words, *factory girls;* but *they* form but a small part of the community, and theirs are not the opinions which Mr. Brownson intended to represent. . . .

[*The prejudice against factory girls was connected to the degraded and exploited conditions of European workers, the angry letter writer asserted. "Yankee girls," she said, are independent, and although the work is hard, the wages are better than those in other kinds of employment. It is no wonder, she concluded, that so many intelligent, worthy, and virtuous young women have been drawn to Lowell.*]

The erroneous idea, wherever it exists, must be done away, that there is in factories but one sort of girls, and *that* the baser and degraded sort. There are among us *all* sorts of girls. I believe that there are few occupations which can exhibit so many gradations of piety and intelligence; but the majority may at least lay claim to as much of the former as females in other stations of life. . . . The Improvement Circles, the Lyceum and Institute, the social religious meetings, the Circulating and other libraries, can bear testimony that the little time they have is spent in a better manner. Our well filled churches and lecture halls and the high character of our clergymen and lecturers, will testify that the state of morals and intelligence is not low.

Mr. Brownson, I suppose, would not judge of our moral characters by our church-going tendencies; but as many do, a word on this subject may not be amiss. That there are many in Lowell who do not regularly attend any meeting, is as true as the correspondent of the Boston Times once represented it; but for this there are various reasons. . . .

And now, if Mr. Brownson is a *man,* he will endeavor to retrieve the injury he has done; he will resolve that "the dark shall be light, and the wrong made right," and the assertion he has publicly made will be as publicly retracted. If he still doubts upon the subject let him come among us: let him make himself as well acquainted with us as our pastors and superintendents are; and though he will find error, ignorance, and folly among us, (and where would he find them not?) yet he would not see worthy and virtuous girls consigned to infamy, because they work in a factory.

A FACTORY GIRL

10. A Familiar Letter.

Friends and Associates:—

With indescribable emotions of pleasure, mingled with feelings of deepest gratitude to Him who is the Author of every good and perfect gift, I have perused the second and third numbers of the Lowell Offering.

As a laborer among you, (tho' least of all) I rejoice that the time has arrived when a class of laboring females (who have long been made a reproach and byword, by those whom fortune or pride has placed above the avocation by which we have subjected ourselves to the sneers and scoffs of the idle, ignorant and envious part of community,) are bursting asunder the captive chains of prejudice. . . .

I know it has been affirmed, to the sorrow of many a would-be lady, that factory girls and ladies could not be distinguished by their apparel. What a lamentable evil! and no doubt it would be a source of much gratitude to such, if the awful name of "factory girl!" were branded on the forehead of every female who is, or ever was, employed in the Mills. Appalling as the name may sound in the delicate ears of a sensitive lady, as she contrasts the music of her piano with the rumblings of the factory machinery, we would not shrink from such a token of our calling, could the treasures of the mind be there displayed, and merit, in her own unbiased form be stamped there also. . . .

Yours, in the bonds of affection,
DOROTHEA

11. Gold Watches.

It is now nearly a year since an article appeared in the Ladies' Book, in the form of a tale, though it partakes more of the character of an essay. It was written by Mrs. Hale, and exhibits her usual judgment and talent. Her object evidently was to correct the many erroneous impressions which exist in society, with regard to the folly of extravagance in dress, and all outward show. I was much pleased with all of it, with the exception of a single sentence. Speaking of the impossibility of considering dress a mark of distinction, she observed,—(addressing herself, I presume, to the *ladies* of New England,)—"How stands the difference now? Many of the factory girls wear gold watches, and an imitation, at least, of all the ornaments which grace the daughters of our most opulent citizens."

O the times! O the manners! Alas! how very sadly the world has changed! The time was when the *lady* could be distinguished from the *no-lady* by her dress, as far as the eye could reach; but now, you might stand in the same room, and judging by their outward appearance, you could not tell "which was which." Even gold watches are now no *sure* indication—for they have been worn by the lowest, even by "many of the factory girls." No *lady* need carry one now, for any other than the simple purpose of easily ascertaining the time of day, or night, if she so please! . . .

Those who do not labor for their living, have more time for the improvement of their minds, for the cultivation of conversational powers, and graceful manners; but if, with these advantages, they still need richer dress to distinguish them from *us,* the fault must be their own, and they should at least learn to honor merit, and acknowledge talent wherever they see it. . . .

And now I will address myself to my sister operatives in the Lowell factories. Good advice should be taken, from whatever quarter it may come, whether from friend or foe; and part of the advice which Mrs. Hale has given to the readers of the Ladies' Book, may be of advantage to us. Is there not among us, as a class, too much of this striving for distinction in dress? Is it not the only aim and object of too many of us, to wear something a little better than others can obtain? Do we not sometimes see the girl who has half a dozen silk gowns, toss her head, as if she felt herself six times better than her neighbor who has none? . . .

We all have many opportunities for the exercise of the kindly affections, and more than most females. We should look upon one another something as a band of orphans should do. We are fatherless and motherless: we are alone, and surrounded by temptation. Let us caution each other; let us watch over and endeavor to improve each other; and both at our boarding-houses and in the Mill, let us strive to promote each other's comfort and happiness. Above all, let us endeavor to improve ourselves by making good use of the many advantages we here possess. I say let us at least strive to do this; and if we succeed, it will finally be acknowledged that Factory Girls shine forth in ornaments far more valuable than *Gold Watches.*

A FACTORY GIRL

Source 12 from *Lowell Offering,* Series II, Vol. II (1842), p. 380.

12. Editor's Valedictory.

It has been the object of the editor to encourage the cultivation of talent, and thus open and enlarge the sources of enjoyment in the midst of a toilsome life. . . .

We hoped ere this to have seen a spacious room, with a Library, &c., established on each Corporation, for the accommodation of the female operatives in the evenings. The example, we trust, will shortly be set by the

Merrimack. And why should not bathing-rooms be fitted up in the basement of each Mill? The expense would not be felt by the Company, and the means of health and comfort thus provided, would be gratefully acknowledged. We suggest, in addition, a better ventilation of the boarding-houses. Diminution of the hours of mill-labor, and the entire abrogation of premiums to Overseers, should also be included in the list of improvements.

There is another matter, some time since presented to the operatives, and now repeated, namely, the payment of a small sum monthly, say 8 or 10 cents, to consitute a fund for the relief of the sick. The amount might be deducted by the pay-master, as agent of the Superintendent. The details of the plan could readily be agreed upon. Two cents each week would surely be well spent as insurance against the expenses of sickness, to be fixed at about three dollars weekly—to be received, not as *charity,* but as a lawful demand.

Source 13 from *Lowell Offering,* Series II, Vol. V (1845), p. 96.

13. Editorial: The Ten-Hour Movement.

[*The editor begins by reviewing the work of the Massachusetts legislature's Committee upon the Hours of Labor. Although she understands why the demand for a ten-hour workday was not accepted, she believes there were other improvements that might have been made.*]

It seems to have been generally conceded, that the time allotted to meals is very short—where the operatives have tolerable appetites: and this is usually the case with persons who *work so regularly* and indefatigably. Why not have compromised then with the petitioners, and allowed them one hour for dinner through the year, and three-quarters of an hour for breakfast? The dinner *hour* is given in some manufacturing places, therefore the plea with regard to competition is not unanswerable. We believe also that Lowell is expected to take the lead in all improvements of this nature, and, should she amend her present system, it is more probable that she would be imitated than successfully contended against. . . .

[*The editor then addresses employers' argument that there are girls waiting at the factory gate before the work bell rings, eager to get in and begin work. The author concedes that some girls compete with each other for the overseer's favors. But what of the others? she asks.*]

. . . They feel that they are unable to work all these hours, and "work upon the stretch," as they say. They are older, or weaker, or more heavily moulded, or unwilling, if not unable. Therefore they are not favorites with their overseer. They are not so "profitable servants," and the kind look and word, or obliging act, is not so often bestowed upon them. This is one instance where the testimony is liable to misconstruction, and had we space, we might find many more.

The Legislature seem to have doubted the propriety of their commencing action upon this subject. Where should it commence? How is it to be done? When, where, and by whom? All, connected with manufacturing establishments, feel confident that, "as surely as there is benevolence and justice in the heart of man," this wrong will be righted. But objections are brought against every movement. . . .

Source 14 from *Lowell Offering,* Series II, Vol. I (1841), p. 32. Courtesy of the American Textile History Museum.

14. "Song of the Spinners."

SONG OF THE SPINNERS.

1. The day is o'er, nor lon-ger we toil and spin; For ev'ning's hush withdraws from the dai-ly din. And now we sing, with gladsome hearts, The theme of the spinner's song, That la-bor to lei-sure a zest imparts, Unknown to the i - - dle throng.

2. We spin all day, and then, in the time for rest, Sweet peace is found, A joyous and welcome guest. Des - pite of toil we all agree, or out of the Mills, or in, De-pen-dent on others we ne'er will be. So long as we're a-ble to spin.

Source 15 from Lucy Larcom, *A New England Girlhood* (Boston: Houghton Mifflin, 1889).

15. Selection from *A New England Girlhood.*

[*After her husband's death, Lucy Larcom's mother moved to Lowell to run a board-inghouse. Because her mother could not earn enough to support the family, Lucy, age eleven, and her older sister went to work in the mills.*]

So I went to my first day's work in the mill with a light heart. The novelty of it made it seem easy, and it really was not hard, just to change the bobbins on the spinning-frames every three quarters of an hour or so, with half a dozen other little girls who were doing the same thing. When I came back at night, the family began to pity me for my long, tiresome day's work, but I laughed, and said,—

"Why, it is nothing but fun. It is just like play."

And for a little while it was only a new amusement; I liked it better than going to school and "making believe" I was learning when I was not. And there was a great deal of play mixed with it. We were not occupied more than half the time. The intervals were spent frolicking around among the spinning-frames, teasing and talking to the older girls, or entertaining ourselves with games and stories in a corner, or exploring, with the over-seer's permission, the mysteries of the carding-room, the dressing-room, and the weaving-room. . . .

There were compensations for being shut in to daily toil so early. The mill itself had its lessons for us. But it was not, and could not be, the right sort of life for a child, and we were happy in the knowledge that, at the longest, our employment was only to be temporary. . . .

[*Lucy loved elementary school and wanted to continue her studies, but her family needed her mill wages.*]

In the older times it was seldom said to little girls, as it always has been said to boys, that they ought to have some definite plan, while they were children, what to be and do when they were grown up. There was usually but one path open before them, to become good wives and housekeepers. And the ambition of most girls was to follow their mothers' footsteps in this direction; a natural and laudable ambition. But girls, as well as boys, must often have been conscious of their own peculiar capabilities,—must have desired to cultivate and make use of their individual powers. When I was growing up, they had already begun to be encouraged to do so. We were often told that it was our duty to develop any talent we might possess, or at least learn how to do some one thing which the world needed, or which would make it a pleasanter world. . . .

At this time I had learned to do a spinner's work, and I obtained permission to tend some frames that stood directly in front of the river-windows, with only them and the wall behind me, extending half the length of the mill,—and one young woman beside me, at the farther end of the row. She was a sober, mature person, who scarcely thought it worth her while to speak often to a child like me; and I was, when with strangers, rather a reserved girl; so I kept myself occupied with the river, my work, and my thoughts. . . .

The printed regulations forbade us to bring books into the mill, so I made my window-seat into a small library of poetry, pasting its side all over with newspaper clippings. In those days we had only weekly papers, and they had always a "poet's corner," where standard writers were well represented, with anonymous ones, also. I was not, of course, much of a critic. I chose my verses for their sentiment, and because I wanted to commit them to memory; sometimes it was a long poem, sometimes a hymn, sometimes only a stray verse. . . .

Some of the girls could not believe that the Bible was meant to be counted among forbidden books. We all thought that the Scriptures had a right to go wherever we went, and that if we needed them anywhere, it was at our work. I evaded the law by carrying some leaves from a torn Testament in my pocket.

[*In spite of the regulations, girls brought poetry and plants into the factory.*]

One great advantage which came to these many stranger girls through being brought together, away from their own homes, was that it taught them to go out of themselves, and enter into the lives of others. Home-life, when one always stays at home, is necessarily narrowing. That is one reason why so many women are petty and unthoughtful of any except their own family's interests. We have hardly begun to live until we can take in the idea of the whole human family as the one to which we truly belong. To me, it was an incalculable help to find myself among so many working-girls, all of us thrown upon our own resources, but thrown much more upon each others' sympathies. . . .

Source 16 courtesy of the Mildred Tunis Tracey Memorial Library, New London, New Hampshire.

16. A "Typical" Factory Girl, Delia Page, at Age 18 or 19 (c. 1860).

Source 17 courtesy of the American Textile History Museum.

17. Two Weavers (c. 1860).

Sources 18 through 22 from Thomas Dublin, ed., *Farm to Factory: Women's Letters, 1830–1860* (New York: Columbia University Press, 1981), pp. 42, 100–104, 170–172.

18. Letter from Sarah Hodgdon.

[In 1830, Sarah Hodgdon, age sixteen, and two friends went to Lowell to work in the textile mills. After approximately ten years of working in various factories, Hodgdon married a shoemaker from her home town. This is one of her early letters to her mother.]

[June 1830]

Dear mother

I take this oppertunity to write to you to informe you that I have gone into the mill and like [it] very well. I was here one week and three days before I went into the mill to work for my board. We boord t[o]gether. I like my boording place very well. I enjoy my health very well. I do not enjoy my mind so well as it is my desire to. I cant go to any meetings except I hire a seat therefore I have to stay home on that account.[7] I desire you pay that it may not be said of me when I come home that I have sold my soul for the gay vanitys of this world. Give my love to my father and tell him not to forget me and to my dear sister and to my brothers and to my grammother tell her I do not forget her and to my Aunts and to all my enquiring friends. I want that you should write to me as soon as you can and when you write to me I want that you should write to me the particulars about sister and Aunt Betsy. Dont fail writing. I bege you not to let this scrabling be seen.

Sarah Hodgdon

Mary Hodgdon

19. Letter from Mary Paul.

[Mary Paul left home in 1845 at age fifteen. She worked briefly and unsuccessfully as a domestic servant and then went to Lowell as a factory girl for four years. After leaving the mills, she returned home for a short while and then worked as a seamstress. Next she joined a utopian community, and finally she took a job as a housekeeper. In 1857, Paul married the son of the woman who ran the boarding-house where she had lived in Lowell.]

7. Urban churches in this period often charged people who attended services a fee called pew rent.

Saturday, Sept. 13th 1845

Dear Father

I received your letter this afternoon by Wm Griffith. . . . I am very glad you sent my shoes. They fit very well indeed they [are] large enough.

I want you to consent to let me go to Lowell if you can. I think it would be much better for me than to stay about here. I could earn more to begin with than I can any where about here. I am in need of clothes which I cannot get if I stay about here and for that reason I want to go to Lowell or some other place. We all think if I could go with some steady girl that I might do well. I want you to think of it and make up your mind. Mercy Jane Griffith is going to start in four or five weeks. Aunt Miller and Aunt Sarah think it would be a good chance for me to go if you would consent—which I want you to do if possible. I want to see you and talk with you about it.

Aunt Sarah gains slowly.

Mary

Bela Paul

20. Letter from Mary Paul.

Lowell Dec 21st 1845

Dear Father

I received your letter on Thursday the 14th with much pleasure. I am well which is one comfort. My life and health are spared while others are cut off. Last Thursday one girl fell down and broke her neck which caused instant death. She was going in or coming out of the mill and slipped down it being very icy. The same day a man was killed by the cars. Another had nearly all of his ribs broken. Another was nearly killed by falling down and having a bale of cotton fall on him. Last Tuesday we were paid. In all I had six dollars and sixty cents paid four dollars and sixty-eight cents for board. With the rest I got me a pair of rubbers and a pair of 50.cts shoes. . . . I get along very well with my work. I can doff[8] as fast as any girl in our room. I think I shall have frames before long. The usual time allowed for learning is six months but I think I shall have frames before I have been in three as I get along so fast. I think that the factory is the best place for me and if any girl wants employment I advise them to come to Lowell. Tell Harriet

8. A doffer replaced empty bobbins on the spinning frames with full ones.

that though she does not hear from me she is not forgotten. I have little time to devote to writing that I cannot write all I want to. . . .

This from
Mary S Paul

Bela Paul
Henry S Paul

21. Letter to Delia Page.[9]

[Delia Page lived with a foster family, the Trussells, because she did not get along well with her stepmother. In 1859, at age eighteen, she went to work at a textile mill in Manchester, New Hampshire, where she fell in love with a mill worker who had evidently deserted his wife and child in Lowell. When reports of Delia's "affair" reached home, her foster family wrote her urgent letters trying to persuade her to reconsider. Eventually, in 1866, she married an eligible, respectable single man.]

New London Sept. 7, 1860

Dear Delia,

I should thank you for your very good letter. I am glad to know your health is good. I trust I shall ever feel a deep interest in your welfare.

You say you are not so much in love as we imagine; if so I am very glad of it. Not that I should not be willing you should love a worthy object but the one referred to is no doubt an *unworthy* one; and should you fix you[r] affections on him, it will cause you sorrow such as you never knew; indeed we believe it would be *your ruin*. We have no reason to think, his pretensions notwithstanding, that he has any *real love for you*. Your father Trussell has told or rather written you what he has learned about him. I fear it will be hard for you to believe it, but if you will take the trouble to inquire, I think you will find it all true. He probably is incapable of even friendship, and in his apparent regard for you, is actuated by *low, base, selfish* motives.

I think you will sooner or later come to this conclusion respecting him. The sooner the better. Your reputation your happiness all you hold dear are I fear at stake. You have done well, let not your high hopes be blasted. Do the best you can, keep no company but good and you stand fair to get a good husband, one who has a real regard for you. But if you keep this man's company, the virtuous must shun you. You will not like to read this. My only excuse for writing is that I am very anxious about you. If my anxiety

9. Delia Page's photograph is shown in Source 16.

is unfounded so much the better. Unfounded it cannot be if you are keeping the company of an unprincipled libertine.

Your affectionate Mother Trussell

22. Letter to Delia Page.

[Sept. 7 1860]

My Dear Delia,

I am going to trouble you a little longer (I speak for the whole family now). In your situation you must necessarily form many new acquaintance[s] and amongst them there will be not a few who will assure you of their friendship and seek your confidence. The less worthy they are the more earnestly they will seek to convince you of their sincerity. You spoke of one girl whom you highly prised. I hope she is all that you think her to be. If so you are certainly fortunate in making her acquaintance.

But the best have failings & I should hardly expect one of her age a safe counciler in all cases. You must in fact rely upon a principal of morality within your own bosom and if you [are] at a loss you may depend upon the council of Mrs. Piper.[10] A safe way is not to allow yourself to say or do anything that you would not be willing anyone should know if necessary. You will say Humpf think I cant take care of myself. I have seen many who thought so and found their mistake when ruined. My dear girl. We fear much for those we love much, or the fear is in porportion [sic] to the Love. And although I have no reason to think that you go out nights or engage in anything that will injure your health or morrals [sic] yet the love I have for you leads me to fear lest among so much that is pleasant but evil you may be injured before you are aware of danger.

And now my Dear Girl I will finish by telling you what you must do for me.

You must take care of my little factory girl. Dont let her expose her health if you do she will be sick and loose [sic] all she has earned. Don't let her do any thing any time that she would be ashamed to have her father know. If you do she may loose her charracter [sic]. Try to have her improve some every day that she may be the wealthiest most respected & best beloved of all her sisters, brothers & kindred & so be fitted to make the best of husbands the best of wives.

[Luther M Trussell]

10. The Pipers were Trussell family friends who lived in Manchester.

❈ QUESTIONS TO CONSIDER ❈

Why did Brownson (Source 1) believe that slaves were better off than free laborers? What did he imply about women who worked? What major advantages did Reverend Mills observe in the Lowell system (Source 2)? In what important ways did the system (the factories and the boardinghouses) regulate the girls' lives? How did it protect the morals of its female employees? Of course, not all girls lived up to these standards. What did they do? How were they punished? Do you think Reverend Mills presented a relatively unbiased view? Why or why not? In what ways did the author of the article in *Voice of Industry* (Source 4) believe factory girls were being exploited?

Look carefully at the title page (Source 5) and the first editorial of the *Lowell Offering* (Source 6). What do they tell you about the factory girls, their interests, and their concerns? Was C.B. (Source 7) upholding the cult of true womanhood in her article about the dignity of labor? How did "home" in the boardinghouse (Source 8) differ from the girls' real homes? Based on what you read in Reverend Mills's account, in what ways might a boardinghouse have been similar to the girls' real homes?

The next three letters were written by girls who were rather angry. How did "a factory girl" (Source 9) try to disprove Brownson's view? What fears and anxieties do this letter and the one from Dorothea (Source 10) reveal? What were these two girls trying to prove? The third letter writer (Source 11) retained her sense of humor, but she also was upset. In this case, the offensive remark to which she referred appeared in *Godey's Lady's Book,* the most popular American women's magazine of the period, and was written by the highly respected Sarah Josepha Hale, the magazine's editor and author of "Mary Had a Little Lamb." What had Mrs. Hale written? What was the factory girl's response? What advice did she give her coworkers about fashion? About being a true woman? Both the editor's valedictory and the editorial about the ten-hour-day petitions (Sources 12 and 13) want changes. What were they? How does the editor believe these changes can be achieved? Even "Song of the Spinners" (Source 14) contains a message. What do the lyrics tell you about the spinners' values and attitudes toward work?

What were the other realities of factory girls' lives? What does the bell schedule (Source 3) tell you? How would you describe the image that the pictures of the mill girls present (Sources 16 and 17)? The mill girls' letters make them seem very real to us, but we must not take them completely at face value. After all, they were often writing to their parents! What hopes (and fears) does the correspondence between the mill girls and their families (Sources 18 through 22) express? Why did Lucy Larcom (Source 15) have to go to work in the mills when she was so young? How did she feel about the work when she was a child? What contrast did she draw between young boys' and young girls' upbringing in the early nineteenth century? Did she and the other girls always obey the factory rules? What advantages did she discover in her factory experience? What were the disadvantages? Be careful not to overgeneralize or rely too heavily on the girls' letters or Larcom's memoir.

Now that you are thoroughly familiar with the ideas about how the working girls of Lowell were supposed to behave and the realities of the system under which they lived, you are ready to frame an answer to the central question: How did people react when the needs of a modernizing economy came into conflict with the ideas about women's place in society?

❋ EPILOGUE ❋

The Lowell system was a very real attempt to prevent the spread of the evils associated with the factory system and to make work in the textile mills "respectable" for young New England women. Working conditions in Lowell were considerably better than in most other New England mill towns. However, several major strikes (or "turnouts," as they were called) occurred in the Lowell mills in the mid-1830s, and by the mid-1840s Lowell began to experience serious labor problems. To remain competitive yet at the same time maximize profits, companies introduced the "speedup" (a much faster work pace) and the "stretch-out" (one worker was put in charge of more machinery—sometimes as many as four looms). The mills also cut wages, even though boardinghouse rents were rising. In Lowell, workers first tried to have the length of the workday reduced and, as did many other American workers, united in support of the Ten-Hour Movement. When women workers joined such protests, they further challenged the ideas embodied in the cult of true womanhood, especially that of submissiveness.

Even before the strikes, the Lowell system was breaking down, as more and more mills, far larger than their predecessors, were built. Construction of private housing (especially tenements) expanded, and a much smaller proportion of mill hands lived in boardinghouses. Both housing and neighborhoods became badly overcrowded. By 1850, mill owners were looking for still other ways besides the speedup and stretch-out to reduce the cost of labor. They found their answer in the waves of Irish immigrating to America to escape the economic hardships so widespread in their own country. Fewer and fewer "Yankee girls" were recruited for work in the textile mills. At one Lowell company, the number of native-born girls declined from 737 in 1836 to 324 in 1860, although the total number of female workers remained constant. Irish men, women, and increasing numbers of children filled the gap, because as wages declined, a family income became a necessity.

By 1860, what Reverend Mills had characterized as "the moral and intellectual advantages" of the Lowell system had come to an end. Indeed, many Americans could see little or no difference between our own factory towns and those of Europe.

CHAPTER

8

The "Peculiar Institution": Slaves Tell Their Own Story

THE PROBLEM

With the establishment of its new government in 1789, the United States became a virtual magnet for foreign travelers, perhaps never more so than during the three decades immediately preceding our Civil War. Middle to upper class, interested in everything from politics to prison reform to botanical specimens to the position of women in American society, these curious travelers fanned out across the United States, and almost all wrote about their observations in letters, pamphlets, and books widely read on both sides of the ocean. Regardless of their special interests, however, few travelers failed to notice—and comment on—the "peculiar institution" of African American slavery.

As were many nineteenth-century women writers, English author Harriet Martineau was especially interested in those aspects of American society that affected women and children. She was appalled by the slave system, believing it degraded marriage by allowing southern white men to exploit female slaves sexually, a practice that often produced mulatto children born into slavery.

The young Frenchman Alexis de Tocqueville came to study the American penitentiary system and stayed to investigate politics and society. In his book *Democracy in America* (1842), Tocqueville expressed his belief that American slaves had completely lost their African culture—their customs, languages, religions, and even the memories of their countries. An English novelist who was enormously popular in the United States, the

CHAPTER 8

THE "PECULIAR
INSTITUTION":
SLAVES TELL
THEIR OWN
STORY

crusty Charles Dickens, also visited in 1842. He spent very little time in the South but collected (and published) advertisements for runaway slaves that contained gruesome descriptions of their burns, brandings, scars, and iron cuffs and collars. As Dickens departed for a steamboat trip to the West, he wrote that he left "with a grateful heart that I was not doomed to live where slavery was, and had never had my senses blunted to its wrongs and horrors in a slave-rocked cradle."[1]

In the turbulent 1850s, Fredrika Bremer, a Swedish novelist, traveled throughout the United States for two years and spent considerable time in South Carolina, Georgia, and Louisiana. After her first encounters with African Americans in Charleston, Bremer wrote to her sister that "they are ugly, but appear for the most part cheerful and well-fed."[2] Her subsequent trips to the plantations of the backcountry, however, increased her sympathy for slaves and her distrust of white southerners' assertions that "slaves are the happiest people in the world."[3] In fact, by the end of her stay, Bremer was praising the slaves' morality, patience, talents, and religious practices.

These travelers—and many more—added their opinions to the growing literature about the nature of American slavery and its effects. But the overwhelming majority of this literature was written by white people. What did the slaves themselves think? How did they express their feelings about the peculiar institution of slavery?

✳ BACKGROUND ✳

By the time of the American Revolution, what had begun in 1619 as a trickle of Africans intended to supplement the farm labor of indentured servants from England had swelled to a slave population of approximately 500,000 people, the majority concentrated on tobacco, rice, and cotton plantations in the South. Moreover, as the African American population grew, what apparently had been a fairly loose and unregimented labor system gradually evolved into an increasingly harsh, rigid, and complete system of chattel slavery that tried to control nearly every aspect of the slaves' lives. By 1775, African American slavery had become a significant (some would have said indispensable) part of southern life.

The American Revolution did not reverse those trends. Although northern states in which African American slavery was not so deeply rooted began instituting gradual emancipation, after the Revolution, the slave system—as well as its harshness—increased in

1. Charles Dickens, *American Notes and Pictures from Italy* (London: Oxford University Press, 1957), p. 137.

2. Fredrika Bremer, *America of the Fifties: Letters of Fredrika Bremer,* ed. Adolph B. Benson (New York: American Scandinavian Foundation, 1924), p. 96.
3. Ibid., p. 100.

the South. The invention of the cotton gin, which enabled seeds to be removed from the easily grown short staple cotton, permitted southerners to cultivate cotton on the uplands, thereby spurring the westward movement of the plantation system and slavery. As a result, slavery expanded along with settlement into nearly every area of the South: the Gulf region, Tennessee, Kentucky, and ultimately Texas. Simultaneously, the slave population burgeoned, roughly doubling every thirty years (from approximately 700,000 in 1790 to 1.5 million in 1820 to more than 3.2 million in 1850). Because importation of slaves from Africa was banned in 1808 (although there was some illegal slave smuggling), most further gains in the slave population were from natural increase.

But as the slave population grew, the fears and anxieties of southern whites grew correspondingly. In 1793, a slave rebellion in the Caribbean caused tremendous consternation in the white South. Rumors of uprisings plotted by slaves were numerous. And the actual rebellion of Nat Turner in Virginia in 1831 (in which fifty-five whites were killed, many of them while asleep) only increased white insecurities and dread. In response, southern states passed a series of laws that made the system of slavery even more restrictive. Toward the end of his life, Thomas Jefferson (who did not live to see Nat Turner's uprising) agonized:

But as it is, we have the wolf by the ears, and we can neither hold him, nor safely let him go. Justice is in one scale, and self-preservation in the other. . . .

By this time, however, Jefferson was nearly alone among white southerners. Most did not question the assertion that slavery was a necessity, that it was good for both the slave and the owner, and that it must be preserved at any cost.

It often has been pointed out that the majority of white southerners did not own slaves. In fact, the proportion of white southern families who did own slaves was actually declining in the nineteenth century, from one-third in 1830 to roughly one-fourth by 1860. Moreover, nearly three-fourths of these slaveholders owned fewer than ten slaves. Slaveholders, then, were a distinct minority of the white southern population, and those slaveholders with large plantations and hundreds of slaves were an exceedingly small group.

How, then, did the peculiar institution of slavery, as one southerner called it, become so embedded in the Old South? First, even though only a minority of southern whites owned slaves, nearly all southern whites were somehow touched by the institution of slavery. Fear of black uprisings prompted many nonslaveholders to support an increasingly rigid slave system that included night patrols, written passes for slaves away from plantations, supervised religious services for slaves, laws prohibiting teaching slaves to read or write, and other measures to keep slaves ignorant, dependent, and always under the eyes of whites. Many nonslaveholders also were afraid that emancipation would bring them into direct economic com-

CHAPTER 8

THE "PECULIAR
INSTITUTION":
SLAVES TELL
THEIR OWN
STORY

petition with blacks, who, it was assumed, would drive down wages. Finally, although large planters represented only a fraction of the white population, they virtually controlled the economic, social, and political institutions and were not about to injure either themselves or their status by eliminating the slave system that essentially supported them.

To defend their peculiar institution, white southerners constructed a remarkably complete and diverse set of arguments. Slavery, they maintained, was actually a far more humane system than northern capitalism. After all, slaves were fed, clothed, sheltered, cared for when they were ill, and supported in their old age, whereas northern factory workers were paid pitifully low wages, used, and then discarded when no longer useful. Furthermore, many white southerners maintained that slavery was a positive good because it had introduced the "barbarous" Africans to civilized American ways and, more importantly, to Christianity. Other southern whites stressed what they believed was the childlike, dependent nature of African Americans, insisting that they could never cope with life outside the paternalistic and "benevolent" institution of slavery. In such an atmosphere, in which many of the white southern intellectual efforts went into the defense of slavery, dissent and freedom of thought were not welcome. Hence those white southerners who disagreed and might have challenged the South's dependence on slavery remained silent, were hushed up, or decided to leave the region. In many ways, then, the enslavement of Afri-

can Americans partly rested on the limitation of rights and freedoms for southern whites as well.

But how did the slaves react to an economic and social system that meant that neither they nor their children would ever experience freedom? Most white southerners assumed that slaves were happy and content. Northern abolitionists (a minority of the white population) believed that slaves continually yearned for freedom. Both groups used oceans of ink to justify and support their claims. But evidence of how the slaves felt and thought is woefully sparse. Given the restrictive nature of the slave system (which included enforced illiteracy among slaves), this pitiful lack of evidence is hardly surprising.

How, then, can we learn how slaves felt and thought about the peculiar institution? Slave uprisings were few, but does that mean most slaves were happy with their lot? Runaways were common, and some, such as Frederick Douglass and Harriet Jacobs, actually reached the North and wrote about their experiences as slaves. Yet how typical were their experiences? Most slaves were born, lived, and died in servitude, did not participate in organized revolts, and did not run away. How did they feel about the system of slavery?

Although most slaves did not read or write, did not participate in organized revolts, and did not attempt to run away, they did leave a remarkable amount of evidence that can help us understand their thoughts and feelings. Yet we must be imaginative in how we approach and use that evidence.

In an earlier chapter, you discovered that statistical information (about births, deaths, age at marriage, farm size, inheritance, tax rolls, and so forth) can reveal a great deal about ordinary people, such as the colonists on the eve of the American Revolution. Such demographic evidence can help the historian form a picture of who these people were and the socioeconomic trends of the time, even if the people themselves were not aware of those trends. In this exercise, you will be using another kind of evidence and asking different questions. Your evidence will not come from white southerners (whose stake in maintaining slavery was enormous), foreign travelers (whose own cultural biases often influenced what they reported), or even white abolitionists in the North (whose urgent need to eradicate the "sin" of slavery sometimes led them to gross exaggerations for propaganda purposes). You will be using anecdotes, stories, and songs from the rich oral tradition of African American slaves, supplemented by the narratives of two runaway slaves, to investigate the human dimensions of the peculiar institution.

Some of the oral evidence was collected and transcribed by people soon after emancipation. However, much of the evidence did not come to light until many years later, when the former slaves who were still alive were very old men and women. In fact, not until the 1920s did concerted efforts to preserve the reminiscences of these people begin. In the 1920s, Fisk University collected a good deal of evidence. In the 1930s, the government-financed Federal Writers' Project accumulated more than two thousand narratives from ex-slaves in every southern state except Louisiana and deposited them in the Library of Congress in Washington, D.C.

Much of the evidence, however, is in the form of songs and stories that slaves created and told to one another. Like the narratives of former slaves, these sources also must be used with imagination and care.

The central question you are to answer is this: How did the slaves themselves view the peculiar institution? How did they endure under a labor system that, at its very best, was still based on the total ownership of one human being by another?

✳ THE METHOD ✳

Historians must always try to be aware of the limitations of their evidence. In the Federal Writers' Project, most of the former slaves were in their eighties or nineties (quite a few were older than one hundred) at the time they were interviewed. In other words, most of the interviewees had been children or young people in 1860. It is also important to know that although some of the interviewers were black, the overwhelming majority were white. Last, although many of the former slaves had moved to an-

CHAPTER 8

THE "PECULIAR
INSTITUTION":
SLAVES TELL
THEIR OWN
STORY

other location or a different state after the Civil War, many others were still living in the same county.

As historian Ira Berlin has pointed out in his recent edited collection of slave narratives,[4] former slaves were always patronized and sometimes intimidated by local white interviewers. Once in a while, the actual interviews were written up in a stereotypical black dialect form and occasionally the content itself was edited by the interviewers until the Federal Writers' Project issued directives to stop these practices. But Berlin also notes that many, perhaps most, elderly blacks did not fear retaliation, were eager to tell their stories, and answered obliquely or indirectly when the interviewers' questions touched on sensitive racial issues. For example, former slaves might say that they themselves were treated all right, but then tell about "other situations" elsewhere where slaves were badly mistreated. For an excellect example of an oblique answer, notice how a former slave responds to a question about whether slavery was "good" for the slaves by telling a story about a raccoon and a dog (Source 3).

In fact, like all historical evidence, slave narratives have both strengths and weaknesses. They are firsthand reports that when carefully evaluated, corroborated by other testimony, and supported by additional evidence can provide insight into the last years of slavery in the United States from the viewpoint of the slaves themselves.

4. Ira Berlin et al., eds. *Remembering Slavery* (New York: New Press, 1998).

These narratives reveal much about these people's thoughts and feelings about slavery. Although some of the stories or anecdotes may not actually be true, they can be taken as representative of what the former slaves wished had happened or what they really thought about an incident. Therefore, often you must pull the true meaning from a narrative, inferring what the interviewee meant as well as what he or she said.

As for slave songs and other contemporary evidence, slaves often hid their true meanings through the use of symbols, metaphors, and allegories. Here again, you must be able to read between the lines, extracting thoughts, attitudes, and feelings that were purposely hidden or concealed from all but other slaves.

Included in the evidence are two accounts of runaway slaves who escaped to the North before the Civil War. Frederick Bailey (who later changed his name to Douglass) ran away when he was about nineteen years old, but he was captured and returned. Two years later, he was able to escape, and he moved to Massachusetts, where he worked as a laborer. After joining an antislavery society and becoming a successful speaker, he published his autobiography (1845) and edited his own abolitionist newspaper, the *North Star.* Harriet Jacobs (who used the pen name Linda Brent) was twenty-seven years old when she ran away in 1845, but her narrative was not published until the beginning of the Civil War. Throughout her story, Jacobs used fictitious names and places to protect those who had helped her and to conceal the escape route she had used.

Both Douglass and Jacobs were self-educated people who wrote their own books, although the abolitionist writer Lydia Maria Child made minor editorial revisions in Jacobs's manuscript.

As you examine each piece of evidence, jot down enough notes to allow you to recall that piece of evidence later. But also, perhaps in a separate column, write down the *attitude* that each piece of evidence communicates about the peculiar institution of slavery. What is the hidden message?

After you have examined each piece of evidence, look back over your notes. What attitudes about slavery stand out? What did the slaves think about the slave system?

✳ THE EVIDENCE ✳

Sources 1 through 16 from B. A. Botkin, Federal Writers' Project, *Lay My Burden Down: A Folk History of Slavery* (Chicago: University of Chicago Press, 1945), pp. 4–5, 7, 14, 22–23, 25, 26, 27, 33–34, 53, 55, 91, 106, 121, 124.

1. Hog-Killing Time.

. . . I remember Mammy told me about one master who almost starved his slaves. Mighty stingy, I reckon he was.

Some of them slaves was so poorly thin they ribs would kinda rustle against each other like corn stalks a-drying in the hot winds. But they gets even one hog-killing time, and it was funny, too, Mammy said.

They was seven hogs, fat and ready for fall hog-killing time. Just the day before Old Master told off they was to be killed, something happened to all them porkers. One of the field boys found them and come a-telling the master: "The hogs is all died, now they won't be any meats for the winter."

When the master gets to where at the hogs is laying, they's a lot of Negroes standing round looking sorrow-eyed at the wasted meat. The master asks: "What's the illness with 'em?"

"Malitis," they tells him, and they acts like they don't want to touch the hogs. Master says to dress them anyway for they ain't no more meat on the place.

He says to keep all the meat for the slave families, but that's because he's afraid to eat it hisself account of the hogs' got malitis.

"Don't you all know what is malitis?" Mammy would ask the children when she was telling of the seven fat hogs and seventy lean slaves. And she would laugh, remembering how they fooled Old Master so's to get all them good meats.

CHAPTER 8

THE "PECULIAR
INSTITUTION":
SLAVES TELL
THEIR OWN
STORY

"One of the strongest Negroes got up early in the morning," Mammy would explain, "long 'fore the rising horn called the slaves from their cabins. He skitted to the hog pen with a heavy mallet in his hand. When he tapped Mister Hog 'tween the eyes with the mallet, 'malitis' set in mighty quick, but it was a uncommon 'disease,' even with hungry Negroes around all the time."

2. The Old Parrot.

The mistress had an old parrot, and one day I was in the kitchen making cookies, and I decided I wanted some of them, so I tooks me out some and put them on a chair; and when I did this the mistress entered the door. I picks up a cushion and throws [it] over the pile of cookies on the chair, and Mistress came near the chair and the old parrot cries out, "Mistress burn, Mistress burn." Then the mistress looks under the cushion, and she had me whupped, but the next day I killed the parrot, and she often wondered who or what killed the bird.

3. The Coon and the Dog.

Every time I think of slavery and if it done the race any good, I think of the story of the coon and dog who met. The coon said to the dog, "Why is it you're so fat and I am so poor, and we is both animals?" The dog said: "I lay round Master's house and let him kick me and he gives me a piece of bread right on." Said the coon to the dog: "Better, then, that I stay poor." Them's my sentiment. I'm like the coon, I don't believe in 'buse.

4. The Partridge and the Fox.

. . . A partridge and a fox 'greed to kill a beef. They kilt and skinned it. Before they divide it, the fox said, "My wife says send her some beef for soup." So he took a piece of it and carried it down the hill, then come back and said, "My wife wants more beef for soup." He kept this up till all the beef was gone 'cept the liver. The fox come back, and the partridge says, "Now let's cook this liver and both of us eat it." The partridge cooked the liver, et its parts right quick, and then fell over like it was sick. The fox got scared and said that beef is pizen, and he ran down the hill and started bringing the beef back. And when he brought it all back, he left, and the partridge had all the beef.

5. The Rabbit and the Tortoise.

I want to tell you one story 'bout the rabbit. The rabbit and the tortoise had a race. The tortoise git a lot of tortoises and put 'em 'long the way. Ever' now and then a tortoise crawl 'long the way, and the rabbit say, "How you now, Br'er Tortoise?" And he say, "Slow and sure, but my legs very short." When they git tired, the tortoise win 'cause he there, but he never run the race, 'cause he had tortoises strowed out all 'long the way. The tortoise had other tortoises help him.

6. Same Old Thing.

The niggers didn't go to the church building; the preacher came and preached to them in their quarters. He'd just say, "Serve your masters. Don't steal your master's turkey. Don't steal your master's chickens. Don't steal your master's hogs. Don't steal your master's meat. Do whatsomever your master tells you to do." Same old thing all the time.

7. Freedom.

I been preaching the gospel and farming since slavery time. I jined the church 'most 83 years ago when I was Major Gaud's slave, and they baptizes me in the spring branch close to where I finds the Lord. When I starts preaching I couldn't read or write and had to preach what Master told me, and he say tell them niggers iffen they obeys the master they goes to Heaven; but I knowed there's something better for them, but daren't tell them 'cept on the sly. That I done lots. I tells 'em iffen they keeps praying, the Lord will set 'em free.

8. Prayers.

My master used to ask us children, "Do your folks pray at night?" We said "No," 'cause our folks had told us what to say. But the Lord have mercy,

CHAPTER 8

THE "PECULIAR
INSTITUTION":
SLAVES TELL
THEIR OWN
STORY

there was plenty of that going on. They'd pray, "Lord, deliver us from under bondage."

9. Hoodoo Doctor.

My wife was sick, down, couldn't do nothing. Someone got to telling her about Cain Robertson. Cain Robertson was a hoodoo doctor in Georgia. They [say] there wasn't nothing Cain couldn't do. She says, "Go and see Cain and have him come up here."

I says, "There ain't no use to send for Cain. Cain ain't coming up here because they say he is a 'two-head' nigger." (They called all them hoodoo men "two-head" niggers; I don't know why they called them two-head.) "And you know he knows the white folks will put him in jail if he comes to town."

But she says, "You go and get him."

So I went.

I left him at the house, and when I came back in, he said, "I looked at your wife and she had one of them spells while I was there. I'm afraid to tackle this thing because she has been poisoned, and it's been going on a long time. And if she dies, they'll say I killed her, and they already don't like me and looking for an excuse to do something to me."

My wife overheard him and says, "You go on, you got to do something."

So he made me go to town and get a pint of corn whiskey. When I brought it back he drunk a half of it at one gulp, and I started to knock him down. I'd thought he'd get drunk with my wife lying there sick.

Then he said, "I'll have to see your wife's stomach." Then he scratched it, and put three little horns on the place he scratched. Then he took another drink of whiskey and waited about ten minutes. When he took them off her stomach, they were full of blood. He put them in the basin in some water and sprinkled some powder on them, and in about ten minutes more he made me get them and they were full of clear water and there was a lot of little things that looked like wiggle tails swimming around it.

He told me when my wife got well to walk in a certain direction a certain distance, and the woman that caused all the trouble would come to my house and start a fuss with me.

I said, "Can't you put this same thing back on her?"

He said, "Yes, but it would kill my hand." He meant that he had a curing hand and that if he made anybody sick or killed them, all his power to cure would go from him.

I showed the stuff he took out of my wife's stomach to old Doc Matthews, and he said, "You can get anything into a person by putting it in them." He asked me how I found out about it, and how it was taken out, and who did it.

I told him all about it, and he said, "I'm going to see that that nigger practices anywhere in this town he wants to and nobody bothers him." And he did.

10. Buck Brasefield.

They was pretty good to us, but old Mr. Buck Brasefield, what had a plantation 'jining us'n, was so mean to his'n that 'twa'n't nothing for 'em to run away. One nigger, Rich Parker, runned off one time, and whilst he gone he seed a hoodoo man, so when he got back Mr. Brasefield took sick and stayed sick two or three weeks. Some of the darkies told him, "Rich been to the hoodoo doctor." So Mr. Brasefield got up outen that bed and come a-yelling in the field, "You thought you had old Buck, but by God he rose again." Them niggers was so scared they squatted in the field just like partridges, and some of 'em whispered, "I wish to God he had-a died."

11. The White Lady's Quilts.

Now I'll tell you another incident. This was in slave times. My mother was a great hand for nice quilts. There was a white lady had died, and they were going to have a sale. Now this is true stuff. They had the sale, and Mother went and bought two quilts. And let me tell you, we couldn't sleep under 'em. What happened? Well, they'd pinch your toes till you couldn't stand it. I was just a boy and I was sleeping with my mother when it happened. Now that's straight stuff. What do I think was the cause? Well, I think that white lady didn't want no nigger to have them quilts. I don't know what Mother did with 'em, but that white lady just wouldn't let her have 'em.

12. Papa's Death.

My papa was strong. He never had a licking in his life. He helped the master, but one day the master says, "Si, you got to have a whopping," and my poppa says, "I never had a whopping and you can't whop me." And the master says, "But I can kill you," and he shot my papa down. My mama took him in the cabin and put him on a pallet. He died.

[189]

CHAPTER 8

THE "PECULIAR
INSTITUTION":
SLAVES TELL
THEIR OWN
STORY

13. Forbidden Knowledge.

None of us was 'lowed to see a book or try to learn. They say we git smarter than they was if we learn anything, but we slips around and gits hold of that Webster's old blue-back speller and we hides it till 'way in the night and then we lights a little pine torch, and studies that spelling book. We learn it too. I can read some now and write a little too.

They wasn't no church for the slaves, but we goes to the white folks' arbor on Sunday evening, and a white man he gits up there to preach to the niggers. He say, "Now I takes my text, which is, Nigger obey your master and your mistress, 'cause what you git from them here in this world am all you ever going to git, 'cause you just like the hogs and the other animals—when you dies you ain't no more, after you been throwed in that hole." I guess we believed that for a while 'cause we didn't have no way finding out different. We didn't see no Bibles.

14. Broken Families.

I seen children sold off and the mammy not sold, and sometimes the mammy sold and a little baby kept on the place and give to another woman to raise. Them white folks didn't care nothing 'bout how the slaves grieved when they tore up a family.

15. Burning in Hell.

We was scared of Solomon and his whip, though, and he didn't like frolicking. He didn't like for us niggers to pray, either. We never heard of no church, but us have praying in the cabins. We'd set on the floor and pray with our heads down low and sing low, but if Solomon heared he'd come and beat on the wall with the stock of his whip. He'd say, "I'll come in there and tear the hide off you backs." But some the old niggers tell us we got to pray to God that He don't think different of the blacks and the whites. I know that Solomon is burning in hell today, and it pleasures me to know it.

16. Marriage.

After while I taken a notion to marry and Massa and Missy marries us same as all the niggers. They stands inside the house with a broom held crosswise of the door and we stands outside. Missy puts a little wreath on my head they kept there, and we steps over the broom into the house. Now, that's all they was to the marrying. After freedom I gits married and has it put in the book by a preacher.

Sources 17 and 18 from Gilbert Osofsky, comp., *Puttin' on Ole Massa* (New York: Harper & Row, 1969), p. 22.

17. Pompey.

Pompey, how do I look?
O, massa, mighty.
What do you mean "mighty," Pompey?
Why, massa, you look noble.
What do you mean by "noble"?
Why, sar, you just look like one *lion.*
Why, Pompey, where have you ever seen a lion?
I see one down in yonder field the other day, massa.
Pompey, you foolish fellow, that was a *jackass.*
Was it, massa? Well you look just like him.

18. A Grave for Old Master.

Two slaves were sent out to dig a grave for old master. They dug it very deep. As I passed by I asked Jess and Bob what in the world they dug it so deep for. It was down six or seven feet. I told them there would be a fuss about it, and they had better fill it up some. Jess said it suited him exactly. Bob said he would not fill it up; he wanted to get the old man as near *home* as possible. When we got a stone to put on his grave, we hauled the largest we could find, so as to fasten him down as strong as possible.

Sources 19 through 21 from Lawrence W. Levine, "Slave Songs and Slave Consciousness: An Exploration in Neglected Sources," in *Anonymous Americans: Explorations in Nineteenth Century Social History,* ed. Tamara K. Hareven (Englewood Cliffs, N.J.: Prentice Hall, 1971), pp. 112, 113, 121.

19.

We raise de wheat,
Dey gib us de corn;

CHAPTER 8

THE "PECULIAR
INSTITUTION":
SLAVES TELL
THEIR OWN
STORY

We bake de bread,
Dey gib us de crust;
We sif de meal,
Dey gib us de huss;
We [peel] de meat,
Dey gib us de skin;
And dat's de way
Dey take us in;
We skim de pot,
Dey gib us de liquor,
And say dat's good enough for nigger.

20.

My old Mistiss promise me,
W'en she died, she'd set me free,
She lived so long dat 'er head got bal',
An, she give out'n de notion a dyin' at all.

21.

He delivered Daniel from the lion's den,
Jonah from de belly ob de whale,
And de Hebrew children from de fiery furnace,
And why not every man?

Sources 22 and 23 from Sterling Stuckey, "Through the Prism of Folklore: The
Black Ethos in Slavery," *Massachusetts Review* 9 (1968): 421, 422.

22.

When I get to heaven, gwine be at ease,
Me and my God gonna do as we please.
Gonna chatter with the Father, argue with the Son,
Tell um 'bout the world I just come from.

23.

[*A song about Samson and Delilah*]

He said, 'An' if I had-'n my way,'
He said, 'An' if I had-'n my way,'
He said, 'An' if I had-'n my way,
I'd tear the build-in' down!'

Source 24 from Frederick Douglass, *Narrative of the Life of Frederick Douglass* (New York: Anchor Books, Doubleday, 1963), pp. 1–3, 13–15, 36–37, 40–41, 44–46, 74–75.

24. Excerpts from the Autobiography of Frederick Douglass.

I was born in Tuckahoe, near Hillsborough, and about twelve miles from Easton, in Talbot county, Maryland. I have no accurate knowledge of my age, never having seen any authentic record containing it. By far the larger part of the slaves know as little of their ages as horses know of theirs, and it is the wish of most masters within my knowledge to keep their slaves thus ignorant. I do not remember to have ever met a slave who could tell of his birthday. They seldom come nearer to it than planting-time, harvesting-time, cherry-time, spring-time, or fall-time. . . . The nearest estimate I can give makes me now between twenty-seven and twenty-eight years of age. I come to this, from hearing my master say, some time during 1835, I was about seventeen years old.

My mother was named Harriet Bailey. She was the daughter of Isaac and Betsey Bailey, both colored, and quite dark. My mother was a darker complexion than either my grandmother or grandfather.

My father was a white man. He was admitted to be such by all I ever heard speak of my parentage. The opinion was also whispered that my master was my father; but of the correctness of this opinion, I know nothing; the means of knowing was withheld from me. . . .

[*His mother, a field hand, lived twelve miles away and could visit him only at night.*]

. . . I do not recollect of ever seeing my mother by the light of day. She was with me in the night. She would lie down with me, and get me to sleep, but long before I waked she was gone. Very little communication ever took place between us. Death soon ended what little we could have while she lived, and with it her hardships and suffering. She died when I was about

[193]

CHAPTER 8

THE "PECULIAR
INSTITUTION":
SLAVES TELL
THEIR OWN
STORY

seven years old, on one of my master's farms, near Lee's Mill. I was not allowed to be present during her illness, at her death, or burial. She was gone long before I knew any thing about it. Never having enjoyed, to any considerable extent, her soothing presence, her tender and watchful care, I received the tidings of her death with much the same emotions I should have probably felt at the death of a stranger. . . .

The slaves selected to go to the Great House Farm,[5] for the monthly allowance for themselves and their fellow-slaves, were peculiarly enthusiastic. While on their way, they would make the dense old woods, for miles around, reverberate with their wild songs, revealing at once the highest joy and the deepest sadness. They would compose and sing as they went along, consulting neither time nor tune. The thought that came up, came out—if not in the word, in the sound;—and as frequently in the one as in the other. . . .

I did not, when a slave, understand the deep meaning of those rude and apparently incoherent songs. I was myself within the circle; so that I neither saw nor heard as those without might see and hear. They told a tale of woe which was then altogether beyond my feeble comprehension; they were tones loud, long, and deep; they breathed the prayer and complaint of souls boiling over with the bitterest anguish. Every tone was a testimony against slavery, and a prayer to God for deliverance from chains.

I have often been utterly astonished, since I came to the north, to find persons who could speak of the singing, among slaves, as evidence of their contentment and happiness. It is impossible to conceive of a greater mistake. Slaves sing most when they are most unhappy. The songs of the slave represent the sorrows of his heart; and he is relieved by them, only as an aching heart is relieved by its tears. At least, such is my experience. I have often sung to drown my sorrow, but seldom to express my happiness. Crying for joy, and singing for joy, were alike uncommon to me while in the jaws of slavery. . . .

[*Douglass was hired out as a young boy and went to live in Baltimore. His mistress began to teach him the alphabet, but when her husband found out he forbade her to continue. After Douglass overheard his master's arguments against teaching slaves to read and write, he came to believe that education could help him gain his freedom.*]

The plan which I adopted, and the one by which I was most successful, was that of making friends of all the little white boys whom I met in the street. As many of these as I could, I converted into teachers. With their kindly aid, obtained at different times and in different places, I finally

5. Great House farm was the huge "home plantation" that belonged to Douglass's owner.

succeeded in learning to read. When I was sent on errands, I always took my book with me, and by doing one part of my errand quickly, I found time to get a lesson before my return. I used also to carry bread with me, enough of which was always in the house, and to which I was always welcome; for I was much better off in this regard than many of the poor white children in our neighborhood. This bread I used to bestow upon hungry little urchins, who, in return, would give me that more valuable bread of knowledge. I am strongly tempted to give the names of two or three of those little boys, as a testimonial of the gratitude and affection I bear them; but prudence forbids;—not that it would injure me, but it might embarrass them; for it is almost an unpardonable offence to teach slaves to read in this Christian country. . . .

I was now about twelve years old, and the thought of being a *slave for life* began to bear heavily upon my heart. . . . After a patient waiting, I got one of our city papers, containing an account of the number of petitions from the north, praying for the abolition of slavery in the District of Columbia, and of the slave trade between the States. From this time I understood the words *abolition* and *abolitionist,* and always drew near when that word was spoken, expecting to hear something of importance to myself and fellow-slaves. The light broke in upon me by degrees. . . .

[*After talking with two Irish laborers who advised him to run away, Douglass determined to do so.*]

. . . I looked forward to a time at which it would be safe for me to escape. I was too young to think of doing so immediately; besides, I wished to learn how to write, as I might have occasion to write my own pass.[6] I consoled myself with the hope that I should one day find a good chance. Meanwhile, I would learn to write. . . .

[*Douglass first copied the letters written on the planks of wood used in ship construction. Later, he dared small boys in the neighborhood to prove that they could spell better than he could; in that way, he began to learn how to write.*]

. . . During this time, my copy-book was the board fence, brick wall, and pavement; my pen and ink was a lump of chalk. With these, I learned mainly how to write. I then commenced and continued copying the Italics in Webster's Spelling Book, until I could make them all without looking on the book. By this time, my little Master Thomas had gone to school, and learned how to write, and had written over a number of copy-books. These had been brought home, and shown to some of our near neighbors, and then laid

6. In many areas, slaves were required to carry written passes stating that they had permission from their owners to travel to a certain place.

CHAPTER 8

THE "PECULIAR
INSTITUTION":
SLAVES TELL
THEIR OWN
STORY

aside. My mistress used to go to class meeting at the Wilk Street meeting-house every Monday afternoon, and leave me to take care of the house. When left thus, I used to spend the time in writing in the spaces left in Master Thomas's copy-book, copying what he had written. I continued to do this until I could write a hand very similar to that of Master Thomas. Thus, after a long, tedious effort for years, I finally succeeded in learning how to write. . . .

[After the death of his owner, Douglass was recalled to the plantation and put to work as a field hand. Because of his rebellious attitude, he was then sent to work for a notorious "slave-breaker" named Covey. When Covey tried to whip Douglass, who was then about sixteen years old, Douglass fought back.]

We were at it for nearly two hours. Covey at length let me go, puffing and blowing at a great rate, saying that if I had not resisted, he would not have whipped me half so much. The truth was, that he had not whipped me at all. I considered him as getting entirely the worst end of the bargain; for he had drawn no blood from me, but I had from him. The whole six months afterwards, that I spent with Mr. Covey, he never laid the weight of his finger upon me in anger. He would occasionally say, he didn't want to get hold of me again. "No," thought I, "you need not; for you will come off worse than you did before." . . .

[This fight was a turning point for Douglass, who felt his self-confidence increase greatly along with his desire to be free. Although he was a slave for four more years, he was never again whipped.]

It was for a long time a matter of surprise to me why Mr. Covey did not immediately have me taken by the constable to the whipping-post, and there regularly whipped for the crime of raising my hand against a white man in defense of myself. And the only explanation I can now think of does not entirely satisfy me; but such as it is, I will give it. Mr. Covey enjoyed the most unbounded reputation for being a first-rate overseer and negro-breaker. It was of considerable importance to him. That reputation was at stake; and had he sent me—a boy about sixteen years old—to the public whipping-post, his reputation would have been lost; so, to save his reputation, he suffered me to go unpunished. . . .

[During the Civil War, Douglass actively recruited African American soldiers for the Union, and he worked steadfastly after the war for African American civil rights. Douglass also held a series of federal jobs that culminated in his appointment as the U.S. minister to Haiti in 1888. He died in 1895 at the age of seventy-eight.]

Source 25 from Linda Brent, *Incidents in the Life of a Slave Girl* (New York: Harcourt Brace Jovanovich, 1973), pp. xiii–xiv, 7, 9–10, 26–28, 48–49, 54–55, 179, 201–203, 207.

25. Excerpts from the Autobiography of Linda Brent (Harriet Jacobs).

I wish I were more competent to the task I have undertaken. But I trust my readers will excuse deficiencies in consideration of circumstances. I was born and reared in Slavery; and I remained in a Slave State twenty-seven years. Since I have been at the North, it has been necessary for me to work diligently for my own support, and the education of my children. This has not left me much leisure to make up for the loss of early opportunities to improve myself; and it has compelled me to write these pages at irregular intervals, whenever I could snatch an hour from household duties. . . .

[*Brent explains that she hopes her story will help northern women realize the suffering of southern slave women.*]

I was born a slave; but I never knew it till six years of happy childhood had passed away. My father was a carpenter, and considered so intelligent and skilful in his trade, that when buildings out of the common line were to be erected, he was sent for from long distances, to be head workman. On condition of paying his mistress two hundred dollars a year, and supporting himself, he was allowed to work at his trade, and manage his own affairs. His strongest wish was to purchase his children; but, though he several times offered his hard earnings for that purpose, he never succeeded. In complexion my parents were a light shade of brownish yellow, and were termed mulattoes. They lived together in a comfortable home; and, though we were all slaves, I was so fondly shielded that I never dreamed I was a piece of merchandise, trusted to them for safe keeping, and liable to be demanded of them at any moment. I had one brother, William, who was two years younger than myself—a bright, affectionate child. I had also a great treasure in my maternal grandmother, who was a remarkable woman in many respects. . . .

[*When Linda Brent was six years old, her mother died, and a few years later the kind mistress to whom Brent's family belonged also died. In the will, Brent was bequeathed to the mistress's five-year-old niece, Miss Emily Flint. At the same time, Linda Brent's brother William was purchased by Dr. Flint, Emily's father.*]

My grandmother's mistress had always promised her that, at her death, she would be free; and it was said that in her will she made good the

CHAPTER 8

THE "PECULIAR
INSTITUTION":
SLAVES TELL
THEIR OWN
STORY

promise. But when the estate was settled, Dr. Flint told the faithful old servant that, under existing circumstances, it was necessary she should be sold. . . .

[*Brent's grandmother, widely respected in the community, was put up for sale at a local auction.*]

. . . Without saying a word, she quietly awaited her fate. No one bid for her. At last, a feeble voice said, "Fifty dollars." It came from a maiden lady, seventy years old, the sister of my grandmother's deceased mistress. She had lived forty years under the same roof with my grandmother; she knew how faithfully she had served her owners, and how cruelly she had been defrauded of her rights; and she resolved to protect her. The auctioneer waited for a higher bid; but her wishes were respected; no one bid above her. She could neither read nor write; and when the bill of sale was made out, she signed it with a cross. But what consequence was that, when she had a big heart overflowing with human kindness? She gave the old servant her freedom. . . .

During the first years of my service in Dr. Flint's family, I was accustomed to share some indulgences with the children of my mistress. Though this seemed to me no more than right, I was grateful for it, and tried to merit the kindness by the faithful discharge of my duties. But I now entered on my fifteenth year—a sad epoch in the life of a slave girl. My master began to whisper foul words in my ear. Young as I was, I could not remain ignorant of their import. I tried to treat them with indifference or contempt. The master's age, my extreme youth, and the fear that his conduct would be reported to my grandmother, made him bear this treatment for many months. He was a crafty man, and resorted to many means to accomplish his purposes. . . . The mistress, who ought to protect the helpless victim, has no other feelings towards her but those of jealousy and rage. . . . Even the little child, who is accustomed to wait on her mistress and her children, will learn, before she is twelve years old, why it is that her mistress hates such and such a one among the slaves. . . . She listens to violent outbreaks of jealous passion, and cannot help understanding what is the cause. She will become prematurely knowing in evil things. Soon she will learn to tremble when she hears her master's footfall. She will be compelled to realize that she is no longer a child. If God has bestowed beauty upon her, it will prove her greatest curse. That which commands admiration in the white woman only hastens the degradation of the female slave. . . .

[*Afraid to tell her grandmother about Dr. Flint's advances, Brent kept silent. But Flint was enraged when he found out that Brent had fallen in love with a young,*] *free, African American carpenter. The doctor redoubled his efforts to seduce Brent and told her terrible stories about what happened to slaves who tried to run away. For a long time, she was afraid to try to escape because of stories such as the one she recounts here.*]

In my childhood I knew a valuable slave, named Charity, and loved her, as all children did. Her young mistress married, and took her to Louisiana. Her little boy, James, was sold to a good sort of master. He became involved in debt, and James was sold again to a wealthy slaveholder, noted for his cruelty. With this man he grew up to manhood, receiving the treatment of a dog. After a severe whipping, to save himself from further infliction of the lash, with which he was threatened, he took to the woods. He was in a most miserable condition—cut by the cowskin, half naked, half starved, and without the means of procuring a crust of bread.

Some weeks after his escape, he was captured, tied, and carried back to his master's plantation. This man considered punishment in his jail, on bread and water, after receiving hundreds of lashes, too mild for the poor slave's offence. Therefore he decided, after the overseer should have whipped him to his satisfaction, to have him placed between the screws of the cotton gin, to stay as long as he had been in the woods. This wretched creature was cut with the whip from his head to his feet, then washed with strong brine, to prevent the flesh from mortifying. . . . He was then put into the cotton gin, which was screwed down, only allowing him room to turn on his side when he could not lie on his back. Every morning a slave was sent with a piece of bread and bowl of water, which were placed within reach of the poor fellow. The slave was charged, under penalty of severe punishment, not to speak to him.

Four days passed, and the slave continued to carry the bread and water. On the second morning, he found the bread gone, but the water untouched. When he had been in the press four days and five nights, the slave informed his master that the water had not been used for four mornings, and that a horrible stench came from the gin house. The overseer was sent to examine into it. When the press was unscrewed, the dead body was found partly eaten by rats and vermin. . . .

[*Dr. Flint's jealous wife watched his behavior very closely, so Flint decided to build a small cabin out in the woods for Brent, who was now sixteen years old. Still afraid to run away, she became desperate.*]

And now, reader, I come to a period in my unhappy life, which I would gladly forget if I could. The remembrance fills me with sorrow and shame. . . . The influences of slavery had had the same effect on me that they had

CHAPTER 8

THE "PECULIAR
INSTITUTION":
SLAVES TELL
THEIR OWN
STORY

on other young girls; they had made me prematurely knowing, concerning the evil ways of the world. I knew what I did, and I did it with deliberate calculation. . . .

I have told you that Dr. Flint's persecutions and his wife's jealousy had given rise to some gossip in the neighborhood. Among others, it chanced that a white unmarried gentleman had obtained some knowledge of the circumstances in which I was placed. He knew my grandmother, and often spoke to me in the street. He became interested for me, and asked questions about my master, which I answered in part. He expressed a great deal of sympathy, and a wish to aid me. He constantly sought opportunities to see me, and wrote to me frequently. I was a poor slave girl, only fifteen years old.

So much attention from a superior person was, of course, flattering; for human nature is the same in all. I also felt grateful for his sympathy, and encouraged by his kind words. It seemed to me a great thing to have such a friend. By degrees, a more tender feeling crept into my heart. He was an educated and eloquent gentleman; too eloquent, alas, for the poor slave girl who trusted in him. Of course I saw whither all this was tending. I knew the impassable gulf between us; but to be an object of interest to a man who is not married, and who is not her master, is agreeable to the pride and feelings of a slave, if her miserable situation has left her any pride or sentiment. It seems less degrading to give one's self, than to submit to compulsion. There is something akin to freedom in having a lover who has no control over you, except that which he gains by kindness and attachment. A master may treat you as rudely as he pleases, and you dare not speak; moreover, the wrong does not seem so great with an unmarried man, as with one who has a wife to be made unhappy. There may be sophistry in all this; but the condition of a slave confuses all principles of morality, and, in fact, renders the practice of them impossible.

[*Brent had two children, Benjy and Ellen, as a result of her relationship with Mr. Sands, the white "gentleman." Sands and Brent's grandmother tried to buy Brent, but Dr. Flint rejected all their offers. However, Sands was able (through a trick) to buy his two children and Brent's brother, William. After he was elected to Congress, Sands married a white woman. William escaped to the North, and Brent spent seven years hiding in the tiny attic of a shed attached to her grandmother's house. Finally, Brent and a friend escaped via ship to Philadelphia. She then went to New York City, where she found work as a nursemaid for a kind family, the Bruces, and was reunited with her two children. However, as a fugitive slave, she was not really safe, and she used to read the newspapers every day to see whether Dr. Flint or any of his relatives were visiting New York.*]

But when summer came, the old feeling of insecurity haunted me. It was necessary for me to take little Mary[7] out daily, for exercise and fresh air, and the city was swarming with Southerners, some of whom might recognize me. Hot weather brings out snakes and slaveholders, and I like one class of the venomous creatures as little as I do the other. What a comfort it is, to be free to *say* so! . . .

I kept close watch of the newspapers for arrivals; but one Saturday night, being much occupied, I forgot to examine the Evening Express as usual. I went down into the parlor for it, early in the morning, and found the boy about to kindle a fire with it. I took it from him and examined the list of arrivals. Reader, if you have never been a slave, you cannot imagine the acute sensation at my heart, when I read the names of Mr. and Mrs. Dodge,[8] at a hotel in Courtland Street. It was a third-rate hotel, and that circumstance convinced me of the truth of what I had heard, that they were short of funds and had need of my value, as *they* valued me; and that was by dollar and cents. I hastened with the paper to Mrs. Bruce. Her heart and hand were always open to every one in distress, and she always warmly sympathized with mine. It was impossible to tell how near the enemy was. He might have passed and repassed the house while we were sleeping. He might at that moment be waiting to pounce upon me if I ventured out of doors. I had never seen the husband of my young mistress, and therefore I could not distinguish him from any other stranger. A carriage was hastily ordered; and, closely veiled, I followed Mrs. Bruce, taking the baby again with me into exile. After various turnings and crossings, and returnings, the carriage stopped at the house of one of Mrs. Bruce's friends, where I was kindly received. Mrs. Bruce returned immediately, to instruct the domestics what to say if any one came to inquire for me.

It was lucky for me that the evening paper was not burned up before I had a chance to examine the list of arrivals. It was not long after Mrs. Bruce's return to her house, before several people came to inquire for me. One inquired for me, another asked for my daughter Ellen, and another said he had a letter from my grandmother, which he was requested to deliver in person.

They were told, "She *has* lived here, but she has left."

"How long ago?"

"I don't know, sir."

"Do you know where she went?"

"I do not, sir." And the door was closed. . . .

7. Mary was the Bruces' baby.
8. Emily Flint and her husband.

CHAPTER 8

THE "PECULIAR
INSTITUTION":
SLAVES TELL
THEIR OWN
STORY

[*Mrs. Bruce was finally able to buy Brent from Mr. Dodge, and she immediately gave Brent her freedom.*]

Reader, my story ends with freedom; not in the usual way, with marriage. I and my children are now free! We are as free from the power of slaveholders as are the white people of the north; and though that, according to my ideas, is not saying a great deal, it is a vast improvement in *my* condition. The dream of my life is not yet realized. I do not sit with my children in a home of my own. I still long for a hearthstone of my own, however humble. I wish it for my children's sake far more than for my own. But God so orders circumstances as to keep me with my friend Mrs. Bruce. Love, duty, gratitude, also bind me to her side. It is a privilege to serve her who pities my oppressed people, and who has bestowed the inestimable boon of freedom on me and my children. . . .

[*Harriet Jacobs's story was published in 1861, and during the Civil War she did relief work with the newly freed slaves behind the Union army lines. For several years after the war ended, she worked tirelessly in Georgia to organize orphanages, schools, and nursing homes. Finally, she returned to the North, where she died in 1897 at the age of eighty-four.*]

❊ QUESTIONS TO CONSIDER ❊

The evidence in this chapter falls into three categories: reminiscences from former slaves, culled from interviews conducted in the 1930s (Sources 1 through 18); songs transcribed soon after the Civil War, recalled by runaway slaves, or remembered years after (Sources 19 through 23); and the autobiographies of two slaves who escaped to the North: Frederick Douglass and Harriet Jacobs (Sources 24 and 25).

The evidence contains a number of subtopics, and arrangement into those subtopics may be profitable. For example:

1. How did slaves feel about their masters and/or mistresses?

2. How did slaves feel about their work? Their families? Their religion?
3. How did they feel about freedom?
4. How did slaves feel about themselves?

By regrouping the evidence into subtopics and then using each piece of evidence to answer the question for that subtopic, you should be able to answer the central question: What did slaves (or former slaves) think and feel about the peculiar institution of slavery?

As mentioned, some of the slaves and former slaves chose to be direct in their messages (see, for example, Source 19), but many more chose to communicate their thoughts and feelings more indirectly or obliquely. Several of the symbols and metaphors used are easy to figure out (see Source 23), but others will take considerably more care. The messages are there, however.

Frederick Douglass and Harriet Jacobs wrote their autobiographies for northern readers. Furthermore, both of these runaway slaves were active in abolitionist work. Do these facts mean that this evidence is worthless? Not at all, but the historian must be very careful when analyzing such sources. Which parts of Douglass's and Jacobs's stories seem to be exaggerated or unlikely to be true? What do these writers say about topics such as their work, religious beliefs, and families? Does any other evidence from the interviews, tales, or songs corroborate what Douglass and Jacobs wrote?

❋ EPILOGUE ❋

Even before the Civil War formally ended, thousands of African Americans began casting off the shackles of slavery. Some ran away to meet the advancing Union armies, who often treated them no better than their former masters and mistresses. Others drifted into cities, where they hoped to find work opportunities for themselves and their families. Still others stayed on the land, perhaps hoping to become free farmers. At the end of the war, African Americans were quick to establish their own churches and enrolled in schools established by the Freedmen's Bureau. For most former slaves, the impulse seems to have been to look forward and not backward into the agonizing past of slavery.

Yet memories of slavery were not forgotten and often were passed down orally, from generation to generation. In 1976, Alex Haley's book *Roots* and the twelve-part television miniseries based on it stunned an American public that had assumed that blacks' memories of their origins and of slavery had been for the most part either forgotten or obliterated.[9] Although much of Haley's work contains the author's artistic license, the skeleton of the book was the oral tradition transmitted by his family since the capture of his ancestor Kunta Kinte in West Africa in the late eighteenth century. Not only had Haley's family remembered its African origins, but stories about slavery had not been lost; they had been passed down through the generations.

While Haley was engaged in his twelve years of research and writing, historian Henry Irving Tragle was compiling a documentary history of the Nat Turner rebellion of 1831. Talking to black people in 1968 and 1969 in Southampton County, Virginia, where the rebellion occurred, Tragle discovered that in spite of numerous attempts to obliterate Turner from the area's historical memory, Turner's action had become part of the oral history of the region. As the

9. A condensed version of *Roots* appeared in 1974 in *Reader's Digest*.

CHAPTER 8

THE "PECULIAR
INSTITUTION":
SLAVES TELL
THEIR OWN
STORY

surprised Tragle wrote, "I believe it possible to say with certainty that Nat Turner did exist as a folk-hero to several generations of black men and women who have lived and died in Southampton County since 1831."[10] Again, oral history had persisted and triumphed over time, and professional historians began looking with a new eye on what in the past many had dismissed as unworthy of their attention.

Folk music, customs, religious practices, stories, and artifacts have also received new attention since the 1960s. Increasingly, students of history have been able to reconstruct the lives, thoughts, and feelings of peo-ple once considered inarticulate. Of course, these people were not really inarticulate, but it took imagination to let their evidence speak.

Many people have argued about the impact of slavery on blacks and whites alike, and that question may never be answered fully. What we *do* know is that an enormous amount of historical evidence about slavery exists, from the perspectives of both African Americans and whites. And the memory of that institution lingers. It is part of what one southern white professional historian calls the "burden of southern history," a burden to be overcome but never completely forgotten.

10. Henry Irving Tragle, *The Southampton Slave Revolt of 1831: A Compilation of Source Material* (Amherst: University of Massachusetts Press, 1971), p. 12.

CHAPTER

9

Slavery and Territorial Expansion: The Wilmot Proviso Debate, February 1847

❋ THE PROBLEM ❋

On Saturday morning, August 8, 1846, near the end of the first session of the Twenty-ninth Congress, Speaker John Davis laid before the House of Representatives a message from President James Polk requesting an appropriation of $2 million to be used to negotiate an end to the nearly three-month-old war with Mexico.[1] Caught somewhat off guard, the House members voted to take a two-hour recess (from 3:00 to 5:00 P.M.), after which there would be a limited debate of two hours (each speaker would be held to ten minutes), and

then a vote on the appropriation would be taken.

During the dinner recess, a small group of northern Democrats conceived the idea of amending the appropriation bill to prohibit the introduction of slavery into any territories purchased or taken from Mexico. Word of the scheme must have leaked out, for the House chamber was packed with visitors when the body reconvened at 5:00 P.M., including some members of Polk's cabinet as well as Major General Winfield Scott, a career army officer since the War of 1812 and soon to be a hero in the war with Mexico. Members of the Whig party also must have known of the plan, for Congressman Hugh White of New York called upon his Democratic colleagues to introduce any amend-

1. Originally, Polk had hoped that the Senate would attach the appropriation to a proposed peace treaty. Failing that, the president had the "Two Million Dollar Bill" introduced in the House at the very last minute in order to attract the least amount of attention.

CHAPTER 9

SLAVERY AND
TERRITORIAL
EXPANSION: THE
WILMOT PROVISO
DEBATE,
FEBRUARY 1847

ments to the appropriation bill that would ban slavery from any new territories.

In time, freshman congressman David Wilmot arose to offer the amendment that all had anticipated. Whether Wilmot himself was the author of the amendment remains unclear to this day. We know that he was a member of the small dinner party of Democrats who originated the idea for such an amendment and that it was he who actually introduced it.[2] Modeled on the language of the Northwest Ordinance of 1787 (which prohibited the introduction of slavery into the Northwest Territory), the amendment stated clearly that "neither slavery nor involuntary servitude shall ever exist in any part of said territory, except for crime, whereof the party shall first be duly convicted."[3]

In spite of the nature of the proposed amendment itself and the crowd in the House gallery, the congressmen appeared not to have taken Wilmot's amendment very seriously. Many saw Wilmot's action as an attempt to embarrass President Polk, who increasingly had fallen out of favor with northern Democrats. The president's successful advocacy of a low tariff (the Walker Tariff), his veto of internal improvements (the Rivers and Harbors bill), his championship of a new independent treasury, and his settling of the Oregon boundary dispute on considerably more modest terms than those he had promised during his election campaign had widened the rifts in the Democratic party. To an increasing number of northern Democrats, these actions appeared to show that Polk was unsympathetic to their pro-development, pro-commercial approach to the American economy. Many believed that Wilmot, once a firm supporter of the administration, had introduced his amendment for purely political purposes, possibly because Polk's political appointments had ignored Wilmot and other northern Democrats, especially the Van Buren wing of the Democratic party. Perhaps another reason the amendment did not arouse much hostility was the time limit that had been placed on the debate: two hours, after which a vote had to be taken. Such a short time period did not give much time for a truly inflammatory exchange. Finally, it was reported that not a few House members returned from their dinners intoxicated.[4]

Thus, after a listless debate, the House voted 83–64 in favor of the Proviso, and then 87–64 in favor of the appropriation bill with the Wilmot Proviso attached. In the Senate the following Monday, however, one speaker ran past the adjournment time and the bill was not even voted on.[5] In his diary, Polk referred to the

2. Some have attributed the true authorship of the amendment to Jacob Brinkerhoff (1810–1880), a Democrat congressman from Ohio. See *Congressional Globe*, 29th Congress, 2nd sess. pp. 377, 383; Charles Buxton Going, *David Wilmot, Free-Soiler* (New York, 1924), pp. 122–141. On the crowded gallery, see *New York Herald*, August 11, 1846.
3. *Congressional Globe*, 29th Congress, 1st sess., p. 1217.

4. In his diary, Polk wrote that "several members as I was informed were much excited by drink." See Milo Milton Quaife, *The Diary of James K. Polk During His Presidency, 1845–1849* (Chicago, 1910), Vol. II, p. 74.
5. The clock in the Senate chamber was eight minutes slower than the clock in the House.

Wilmot Proviso as "a mischievous and foolish amendment."[6] Viewing territorial expansion as a unifying principle for Americans, Polk initially seemed both dismayed and puzzled by the introduction of Wilmot's amendment, which threatened the expansionist impulse.

In spite of his comments to the contrary, President Polk was well aware of the terrible consequences that might occur if the debate over slavery would be linked to territorial expansion. As the second session of the Twenty-ninth Congress convened, Polk confided to his diary that a reintroduction of the Wilmot Proviso "will be attended with terrible consequences to the country, and cannot fail to destroy the Democratic Party, if it does not threaten the Union itself."[7] The previous December (on December 23, 1846), Polk had called Wilmot to the White House and extracted from the congressman a promise that Wilmot would not attach his amendment to the appropriation bill or to any bill having to do with a peace treaty with Mexico. It was, however, a promise that Wilmot broke.[8] After considerable legislative maneuvering, on February 8, 1847, Wilmot attempted to reintroduce his amendment to the appropriation bill (by now raised from $2 million to $3 million), and from early

February 1847 to the House of Representatives' vote on the Wilmot Proviso on February 15, the debate took place nearly every day.

This time the House debate was anything but listless, as President Polk's worst fears seemed to be coming true. The Missouri Compromise appeared to have settled the issue of slavery in the territories for a quarter-century. That issue, however, had re-emerged with the Wilmot Proviso, and the rhetoric in the House in 1847 showed clearly that the North and South had grown further and further apart and that a sectional crisis might not be avoidable.

The Evidence section contains excerpts from thirteen of the twenty-one speeches concerning the Wilmot Proviso that were made in the House of Representatives on February 4–13, 1847, plus one speech delivered prior to that time that touches on an important aspect of the debate. Your task in this chapter is to examine and analyze the evidence in order to answer the following questions:

1. What were the major points made by both pro-proviso and anti-proviso speakers?
2. How fundamental were their differences or disagreements?
3. Judging from the congressional debate, how likely does it seem that sectional differences between the North and the South could be smoothed over by compromises (as had been the case in the past)?

Note that while the Wilmot Proviso debate of 1847 brought to the surface the raw tensions caused by the issue of the expansion of slavery into the

Therefore, by the time the Senate had concluded its debate the House already had adjourned, thereby officially ending the first session of the Twenty-ninth Congress.

6. Quaife, *The Diary of James K. Polk,* Vol. II, p. 75.
7. Ibid., Vol. II, p. 303.
8. For the Polk-Wilmot meeting, see ibid., Vol. II, pp. 289–290. For Wilmot's version of the meeting, see *Congressional Globe,* 30th Congress, 2nd sess., appendix, p. 139.

CHAPTER 9

SLAVERY AND
TERRITORIAL
EXPANSION: THE
WILMOT PROVISO
DEBATE,
FEBRUARY 1847

territories, not all northern congress-men favored the Wilmot Proviso, and that neither section (if its congres-sional representatives are any sign) spoke with a united voice on slavery and territorial expansion.

✳ BACKGROUND ✳

Ever since colonial times, Americans had viewed the West as the key to both their individual and collective futures. To land companies and investors, the West held out the promise of great riches, fortunes made in either land speculation or trade. To southern planters who often exhausted the soil growing cash crops like tobacco, it offered the chance to repeat their successes on rich, virgin land. To European immigrants and people from the overpopulated northeastern farming communities, the West was seen as a Garden of Eden where they could make a new start. To Thomas Jefferson, it represented an "Empire of Liberty" that would prevent the rise of unwholesome cities and social conflict in the young republic. Hence it is easy to see why most Americans came to equate national progress with westward expansion. In this atmosphere, the ceding of western lands by the new states to the national government in the 1780s and the Louisiana Purchase of 1803 were seen as the insurers of national greatness. And in a society in which private property was venerated and the acquisition of land had become for many almost a cultural imperative, expansion westward was very nearly inevitable.

Although there were a number of obstacles to westward expansion, at most they proved temporary. The Indian nations offered brisk opposition, but they could fight only a holding action against the more numerous and technologically superior Caucasians. When the United States put its mind to it, the Indians were quickly, and sometimes mercilessly, eradicated or gathered onto reservations, where they were forced to become dependent on the United States government for their existence. For their part, the Spanish (in the Floridas), French (in the Louisiana Territory), and British (in the Northwest) could not bring sufficient military power to bear so far from home and ultimately preferred to either sell or give up through treaty their territorial claims. Even the Republic of Mexico, which did choose to fight, was no match for its expansion-minded neighbor.

The demographic, economic, and social imperatives to expand and the absence of powerful opposition gradually convinced many Americans that westward expansion was both a right and a duty, approved by God for "His people." As one editor explained, it was America's "manifest destiny to overspread the continent allotted by Providence for the free development of our yearly multiplying millions."[9] Another contemporary envisaged a time when

9. *United States Magazine and Democratic Review*, Vol. 17 (1845), p. 5.

the American eagle would have its beak in Canada, its talons in Mexico, and its wings flapping in the two oceans. Although in both statements there is more than a trace of arrogance and feelings of superiority, it is important to note that a vast number of American Caucasians sincerely believed in those claims. After all, in their opinion, westward expansion was their "destiny."

Running parallel to America's westward expansion, however, was the thorny issue of whether or not the institution of slavery should be permitted to follow the American flag westward. That question actually had predated the ratification of the Constitution itself, as the Articles of Confederation government had approved the Northwest Ordinance of 1787, which prohibited the introduction of slavery into the territory that eventually became the states of Ohio (1803), Indiana (1816), Illinois (1818), Michigan (1837), and Wisconsin (1848). But because most southerners did not believe that slavery could grow or prosper in that region, the measure encountered little opposition in the Confederation Congress.

This was not the case with Missouri, the first state to be carved from the enormous Louisiana Territory (acquired from France in 1803). In 1819, Missouri petitioned Congress to be admitted as a slave state, a move that was vigorously opposed by some northern congressmen. In 1819, the nation contained eleven states that prohibited slavery and eleven that allowed it. The admission of Missouri as a slave state, therefore, would tip the balance of power in the Senate in favor of the South. Debates in both the Senate and House of Representatives were heated, and Speaker of the House Henry Clay claimed that he heard the words "disunion" and "civil war" often. At Monticello, retired president Thomas Jefferson feared for the Union.

The Missouri Compromise, in part engineered by Henry Clay, appeared to settle the issue. Maine, formerly a part of Massachusetts, was admitted as a free state, thus preserving the balance in the Senate when Missouri was admitted as a slave state one year later. More significant, Congress drew a line across the remainder of the Louisiana Purchase Territory at 36°30' (the southern boundary of Missouri). North of that line slavery would be prohibited, while it could expand westward south of that boundary.

As many observers recognized at the time, the Missouri Compromise was at best an imperfect and temporary solution. In the early decades of the nineteenth century, thousands of native whites and European immigrants moved west in search of land and opportunity. The population of Ohio mushroomed from 45,000 in 1800 to 1.52 million in 1840, a gain of 3,278 percent. Michigan grew from 5,000 inhabitants in 1810 to over 212,000 in 1840 (+4,140 percent), and Iowa surged from 43,000 in 1840 to 675,000 by 1860 (+1,470 percent). To this almost inexhaustible train of settlers, "manifest destiny" meant small farms and futures for their children, futures unencumbered by the introduction of slavery into their communities.

Although these settlers and their relatives back East cared little about slavery in the Southeast, they feared

CHAPTER 9

SLAVERY AND
TERRITORIAL
EXPANSION: THE
WILMOT PROVISO
DEBATE,
FEBRUARY 1847

that its expansion would threaten their own futures. Moreover, the issue of slavery itself was beginning to intrude itself into other American institutions. In the 1840s, the nation's largest Protestant denominations (Presbyterians, Methodists, and Baptists) all divided along sectional lines, in part over the intrusion of the issue of slavery. Congressmen from the South tried to block the introduction of antislavery petitions and, while few of these settlers would have drafted or signed such a petition, they resented the effort by southern congressmen to limit their right of freedom of speech. Similarly, they were angered by the U.S. Post Office's policy of censoring the mail, so that no abolitionist literature would reach the eyes of the slaves. Again, while most settlers wrote very few letters and almost none either read or sent antislavery pamphlets or literature, they resented the notion that the preservation of slavery meant that *they* would have to give up some of their rights. Hence, while very few white northerners were abolitionists, many were determined that the westward expansion of slavery must be halted.

But slavery was expanding westward as well, by 1830 beyond the Louisiana Territory into Texas, at the time a state of the Republic of Mexico. The chief attraction was land on which to grow cotton, a crop that boomed so rapidly that by 1840 it represented over half of all U.S. exports. In the minds of white southerners, large-scale cotton production required the use of slave labor. Therefore, as white southerners moved into Texas, many brought slaves with them.

Initially, the Mexican government encouraged migration from the United States but then, realizing it was losing control over the area, attempted in 1830 to stop it. And when Mexico attempted to enforce its laws in 1836, the Texans rebelled.

Mexican president Antonio Lopez de Santa Anna attempted to crush the revolt. At the Alamo mission in San Antonio, Santa Anna killed all the defenders (he spared women and children and, according to legend, at least one male native Mexican), stacked their bodies like cordwood, and burned them. Later, Mexican troops shot every defender at Goliad, even though a formal surrender had been arranged with an agreement that survivors would be spared. Ultimately, however, Texans under General Sam Houston prevailed, and by the end of 1836, Texas was an independent nation, the Republic of Texas.

Texans did not want to remain independent but wanted to become part of the United States. For eight years, however, the issue of whether or not to annex Texas to the United States remained unresolved, as both presidents Jackson and Van Buren attempted to avoid both the delicate issue of slavery in the territories and a potential war with Mexico if Texas became part of the Union (Mexico had never recognized the independence of Texas). Finally, on March 1, 1845, Texas was admitted to the United States by joint congressional resolution (the House vote was 120–98).

War with Mexico did come, in May 1846, but less because of the admission of Texas than because President Polk was determined to acquire California from Mexico as well—by purchase if he could or by war if he must. Even after war had broken out, however, Polk still hoped to get California peacefully, and it was in this context that he sent the "Two Million Dollar Bill" to the House of Representatives in August 1846.

Polk's hope of getting the appropriation through the House "without attracting much public attention" was dashed, in part by the Wilmot Proviso.[10] Members of the opposition party (the Whigs) would like nothing better than to embarrass the president. Antislavery sentiment among northern congressmen was growing, in part a reflection of their constituents' fears about the expansion of slavery. Also, as noted earlier, many northern Democrats felt that Polk's administration was excessively prosouthern, as evidenced by the Walker Tariff, the independent treasury, the compromise with Great Britain over Oregon, and the veto of the Rivers and Harbors bill, all of which appeared to be in opposition to a pro-development, pro-commercial approach to the American economy. Thus when Wilmot rose to offer his amendment in the House, there was strong if hardly united support. Indeed, within a year some northern Democrats, New England Whigs, and members of the Liberty party combined in the new Free Soil party, which opposed the expansion of slavery.

Who was this congressman who leant his name to an amendment that he possibly did not author and who reignited the fierce debate over slavery in the territories? David Wilmot (1814–1868) was the son of a Pennsylvania businessman. Admitted to the bar in 1834, Wilmot practiced law and was active in local Democratic party politics. First elected to Congress in 1844, he represented a district largely populated by farmers who had migrated from New England. Vastly overweight due to his love of both food and drink, he referred to his impressive girth in his maiden speech in the House of Representatives, in which he claimed he had attempted to speak earlier but failed, "doubtless from the force of fixed laws, not being able to rise as quick or get up as high, as gentlemen of less gravitating properties than myself."[11] After that he was well known in Congress, more for his oratorical abilities than for his self-discipline or hard work. Whether or not he wrote the proviso that forever bears his name, Wilmot almost surely was chosen to introduce the amendment because of his talents as a speaker and because he had been a firm supporter of Polk and his administration. He had voted in favor of admitting Texas to the Union, in favor of the Walker Tariff (the only Pennsylvania congressman to do so), and in favor of tabling abolitionist petitions. For these reasons, his introduction of an amendment that threatened to sink Polk's

10. See Polk's August 7, 1849, diary entry, in Quaife, *The Diary of James K. Polk,* Vol. II, p. 71. On August 10, Polk confided to his diary the true purpose of the $2 million appropriation: "No Government . . . is strong enough to make a treaty ceding territory and long maintain power unless they could receive . . . money enough to support the army" (ibid., Vol. II, p. 76). What do *you* think Polk meant by that statement?

11. Going, *David Wilmot,* p. 68.

CHAPTER 9

SLAVERY AND
TERRITORIAL
EXPANSION: THE
WILMOT PROVISO
DEBATE,
FEBRUARY 1847

hoped-for $2 million appropriation was all the more dramatic.

Your tasks in this chapter are to summarize the arguments put forth in the February 1847 House debates both in favor of and against the Wilmot Proviso, to assess how fundamental the points of disagreement were, and to judge the extent to which compromises of those differences were likely in 1847. Take notes as you read each selection.

❋ THE METHOD ❋

For your first task in this chapter—to summarize the main points both in favor of and opposed to the Wilmot Proviso—begin by dividing the fourteen excerpts into pro-proviso and anti-proviso groups. Be sure, however, to keep the speeches in their proper order; because this was a *debate,* it is important to note that several congressmen addressed points made by preceding speakers (see Sources 1 and 2, for example).

Almost immediately you will see that the four excerpts from speeches of southern representatives (Sources 2, 6, 11, and 12) have many points in common (as do the four speeches by southern congressmen that have not been included in the Evidence section). What are those similarities? In addition to the points made, are the speeches by southern representatives similar in *tone* or *character* (bellicose, accommodating, friendly, or hostile)? Or are they *dissimilar* in tone or character? Make a list of all the points made by these speakers.

As you will quickly see, the same cannot be said for congressmen from the North. Of the ten speakers representing "free states," three were *against* the Wilmot Proviso (see Sources 4, 5, and 8). On what grounds did these representatives oppose the proviso? In what ways are their arguments similar (or dissimilar) to those made by the speakers from the South?

Now examine and analyze the seven excerpts from those who supported the Wilmot Proviso, including the excerpt from Wilmot himself (Sources 1, 3, 7, 9, 10, 13, and 14). Remember that the Wilmot Proviso referred specifically to the *expansion* of slavery into any territories acquired from Mexico either by treaty or by conquest, and *not* to whether slavery should exist in the United States at all. It is clear, however, that by 1847 some northern congressmen were beginning to take a more determined stand against slavery itself. Which representatives, in your view, took a stronger stand against slavery? Do their speeches offer any clues as to why they had done this?

Having summarized the principal points made both in favor of and opposed to the Wilmot Proviso, you are ready to explain why, in your opinion, compromises over slavery were becoming increasingly difficult. Return to your earlier analysis of the tone of the debate. From your previous study of the 1787 Northwest Ordinance, the 1787 to 1788 debate over the drafting and ratification of the Constitution, and the Missouri controversy of 1819 to 1821, do you detect any significant changes in the tone of the debates over slavery? What are those changes? For example, one sure sign of difficulties in any historical era is the appearance of *conspiracy theories* that are widely circulated and often discussed. Does the debate over the Wilmot Proviso contain any conspiracy theories? Which sources (on each side) show this? How many "conspiracies" can you detect in the excerpts?

As you examine and analyze the February 1847 debate in the House of Representatives, it would be well for you to keep in mind that nineteenth-century American oratorical style generally was extremely stylized and ornate. It was an epoch of overacted melodramas, romantic poetry and musical lyrics, of women and men openly displaying their emotions, and (as you will see) of a very formalized style of public speaking. Interestingly, most typical men and women actually preferred this style of oratory, often sitting for hours listening to a political debate or a particularly polished public speaker. Moreover, without the aid of mechanical amplification (such as an electrically powered public-address system), orators often repeated their main points to make sure they would be lost on no one. Therefore, you will have to read the individual speaker's remarks more slowly and carefully— at least until you become familiar with the oratorical style. As suggested earlier, take notes as you go along.

❋ THE EVIDENCE ❋

Sources 1 through 14 from *Congressional Globe*, 29th Congress, 2nd sess., pp. 181–182, 360–364, 383–386, 401–402; appendix, pp. 134–135, 314–318, 320–323, 331–334, 343–348, 403–406.

1. John Pettit (Democrat, Indiana), January 14, 1847.[12]

. . . Sir, we are told often, and loud, and long, of the dissolution of the Union, and denunciations, broad and bitter, are thrown out against us, if we dare to say we will not lend the power of this Government to the extension of slavery. If I believed that this was an infraction of the Constitution, I should be the last to put unholy hands upon it but believing it only a prudential matter, I shall act as my judgment dictates. We are told

12. On January 4, 1847, Representative Preston King (Democrat, New York) attempted to introduce the appropriation bill with the Wilmot Proviso attached but was ruled out of order. Therefore, although Pettit's remarks were made prior to Wilmot's speech and the warm February debate, they have been included here because the issue they raised was referred to in later speeches.

CHAPTER 9

SLAVERY AND
TERRITORIAL
EXPANSION: THE
WILMOT PROVISO
DEBATE,
FEBRUARY 1847

that separation is the order of the day. Well, my southern brethren! . . . So I say to you; if you are unwilling to stay; if you cannot abide the compact; if you cannot submit to have the will of the majority govern—go. . . .

Let it come; I fear it not. And here I say, you cannot dissolve the Union on any such question. A handful of negroes dissolve this Union! A valuable rope, a strong cord this, that holds us together. The blood of our ancestors, their achievements on many a well-fought field, are all to be forgotten then, and given up for a handful of negro wool! But let me tell you, beware lest the marble the Persian brought to the plains of Marathon be used by Miltiades instead of the invader.[13] No; be careful, let me tell you. You cannot go to your constituents and talk in safety about a dissolution of this Union for such a miserable cause. They will be the first to hang you higher than Haman was hung,[14] if you treat them thus. It cannot be, it will not be a dissolution of this Union on this ground. In the first place, let me say to my southern brethren, you cannot dissolve the Union; in the next place, you don't want to dissolve the Union; and you could not dissolve the Union under any circumstances, or for any purposes of this miserable kind. . . .

2. R. W. Roberts (Democrat, Mississippi), February 4, 1847.[15]

. . . The time has come, and I feel called upon to meet this question of slavery; a question of a more deep and abiding interest to the South, and to the whole nation, could not have been forced upon us, nor a more unpropitious time selected; but, sir, the time has come when this question must be met. We are now to determine upon the wisdom and prudence of the fathers of the Republic, and unpropitious as the time may be, and whatever circumstances may exist adverse to the agitation of so momentous a question, are considerations which are forced to yield to the reckless and maddened spirit which forces the subject upon our immediate action. This goodly heritage of ours, purchased by the blood and treasure of patriotic sires, is committed to us to watch over, to guard and protect. As long as the mind and spirit of our forefathers are regarded, so long will the

13. The Athenians under Miltiades defeated the invading Persians in the Battle of Marathon in 490 B.C. The phrase probably refers to Miltiades using the attempted invasion against his political rivals in Athens.
14. Haman, chief minister to the Persian king Ahasuerus, was hanged from his own gallows when his plot against the Jews was revealed by Esther. The gallows supposedly was fifty cubits high, or approximately eighty-one feet high. See *Esther*, 8:7.
15. R. W. Roberts (1784–1865): planter-lawyer; elected to Congress as a Democrat; served in the House from 1845 to 1849.

Constitution that binds these States, give protection to the life, reputation, and property, of all and every one of its citizens. The East and the West, the North and the South, are alike bound, and owe like allegiance to the Constitution, and claim and are entitled to like equal protection. If the South were to demand from the North that the domestic institutions of limited servitude should be abrogated; that the relative rights growing out of the relation of master and servant, or apprentice, were inimical to their views of right, and should therefore be abolished, she could commit no greater outrage than is attempted to be perpetrated by the North against herself. . . .

[Here Roberts asserted that both southerners and northerners were fighting to acquire territory from Mexico but, if the Wilmot Proviso was approved, only northerners would be allowed to settle in that territory. Even free blacks, Roberts said, would be permitted to settle in the territory, but it would be closed to southerners.]

I would most respectfully inquire what constitutes the evils of slavery, or servitude, about which we have heard so much? Is it the service, or is it the length of the service? Is it the thing itself, or is it the condition annexed? If the former, then they are guilty of the very wrong we are charged with; and their proposition is designed to correct abuses of which the North and the South, and the whole Union is guilty. Surely this is not their meaning, else they would first begin at home, and after purging their own States of the evil, recommend their good example to others. They would, doubtless, before this, have abolished the domestic service, and such a thing as master and bondman, guardian and ward, ceased to be among them.

It is therefore fair to presume, that it is the duration of the service, and *not* service itself, to which they so strenuously object. They favor limited servitude, and defend it upon grounds of expediency and public policy. They agree with us that servitude, in the abstract, is just and proper, but differ with us as to the length of time we may properly avail ourselves of such service. From motives of policy they favor it for a term of years, and in proof of their right to do so, would cite us any amount of authority coming from the source that employs such service, and would point us to the beneficial results that flow from it. Now, suppose a proposition was made here to interfere with this domestic institution: to say to those persons who approve of the wisdom and the policy of the relation, that in certain territory hereafter to be acquired, such institutions shall not exist; that no service or obedience shall be recognised; that the minor, as he is called, shall be free to act as he likes, and subject to no control but the law that binds those who may have attained their majority; that the youth who desires to obtain a knowledge of a trade or business shall owe his master no servitude, but

CHAPTER 9

SLAVERY AND
TERRITORIAL
EXPANSION: THE
WILMOT PROVISO
DEBATE,
FEBRUARY 1847

shall be permitted, and it may be lawful for him at any time to leave that master's employ,—what would be the result? Ah, then their ox would be gored, and the case would be widely different, and we should have any quantity of argument to show the evil of such a proposition. . . .

The gentleman from Indiana, [Mr. PETTIT,] who is, I am sorry to perceive, not now in his seat, had much to say a few day ago about the threats of the South to dissolve the Union. Now, sir, I may be mistaken, but I have yet to know that any gentleman from the South ever, upon any occasion, made any such declaration. I repeat it, sir, if it is so, I have never heard it. He cautioned the South against any attempt to dissolve the Union, as though such sentiment was entertained by any one, and read us a lecture prominent in its cautions to us of Haman's gallows. What he may have done to entitle him to that elevation I know not. I presume, however, he has done nothing to merit it; but be that as it may, I am quite sure that no gentleman from the South has any such elevated notions, and lays no claims whatever to any such conspicuous distinction. But this much I will say, that if the gentlemen who advocate this nefarious, unjust, illegal, Wilmot proviso, and then go South among those whom they have thus defrauded, pilfered and plundered, I am not sure but that they may realize some experience in the elevations which seem so constantly to trouble the visions of some gentlemen. . . .

3. David Wilmot (Democrat, Pennsylvania), February 8, 1847.

[*Wilmot began his speech by reviewing the history of his proviso in the first session of the Twenty-ninth Congress, its passage, and the South's opposition.*]

. . . Her Representatives resisted it; manfully, boldly resisted it. But, sir, it *was passed.* There was then no cry that the Union was to be severed in consequence. The South, like brave men defeated, bowed to the voice and judgment of the nation. No, sir, no cry of disunion then. Why now? The hesitation and the wavering of northern men on this question has encouraged the South to assume a bolder attitude. This cry of disunion proceeds from no resolve of the South. It comes, sir, from the cowardice of the North. Why, in God's name, should the Union be dissolved for this cause? What do we ask? We demand justice and right. If this were a question of compromise, I would yield much. Were it a question of this character, I would go as far as any man. But it is no question for compromise or concession. It is a question of naked and abstract right; and, in the language of my colleague from the Erie district, [Mr. THOMPSON,] sooner shall this right shoulder be drawn from its socket, than I will yield one jot or tittle of the ground upon which I stand. No concession, sir, no compromise. What, I repeat, do we ask? That free territory shall remain free. We demand the neutrality of this Government upon the question of slavery. Is there any complexion of Abolitionism in this, sir? I have stood up at home, and battled, time and again, against the Abolitionists of the North. I have assailed them publicly, upon all occasions, when it was proper to do so. I have met them in their own meetings, and face to face combated them. Any efforts, sir, that may be made, here or elsewhere, to give an Abolition character to this movement, cannot, so far as my district and my people are concerned, have the least effect. Any efforts made to give to me the character of an Abolitionist will fall harmless when they reach my constituents. They know me upon this question. They know me distinctly upon all questions of public interest. My opinions have ever been proclaimed without reserve, and adhered to without change, or the shadow of turning. I stand by the Constitution upon this question. I adhere to its letter and its spirit. I would never invade one single right of the South. So far from it, I stand ready at all times, and upon all occasions, as do nearly the entire North, to sustain the institutions of the South as they exist. When the day of trial comes, as many, many southern men fear it may come, we stand ready, with our money and our blood, to rush to the rescue. When that day comes, sir, the North will stand, shoulder to shoulder with their brethren of the South. We stand by the Constitution and all its compromises.

But, sir, the issue now presented is not whether slavery shall exist unmolested where it now is, but whether it shall be carried to new and distant regions, now free, where the footprint of a slave cannot be found. This, sir, is the issue. Upon it I take my stand, and from it I cannot be frightened or driven by idle charges of abolitionism. I ask not that slavery be abolished. I demand that this Government preserve the integrity of *free territory* against the aggressions of slavery—against its wrongful usurpations. Sir, I was in favor of the annexation of Texas. I supported it with my whole influence and strength. I was willing to take Texas as she was. I sought not to change the character of her institutions. Slavery existed in Texas— planted there, it is true, in defiance of law; still it existed. It gave character to the country. True, it was held out to the North, that at least two of the five States to be formed out of Texas would be free. Yet, sir, the whole of Texas has been given up to slavery. The Democracy of the North, almost to a man, went for annexation. Yes, sir, here was an empire larger than France given up to slavery. Shall further concessions be made by the North? Shall we give up free territory, the inheritance of free labor? Must we yield this also? Never, sir, never, until we ourselves are fit to be slaves. The North may be betrayed by her Representatives, but upon this great question she

[217]

CHAPTER 9

SLAVERY AND
TERRITORIAL
EXPANSION: THE
WILMOT PROVISO
DEBATE,
FEBRUARY 1847

will be true to herself—true to posterity. Defeat! Sir, there can be no defeat. Defeat to-day will but arouse the teeming millions of the North, and lead to a more decisive and triumphant victory to-morrow.

But, sir, we are told, that the joint blood and treasure of the whole country being expended in this acquisition, therefore it should be divided, and slavery allowed to take its share. Sir, the South has her share already; the instalment for slavery was paid in advance. We are fighting this war for Texas and for the South. I affirm it—every intelligent man knows it—Texas is the primary cause of this war. For this, sir, northern treasure is being exhausted, and northern blood poured out upon the plains of Mexico. We are fighting this war cheerfully, not reluctantly—cheerfully fighting this war for Texas; and yet we seek not to change the character of her institutions. Slavery is there: there let it remain. Sir, the whole history of this question is a history of concessions on the part of the North. The money of the North was expended in the purchase of Louisiana, two-thirds of which was given up to slavery. Again, in the purchase of Florida, did slavery gain new acquisitions. Slavery acquired an empire in the annexation of Texas. Three slave States have been admitted out of the Louisiana purchase. The slave State of Florida has been received into the Union; and Texas annexed, with the privilege of making five States out of her territory. What has the North obtained from these vast acquisitions, purchased by the joint treasure and defended by the common blood of the Union? One State, sir—one: young Iowa, just admitted to the Union, and not yet represented on the floor of the Senate. This, sir, is a history of our acquisitions since we became a nation. A history of northern concession—of southern triumphs.

Now, sir, we are told that California is ours; that New Mexico is ours—won by the valor of our arms. They are free. Shall they remain free? Shall these fair provinces be the inheritance and homes of the white labor of freemen or the black labor of slaves? This, sir, is the issue—this the question. The North has the right, and her representatives here have the power. Shall the right prevail? . . .

[*Wilmot then proceeded to state why, in his opinion, the issue could not be deferred until a later time. He feared that if slavery moved into the area, then it would be too late to prohibit it. He then claimed that in any extended war (such as the American Revolution or, possibly, the Mexican War), the North always would provide more troops, since the laboring population of the South could not be trusted to be given arms.*]

Again, contrast Ohio with Kentucky. Why has the former left so far behind the latter, in the race of prosperity and greatness? It is wholly owing to slavery in the one and not in the other. There is always a lack of that energy and enterprise in slave labor, which is to be found in free labor. I verily believe that the laborer of the North, who goes into the wilderness to hew himself out a home, does more work than three slaves, while he consumes or wastes less. Nothing is neglected by him; his eye sees everything that requires attention. It is the enterprise, the diligence, and the economy of free labor, that has built up new empires in the West, while the South has been falling back into decrepitude and decay. Sir, contrast Michigan with Arkansas. Within the last twenty years, the former has assumed a high position among the States of this Union. She exhibits at this day all the elements and resources of a great State; cities, flourishing towns, and highly cultivated fields, with a population that outnumbers three or four times that of Arkansas. Yet, Arkansas has even a better soil, and superior natural advantages. What is the cause of this disparity? It is slavery, sir, and that alone. Slave labor exhausts, and makes barren the fields it cultivates. That labor is only profitable to the master in the production of the staples of cotton, sugar, and tobacco. Crop follows crop, until the fertility of the soil is exhausted, when the old fields are abandoned, new and virgin soil sought out, to be exhausted in the same manner, and in its turn likewise abandoned. Thus, sir, sterility follows its path. Eastern Virginia, unrivalled in the fertility of its soil, and in the geniality of its climate, with navigable rivers and harbors unsurpassed in commercial importance, is this day but little better than a barren waste. The free labor of the North has commenced the work of regeneration, and to this alone can Eastern Virginia look for redemption and renewed prosperity.

Sir, as a friend of the Union, as a lover of my country, and in no spirit of hostility to the South, I offered my amendment. Viewing slavery as I do, I must resist its further extension and propagation on the North American continent. It is an evil, the magnitude and the end of which, no man can see. . . .

4. Stephen Strong (Democrat, New York), February 8, 1847.[16]

Sir, I am in favor of the bill as recommended by the President, and entirely opposed to this proviso. I shall vote for the one, and not for the other. I will oppose this proviso at the present time, come in what shape it may, and whatever garb it may assume. It is ill-timed; out of place; has no

16. Stephen Strong (1791–1866): lawyer and judge; a Democrat who served in the House from 1845 to 1847.

CHAPTER 9

SLAVERY AND
TERRITORIAL
EXPANSION: THE
WILMOT PROVISO
DEBATE,
FEBRUARY 1847

business here; can do no good; and is calculated to produce, as it has produced, nothing but mischief—absolute, unmitigated evil. . . .

[*Strong then accused a group of northern Democrats of using the Wilmot Proviso as a way to embarrass President Polk and gain control of the Democratic party, presumably to oust Polk in 1848 and replace him with another Democrat—probably Martin Van Buren.*]

Mr. Chairman, it does seem to me that the representatives of the people in this House exhibit a very singular spectacle to their constituents, the country, and the world. We have been in session many weeks, and have done literally nothing. Our country is engaged in war; and whatever we may say or do here, that country will decide, *it has decided,* the war to be a righteous and just one. It will *compel* its servants in Congress, sooner or later, to carry out its wishes and its will. Our army, bravely fighting in its defence, needs reinforcements of men, and supplies of clothing, food, and money. Delay is hazardous—it is ruinous; and yet, instead of attending to the business we were sent here to perform, we have been spending our time in useless and protracted debate, in making Presidents, in forming cliques and combinations to promote the ascendency of certain politicians, in manufacturing political capital to send out to the country. I believe the country is getting dissatisfied with us. I understand that public meetings are now being held in the State of New York, composed of all parties, approving the war, and denouncing Congress for its delay to sustain the country by proper and necessary legislation. For one, I plead guilty to the charge; and have no other excuse to offer to my constituents, when I return, than to say I did all I could. One vote alone, in a body like this, is unavailing. I could do no more than vote. We might have done all that was really necessary to be done during the first three weeks of the session. It is questionable, from present indications, whether the last week of it will find our work completed. There are spirits who must either rule or ruin; some who would "rather rule in hell than serve in heaven." Sir, I belong to no cliques. I have no favorite candidate for the Presidency to bring forward, or whose particular interests I wish to promote to the exclusion of all others. I go for the interests and the rights of my country, and the *whole* country, without regard to sectional, political, or personal considerations. Let not our southern friends be unnecessarily alarmed. They will find the Democracy of the North, in the hour of trial, standing by them upon the compromises of the Constitution as formerly, and uniting with them to preserve that charter inviolate. They will find that the country will not only demand a vigorous prosecution of the war, until we obtain an honorable peace, but ample indemnity for all it has cost us. . . .

5. John S. Chipman (Democrat, Michigan), February 8, 1847.[17]

He regretted to hear gentlemen avow upon that floor their readiness to see the federal Union shattered to ten thousand atoms. As he heard the sentiments which had been uttered in that Hall, his blood curdled around his heart. He trembled at the thought of the dissolution of this fair Confederacy. He knew but one ground on which to stand as a patriot, in view of the circumstances in which they were placed: that was upon the ground of compromise, by which these States were united and bound together. In his humble opinion, the preservation of the Union was worth a million times more than the pitiful consideration of a handful of degraded Africans. He repeated, when gentlemen pretending to love their country would place the consideration of the nominal liberation of a handful of degraded Africans in the one scale, and this Union in the other, and make the latter kick the beam, he would not give a fig for their patriotism. Did all this pretended negro patriotism, then, spring from philanthropy or a love of country? What would these pretended philanthropists accomplish, supposing that they should succeed in liberating that handful of degraded Africans? Would they benefit the slave by liberating him, without providing for his colonization? What would they accomplish? They would drive him to a cold climate, uncongenial to his constitution, and force him to a state of degradation immensely lower than his present state—yea, to starvation. They must elevate the slave morally and intellectually first, if they would improve his condition. But how happened it that gentlemen would prohibit slavery from all newly-acquired territory? Whence originated this Wilmot proviso? He wanted that proposition to be fathered where it belonged. He did not want the distinguished Representative from Pennsylvania to have the honor (if it be an honor) or the disgrace (if it be a disgrace) of having concocted such a proposition, unless he was entitled to it. He would directly come down to the origin of it; but let him first repeat what he had said in the outset, that he did not rise to make a speech for the gratification or irritation of either Whig or Democrat. . . .

17. John S. Chipman (1800–1869): attorney; a Democrat who served in the House from 1845 to 1847.

CHAPTER 9

SLAVERY AND
TERRITORIAL
EXPANSION: THE
WILMOT PROVISO
DEBATE,
FEBRUARY 1847

[Chipman then accused the Van Buren wing of the Democrat party with introducing the Wilmot Proviso in order to block Polk's requested appropriation which, Chipman claimed, would extend the war with Mexico and politically damage the President.]

The gentleman from Pennsylvania brought forward a proviso to exclude slavery from all territory which might be acquired; and for that proposition he had the hardihood to claim the support of the Democracy of the North. He (Mr. C.) thanked God that he voted against that Wilmot proviso. It smelt rank of negroism. Now, he held that that proposition, the two million bill, for the purpose of enabling the President to close the war with Mexico, would have passed both Houses of Congress with but little opposition; but then it was—he would not say in midnight conclave—but then it was that the combined delegations of the distinguished Representatives from New York, Ohio, and Pennsylvania, had the audacity to concoct this proviso. Yet these very men boasted of their patriotism, of their philanthropy, which outshone that of other men, of their unexampled love of their species! Away with such philanthropy! Away with all those crocodile tears over a corporal's guard of unfortunate negroes! Instead of patriotism, by such a concentration of sickly philanthropy, they had lost sight of all patriotism—of all love of country. . . .

6. Howell Cobb (Democrat, Georgia), February 9, 1847.[18]

[Cobb began his speech by stating that Wilmot had not offered "a single reason, or showed before the country a single argument" in favor of the proviso. Cobb then questioned the fairness of having both northern and southern men in arms in the Mexican War and yet, if the Wilmot Proviso was to be passed, only northern men could settle in the new territories.]

I may be permitted, sir, to look to others who are associated with him in this view of the subject, and to inquire into the reasons which make this course "the right." I may ask the gentleman from Pennsylvania, if the reason urged by his associate from Ohio constitutes the reason upon which his proposition is founded? That gentleman [Mr. DELANO][19] told us that he himself was opposed to the acquisition of territory, and hence could express no feeling as to the object of the acquisition; but he gave us to understand what would be the effect of acquisition in case the amendment (which met

18. Howell Cobb (1815–1868): attorney; Democratic congressman (1843–1851); governor of Georgia (1851–1853); secretary of the treasury (1857–1860); general in the Confederate army.
19. Columbus Delano (1809–1896): attorney; Whig congressman (1845–1847); became a Republican in 1860; Republican congressman (1865–1869); secretary of the interior (1870–1875).

his cordial approbation) were adopted; and we may attribute that object to those who differ with that gentleman only on the point of the propriety of acquiring this territory. The gentleman [Mr. DELANO] told you, sir, in plain, explicit terms, spoken with the candor of a man, with the frankness due to the position which he occupies before the country, that the effect would be to draw around the southern portion of the United States a cordon of free States, where they "would light up the fires of liberty, to burn the shackles which now bind our slaves in servitude." Does the gentleman from Pennsylvania [Mr. WILMOT] sympathize with his associates? Do the gentlemen who support that amendment respond "Amen" to the sentiment thus broadly announced upon this floor? And does this constitute one of the reasons why this proposition is based upon "the right?"

Sir, it is perhaps not my place or my duty to inquire further into the motives of those who advocate this proposition upon this floor, than they are proper to give themselves. But I am at liberty to inspect [?] the arguments, the inferences of those who advocate the same side of the question, and to hold the one responsible for the other to the extent that they are not inconsistent and are not denied.

I take it for granted, then, that this is the effect with some, the object with others. . . .

Sir, it cannot be. Upon this subject of the institution of slavery—this peculiar subject of sectional jealousy—there is a spirit of compromise running through the Constitution, not confined to isolated paragraphs, but breathing throughout the whole instrument. That spirit of compromise recognised the existence of these sectional interests. The object was to guard them, to protect them, to make the one a check upon the other. The inducement held out to the South, at the time this Constitution was framed, was the spirit of compromise upon this question. She asked, and she had granted to her at that time, such power and such influence as would enable her to be a check upon the North; so that no attempt could ever be made successfully to interfere with the rights of the South. But where is that spirit now? Where is that regard, on the part of the North, for the rights of the South? And where are those rights, when the views presented by the gentlemen who advocate this amendment are carried out? Where is the check which the South was induced by this Constitution to believe she would always be enabled to hold upon her sister States of the North? This amendment provides that no territory which may hereafter be acquired, from whatever quarter, from whatever section of the country it may come, shall ever be made subject to settlement by the people of the slaveholding States. You of the North extend your territory, your government, your power, strength, and influence, day by day, and year by year; but here

CHAPTER 9

SLAVERY AND
TERRITORIAL
EXPANSION: THE
WILMOT PROVISO
DEBATE,
FEBRUARY 1847

stands the South, her limits fixed, bound hand and foot, subject to your mercy, and to such legislation as you may think proper upon the subject of her institutions and her rights to make.

Will the gentleman from Pennsylvania tell me that he stands upon "the right;" and that the South stands upon "the wrong," in view of these considerations? Will the gentleman, and those who are associated with him, tell me that the South is grasping in her policy—that she is seeking to establish her institutions beyond those limits which were contemplated by the framers of our Constitution? That the South is disposed to obtain a power and an influence to which she is not entitled? That the South so clearly occupies the wrong, that she will cheerfully acquiesce in the proposition which the gentleman brings forward, and make that the legislative criterion upon this subject for the government of this Union! . . .

7. George Rathbun (Democrat, New York), February 9, 1847.[20]

This subject (he said) had been agitated here, and they had heard these threats, over and over again, since he had been here; they had been continued since this Capitol was erected, and they began in the Convention which framed the Constitution. The cry then was, that, if you won't permit our property, our slaves, to be represented, we will form no compact, no confederacy; and from that day down to this, upon almost every subject, great and small, this threat had been echoed and reechoed from every part of the South. But gentlemen had no idea of dissolving the Union; and there need be no alarm felt on that subject.

What was the fact now? Why, we were engaged in a war with Mexico; and we intend to take for indemnity—and he thought we ought to take—a part of Mexico, which she could not use, and which we ought to have. And the cry is again raised, if you will not only permit but aid us to carry our slaves into that territory, and allow them to be represented in the Congress of the United States, we will dissolve this Union. Well, sir, is it not a pretty apology for the dissolution of this Union, that the North would not agree to extend the institution of slavery, by the direct action of this Government, over free territory! And not only that; but it is said, to refuse it is a violation of the Constitution. Well, if these gentlemen should go up to his part of the country, and make this declaration among the schoolboys, instead of being alarmed at it, as his colleague [Mr. STRONG] seemed to be, they would laugh

20. George Rathbun (1803–1870): attorney; Democratic congressman (1843–1847).

at the idea. They knew enough about the Constitution to know that it did not require this Government to go abroad and conquer and convert territory now free into slave territory. They could not find it in the Constitution. . . .

[*Rathbun then listed the things that money from the North had acquired for the South, such as the Louisiana Territory, Florida, and Texas. He then asserted that southerners could take their property into the soon-to-be-acquired territory, but that slaves were* persons.]

He [Rathbun] came here to protest against the North being sacrificed, surrendered, betrayed, given over to the tender mercies of those who had governed them too long already. Why, look at the list of the Presidents of this nation: out of fifty-seven years, all but twelve years and one single month had been filled by Presidents from the South. For forty years out of fifty-seven, had the South had a Secretary of State. For forty years about, he believed exactly, had they had the Speaker of this House; and the present Speaker was the only one since 1827 that had not been a southern man. Look at your army, your navy, the officers of the departments, at every thing connected with the administration of the Government; where are they? All in the hands of those who know how to control and govern. It was produced by the institution of slavery. It was because the whole southern portion of the Union was bound together by a cord so strong that no power ever yet had broken it; because it is a universal sympathy and interest, reaching from one extreme of the South to the other, and bringing together all who represent southern interests. Sir, if the wisest man that ever lived had undertaken to form a scheme for political power, no better could have been found in the world—a perfect combination at all times on every question affecting slavery; while the North were divided, and, step by step, had been surrendering, surrendering, surrendering; and the question had now come, should they surrender the last point, and forever? . . .

8. Richard Brodhead (Democrat, Pennsylvania), February 9, 1847.[21]

If we adopt the amendment, we virtually proclaim to the world that this is a war for conquest; and that we are so greedy for territory, that we

21. Richard Brodhead (1811–1863): attorney; Democratic House member (1843–1849); U.S. senator (1851–1857).

CHAPTER 9

SLAVERY AND
TERRITORIAL
EXPANSION: THE
WILMOT PROVISO
DEBATE,
FEBRUARY 1847

prescribe rules for its government before we have acquired the title. We subject ourselves to ridicule, by counting the spoils before the field is won.

If territory is acquired by treaty, it will, of course, be free; and therefore, if slaves are taken into it, they will be entitled to their freedom, upon the great principle that free territory makes free men, and free ships free goods.

Slavery can only exist by positive law; and therefore, as soon as a slave is taken to reside permanently in a free State or Territory, he is a free man. This is one of the great principles of the common law, recognised by the courts of England as well as of the United States. . . .

If the territory will be free when it is annexed, and Congress has no power to make it slave, where is the necessity for the adoption of the amendment? If it should become a State, Congress would have no jurisdiction over it after it should be admitted in the Union. Pennsylvania would have a perfect right to establish slavery to-morrow if she chose to do it. At the close of the last session of Congress, the venerable gentleman from Massachusetts [Mr. ADAMS] expressed views similar to those I entertain. He said: "There are no slaves in California. Slavery has been abolished there; and if we were to make peace, and in that peace to acquire California, there could be no law of slavery established there, unless it was made an article of the treaty itself."

No one has said, and no sensible man supposes, that we will ever get more than New Mexico and California; and most of these provinces are above 36° 30'—the line of the Missouri compromise—above which, it is admitted on all hands, slavery is to be prohibited. All the southern Representatives have offered, this session, to extend that line to the Pacific Ocean; and besides, slave labor could not be profitably employed in either of those places. Neither sugar, rice, cotton, or tobacco, can be profitably cultivated there. The truth is, that climate and soil have more to do with the extension of slavery than anything else. No person need fear that slaves will be taken from the cotton and rice fields of the southern States around Cape Horn, or overland to California. That country must be the home of a maritime people, and the course of settlement must be from the seaboard to the interior.

The amendment is out of *time* and out of *place*—is a *rider*, and has been a firebrand in our midst. When we are engaged in a foreign war, and we should present an undivided front to the enemy, this question of slavery, which has always been an exciting element in our political system, is thrust forward, to excite sectional jealousies, distract our councils, and delay the adoption of the measures recommended by the President for the vigorous prosecution of the war. . . .

Finally, it is not only an abstraction, which cannot possibly affect either the character or the interests of the people of the northern States, but may do great harm in creating a geographical division of parties. When that kind of division takes place, this Union is gone, and with it the protection to persons and property which it affords.

9. James Dixon (Whig, Connecticut), February 9, 1847.[22]

If this great republic is ever, by any terrific convulsion, to be shattered into fragments, it will be in consequence of attempts on the part of the advocates of human slavery to extend its dominion. Other questions admit of compromise and concession; on this, concession has already gone far beyond the limits of a just moderation, and has degenerated into servility. There is no room for farther concession. Its utmost verge has already been passed.

The war in which we are now engaged had its origin in the policy of extending our territorial limits for the avowed purpose of perpetuating slavery. No man pretends to deny that its primary cause was the annexation of Texas. Without that measure the war would not have existed. One of the main arguments advanced by the opponents of annexation, when the scheme was first proposed, was the war which would be its probable consequence. That it was not an inevitable consequence I admit, for after Texas had become a part of this Union the war might still have been avoided. Having now been commenced, questions of the most momentous importance demand our consideration. If there is wisdom in our councils, all its profoundest lessons are now needed to carry the nation safely through the difficulties which encompass her path. To restore peace by the wisest and surest means is our first duty. I deem it to be a duty, scarcely second to this, to provide that the arrogant and encroaching slaveholding oligarchy, which instigated the measure by which we were involved in war, shall not secure, by its final results, their darling object, the further extension of slave territory. . . .

[*Dixon then proceeded to accuse President Polk of creating the war with Mexico to distract people from his backing down on his campaign promise to take all of the Oregon territory up to the 54°40′ latitude.*]

I shall, therefore, vote for this bill, with the proviso of the gentleman from Pennsylvania, [Mr. WILMOT,] prohibiting the existence of slavery in any territory to be acquired by treaty from Mexico. With that proviso, I can

22. James Dixon (1814–1873): attorney; Whig congressman (1845–1849); U.S. senator (1857–1869).

CHAPTER 9

SLAVERY AND
TERRITORIAL
EXPANSION: THE
WILMOT PROVISO
DEBATE,
FEBRUARY 1847

vote for the bill; without it, it cannot have my support, under any circumstances. And this brings me to a subject of immense importance, on which I propose to address some remarks to this committee.

It seems now to be supposed, that the acquisition of territory, in some mode, is to be the result of the war in which we are engaged. The appetite for territorial aggrandizement grows with the food it feeds on, and the enlargement of our borders, by the annexation of Texas, is to be only the precursor of still greater extension.

But by conquest, with my consent, this extension can never take place. I would not wrest from the Mexican Government one foot of her soil, under any of the low, dishonest, dishonorable pretexts by which a war of conquest may be attempted to be justified. If we are to have new territory, let it be peaceably won, not torn from the Mexican republic by conquest. I deny the justice of any such title. . . .

[*Here Dixon asserted that northern public opinion on extending slavery was firm: the people "never will consent to be instrumental in extending slavery over territory where it does not exist." Yet they understand that they cannot disturb slavery where it already exists.*]

The feeling which pervades the North, on the subject of slavery, is not one of sickly sentimentality. While the system of human bondage which prevails at the South, is considered in the highest degree unjust and oppressive to the slave, it is believed to be hardly less injurious to the master. It is, besides, disgraceful to us as a nation; disgraceful to the age in which we live, so far as those of the present age are responsible for its existence and continuance. Circumstances beyond our control have fastened it upon a portion of our country. It is an inherited evil, and no man is farther than I am, from a spirit of uncharitable denunciation of the South, for the existence of a misfortune to which they are born.

The Constitution of the United States, neither in its letter nor its spirit, requires us to consent to the extension of slave territory. We are at liberty to treat it as an open question, to resume the capacity of choice, which, under the Constitution, we have relinquished, where slavery exists by its sanction, and to decide whether, being thus free to choose, we will consent to be made parties to the extension of a deplorable evil. Viewed in this light, can southern gentlemen complain, that while we respect their rights, we revolt at the idea of inflicting upon a land, blessed by Heaven with every natural advantage, a curse which will render all these advantages comparatively worthless?

What, sir, let me ask, is the effect of slavery, wherever it exists? We have examples among our own States, which furnish a reply to this question. Contrast Virginia and Pennsylvania. In natural advantages Virginia is superior to any State in this Union. Her climate is the most favorable to the perfect development of human excellence on the globe. Her cold is not excessive—her heat is not intense. The breezes which sweep over her valleys, softened by the rays of a genial sun, and purified by her mountains and forests, unlike those of other mild climates, bring physical enjoyment, without enervating the frame. Her soil, though exhausted in many portions of the State by a false system of cultivation, is sufficiently fertile. Iron and coal abound in all her hills, and she has water power in abundance. Yet she is a worn-out decaying State. Her people are emigrating to regions less favored by nature. Pennsylvania, with certainly no greater natural wealth, and a harsher, more repulsive climate, has far outstripped her in wealth and population. What has made them to differ? Can any one doubt that slavery is the incubus which has crushed the energies of Virginia and marred her beauty in the very morning of her youth, with the wan decrepitude of old age.

If California is to be ours, shall we inflict a similar doom upon its future inhabitants? . . .

10. Bradford R. Wood (Democrat, New York), February 10, 1847.[23]

. . . No one could regret a sectional division of the country more than myself; but if it should be so, the fault is not ours. Your accusation against the North of arrogance and dictation, is very much like the cry of "stop thief." It is your arrogance, your dictation, not ours, which has produced this state of things. It is you who first made your peculiar institutions an affirmative issue. The Democracy of the North never withheld their votes from any official candidate because he was a southern man with southern principles. It is you who have declared that no northern man shall receive your support unless he shall first renounce his allegiance to our free institutions, and swear fealty to negro slavery. Now, we do not mention the fact that you are, and have been, in the possession of nearly all the distinguished offices of the republic since its existence, because we desire

23. Bradford R. Wood (1800–1889): attorney; Democratic congressman (1845–1847); U.S. minister to Denmark (1861–1865); president of Young Men's Temperance Society (1851).

CHAPTER 9

SLAVERY AND
TERRITORIAL
EXPANSION: THE
WILMOT PROVISO
DEBATE,
FEBRUARY 1847

those offices, but because it shows the nature and dangerous influence of slave-institutions. In my opinion, a scramble for office is a pitiful business; and yet if these offices are honors, they should be equally shared—if burdens, equally borne. If you are not scrambling for them, it is for the reason that, through the influence of your "peculiar institutions," you get them without any effort. Be it so. . . .

[*Wood stated that any congressman from the North who voted in favor of expanding slavery would be voted out of office in the next election: "all, save those who, the subjects of a modified rotten-borough system, will sell themselves for a foreign mission here, a collectorship there. . . ."*]

If there be any such from my own State, who, for such purposes and by such influences, will betray the North, and encircle himself in the arms of the South, let me say to him that an infamy awaits him deeper and blacker than the pit of perdition. While I can respect a southern man for acting consistently, wrong as I may think him, yet for a northern man to be found riveting the chains of the slave, and extending slavery, merits a rebuke I have not language to administer, and deserves a position more degraded than the miserable being whose shackles he would fasten. There is no highminded southern man but will look upon him with contempt. He may use him, but he will despise him. . . .

[*Wood then said that northerners' respect for the First Amendment of the Constitution prevented them from silencing abolition societies: "We shall never trample on the Constitution," he said, implying that the South was doing just that.*]

My eloquent friend from Alabama [Mr. DARGAN] believes that slavery was instituted by Divine Providence; as if "what we were evil in was by a Divine thrusting on," "villains by necessity." The plea of him who sought his father's ruin and his brother's life. The gentleman from South Carolina, [Mr. SIMS,] in a bolder tone, throws over it at once the mantle of Christianity; though its divine Author declared he came to preach "deliverance to the captive," "and to set at liberty them that are bruised," and has taught us that "all things whatsoever ye would that men should do to you, do ye even so to them." Why, sir, the very spirit of Christ, all he said, all he did, are against negro slavery, and its inseparable vices and enormities. If Christianity does, indeed, sanction slavery, why not teach the slave to read his Bible, that he may have the consolations of its precepts to cheer him onward in his degraded and miserable existence? . . .

I might go to Franklin (President as he was of the first Abolition society) for precepts of philosophy, of political and domestic economy; but for precepts of Christianity I would go to the Word of God itself, and I want them not filtered through the minds of men as fallible as myself. And yet, in connexion with this very subject, that Virginia statesman, to whom I have already alluded, has said, "I tremble for my country, when I think of a just God, and that his justice will not sleep forever."[24]

11. Thomas H. Bayly (Democrat, Virginia), February 11, 1847.[25]

This proposition to exclude slavery from all the territories hereafter to be acquired, without any reference to its geographical position, evinces bad faith upon the part of the non-slaveholding States. It is not only a palpable violation of the Constitution, but also of the Missouri compromise. That compromise, as I have already said, was forced upon us by the North. For the sake of peace we have been willing to acquiesce in it. But the very portion of the country which forced it upon us, now insist upon disregarding it against our remonstrance. . . .

With these admissions and these facts staring us in the face, why is this movement made? Sir, there are three classes of persons concerned in it:

First: The mere politician, who is actuated by the hope that, by pandering to the prejudices of a portion of the people of the non-slaveholding States, he can reap an immediate party advantage.

Second: Those who look a little further ahead, and seek to retard, if they cannot prevent, the admission of new slave States, and to stimulate the formation of new non-slaveholding States, with the view of throwing the control of the government entirely into their hands.

Third: The Abolition fanatic.

The first of these have seen the power which the Abolitionists wield in the elections; and to conciliate their support for mere party advantage, they are willing to trample upon the Constitution and disturb our peace.

The second avow that their object is political power. Their calculation is, that if they prohibit slavery in all the territories, the growth of such as are fitted to slave labor will be retarded, and that of such as are not fitted to slave labor would be proportionally stimulated. The result of which would be, non-slaveholdng States would come into the Union so much faster than

24. The actual quotation from Thomas Jefferson is "I tremble for my country when I reflect that God is just: that his justice cannot sleep forever." See Paul Leicester Ford, ed., *The Works of Thomas Jefferson,* Federal Edition (New York, 1904), Vol. IV, p. 83.
25. Thomas H. Bayly (1810–1850): attorney and military officer; Democratic congressman (1844–1856).

CHAPTER 9

SLAVERY AND
TERRITORIAL
EXPANSION: THE
WILMOT PROVISO
DEBATE,
FEBRUARY 1847

slave States, that in a short time the Government would be in the undisputed possession of the non-slaveholding States. The gentleman from New York [Mr. RATHBUN] had the candor to declare that sympathy for the negro had nothing to do with his conduct; and that if we would consent so to amend the Constitution as to abolish slave representation, he would not care how many slave territories we might erect, or how much slavery was extended. His object was, as he avowed, to throw the power of the Government into the hands of the non-slaveholding States. And why did he desire to do this? Because he thought it would be in hands that would guide our destiny more successfully? Oh! no. But that the North might dispense and enjoy the offices and the patronage of the Government!

The third class is the Abolition fanatics, who are bent upon the abolition of slavery at every hazard and by any means, even by deluging the South with blood. . . .

As a faithful sentinel on the watchtower, I warn my countrymen of the danger which is so rapidly approaching. I warn them to suspect—more than suspect, that man, who would try to lull them into a false security. I see the danger in all its hideousness, and I will not betray a confiding constituency, by crying out "all is well," when I know all is *not* well. Sir, the boldness and the strength of the Abolitionists have increased with wonderful rapidity; and I am amazed to see how quiet southern men are. I have had to school myself for this discussion. For more than ten years I have had my eye upon this monster. I have marked his movements well. I have seen the insidious character of them. I have tried to hold them up to my State in all of their atrocity. But I grieve to say they have not awakened the spirit which they should. The increase of the strength of the Abolitionists has been so gradual, that the country has not been sufficiently alive to it. . . .

I warn southern men that we have arrived at a point at which we must take a firm stand, if we ever mean to do it. We have arrived at a point when further concessions to the Abolitionists would be alike dishonorable and fatal. I repeat, if we ever mean to act with firmness, let us do it now.

12. James C. Dobbin (Democrat, North Carolina), February 11, 1847.[26]

. . . The honorable gentleman from New York, [Mr. RATHBUN,] who advocated this proposition, announced to us, in the most solemn and deliberate

26. James C. Dobbin (1814–1857): attorney; Democratic congressman (1845–1847); secretary of the Navy (1853–1857).

manner, that slavery was an evil; that it was a blighting curse, and a great calamity; and, in an eloquent burst of indignation, proclaimed that any northern man who dared here to countenance the extension of slave territory, would be swept away by a tornado from the North. Yea, sir; his eloquence mounted still higher: he said that such a one would be destroyed "by thunder manufactured at the North, second only to the thunder of the Creator himself! . . ."

I do not claim to be as deeply versed in scriptural learning as I ought to be. Perhaps my reading, sir, has been too casual and inattentive; for surely, the part that consigns the slaveholder to perdition on account of the sinfulness of slavery has escaped my attention. I ask gentlemen to point out the scriptural denunciation of slavery. Where, in the Old or New Testament, do you find it? Is it denounced at the time when the white tents of Israel were spread at the foot of the Mount, and the voice of Jehovah, amid the thunderings and lightnings of Sinai, gave the moral law to Moses? Does the honorable gentleman read in that moral law any warning to man against this terrible sin of holding slave property? Does he infer it from that commandment which proclaims the seventh day as, the Sabbath of the Lord, and saith to man, "in it thou shalt not do any work, thy *man-servant* nor thy *maid-servant*?" Does he infer it from that other commandment which saith "thou shalt not covet thy neighbor's house, nor his *man-servant,* nor his *maid-servant,* nor anything that *is* thy neighbor's?" Or is it found in the New Testament, where the Apostle preaches thus: "Servants, be obedient to them that are your masters according to the flesh with fear and trembling?" Is it found in the same Apostle's admonition to masters to act well their part, "knowing that your Master also is in Heaven?" Is it found in the Epistle to Timothy: "Let as many servants as are under the yoke count their own masters worthy of all honor, that the name of God and his doctrine be not blasphemed?"

Sir, fanaticism, fanaticism must yield this point, intelligent piety has yielded it; philosophic Christians have yielded it. Sir, when Moses came to find among the Jews slavery, an institution of the worst sort—slaves who had been taken captive—slaves by crime—slaves by birth—did he denounce it? Did he become an Abolitionist, and proclaim it a crime and sin, and that it must be abolished? No; he only sought to regulate it. And when our Saviour made his advent on earth, what, sir, does history teach us—both sacred and profane history? Did he not find then in existence a *slavery,* the *worst* that the world has ever seen?—a slavery which gave the master a control over the servant greater and more unlimited than we have? Were not human beings then bought and sold? Did our Saviour, in his holy teachings, warn man that he endangered his salvation if he held slave

CHAPTER 9

SLAVERY AND
TERRITORIAL
EXPANSION: THE
WILMOT PROVISO
DEBATE,
FEBRUARY 1847

property? Did he preach the necessity of its abolition? of its sinfulness? Have the honorable gentlemen perused the epistle of Paul to Philemon, which was sent by Onesimus, a *runaway slave?* Paul sent him home to his Christian master; and in his epistle to Philemon, he says of Onesimus, "Whom I would have retained with me; but without thy mind would I do nothing." Sir, if Paul, under Divine inspiration, thought slavery a crime, he would have told Philemon, "Sir, remember you must die, and are accountable to God; take off his shackles, and liberate your slave." No; he recommends him to his mercy, and sent him back to his master, because, he said, he had no authority to keep him—*a very useful lesson, by which our friends in some portions of the Union might profit!* I know it is said the word *servant* does not mean *slave.* I challenge investigation on this subject. The word translated *servant,* in the Greek, is *doulos,* which means *slave,* and is used in contradistinction to words used to mean "a hireling or servant." And I now insist that gentlemen, before they denounce us and consign us to infamy and eternal perdition, invoking the Word of God against us, shall first read that holy book, and know what it contains. . . .

But it is said that these efforts are made to benefit the negro. I hold, Mr. Chairman, that *the black and white races cannot coexist under the same government upon an equal footing.* I challenge anybody to controvert it. I will not go into my own country for proof of this, but will refer to the North, where our friends claim to be, and no doubt many are, actuated in reference to this matter by pure and disinterested motives. Slavery is *technically* abolished there, but servitude exists; and when the legislator, clad in the garb of philanthropy, takes the negro to the hall of legislation, tears his chains from him, and bids him go and be free, he practically stops him at the door and tells him, When you go to the theatre remember you are a black man, and take your seat in an humble place; when you go to church to worship God, remember your color, and *sit not* with the white man, your liberator, but your superior. Dare not intrude at the same table with us. And when you die and are to be buried, your graveyards and ours are to be separate. I do not say this in a spirit of denunciation of the North; far from it; and in every State it may not be true; but it sustains me in the proposition I laid down, that the black and white races cannot coexist under the same government upon an equal footing. The right of suffrage is rarely given to them in the North, and in the State which my friend near me in part represents, (New York,) when the attempt was recently made to give him this right, the proposition was rejected with scorn, by one hundred thousand majority.

But I say, if you attempt to liberate these slaves in our country, in our limited territory, you can do them no good, and you do the whites essential harm. I have seen lately a summary of curious facts prepared by a gentleman who looks into statistics, and these facts indicate clearly that in this country, when you liberate these slaves they are more degraded than when they are slaves, and commit more crime. Diffusion will come nearer promoting ultimate peaceful emancipation than any movement that can be made. And coming to the South, southern gentlemen will bear me out, that the crime committed in the South is by the free negro, not by the slave. And although we have in our midst some free negroes of the best character, yet they do not receive from the white man either the same protection or sympathy that the slave does, whose master protects him both from principle and interest.

The following will serve to show how slightly, if at all, the moral condition of the colored man is improved in the States where he is emancipated; and if this be the picture where the blacks are so few in numbers, what can be expected if our slaves are to be confined to their present territorial limits, and numbering more than three millions, and then emancipated?

In Massachusetts there is one free negro to seventy-four of the white population, and yet *one-sixth* of the convicts are free negroes. In Connecticut there is one free negro to thirty-four of the white population, and yet one-third of the convicts are free negroes. In New York there is one free negro to thirty-five of the white population, and yet one-fourth of the convicts are free negroes. In New Jersey there is one free negro to thirteen of the white population, and yet one-third of the prisoners are free negroes. In Pennsylvania there is one free negro to thirty-four of the white population, and one-third of the prisoners are free negroes.

But gentlemen say they want to elevate the white man at the South; save us, sir, from the elevation to result from turning loose three millions of slaves in our midst. Mr. Chairman, let us take care of ourselves. We know our responsibility to God and man, and we will act in view of it. . . .

13. Paul Dillingham Jr. (Democrat, Vermont), February 12, 1847.[27]

To ascertain the merits or demerits of slavery, he should be obliged to deal somewhat in comparisons; and though it was sometimes said, that "comparisons were odious," he begged all to understand that he used them in no offensive sense, with no wish to give pain, but simply to elicit truth.

27. Paul Dillingham Jr. (1799–1891): attorney; Democratic congressman (1843–1847); governor of Vermont (1865–1866).

CHAPTER 9

SLAVERY AND
TERRITORIAL
EXPANSION: THE
WILMOT PROVISO
DEBATE,
FEBRUARY 1847

At the time of the last census, there were twenty-six States—thirteen free and thirteen slave States. The thirteen free States had an area of territory equal to 332,468 square miles, and the thirteen slave States had one equal to 553,051 square miles—being an excess of slave over free territory of 220,583 square miles. The thirteen free States were entitled to one hundred and thirty-five representatives on this floor; and had the slave States an equal number of inhabitants to the square mile, they, at the same ratio, would have been entitled to two hundred and thirty representatives; but they are, in fact, entitled to but eighty-eight—being forty-seven less than belongs to the free States. Why this disparity? The slave States are as old as the free; they have the best climate on this continent; they are not inferior in soil, in seacoast, harbors, or navigable rivers, to the free States. Does not the difference all arise from the evils inseparable from slavery? Look at some of the States. Virginia, compared with New York or Pennsylvania, with a third more territory than either, but inferior in all things else. Massachusetts has a territory of 7,500 square miles—she has ten representatives here. South Carolina, on the other hand, is as old a State, is a commercial one too: she has a territory of 28,000 square miles, and seven representatives here. South Carolina is most inveterately a slave State: the population of Massachusetts are free.

With some pride, I take my own State, and contrast it with Louisiana. The latter has a territory of 48,221 square miles, through which flows the mighty Mississippi, that father of rivers. On that river, that State has a commercial capital of a hundred thousand inhabitants, and her soil inferior to none for luxuriousness. Before the white man's foot first broke the silence of the forests in my own State, the other had some thousands of inhabitants; and she is now entitled to four representatives here. Vermont, with 10,212 square miles, situated in a high northern latitude, upon the tops of whose green mountains winter hangs her white mantle from the last of October till early May, with no seacoast and no navigable river touching her territory,—she, too, is entitled to her four representatives here. . . .

It was said, however, by southern members, that it would be unkind and unjust to them to restrict slavery to its present limits, even if we have the power; that thereby they will be shut out from all benefit in the acquired territory.

But how, pray, are they to be shut out? We only exclude slavery. Three-fourths of the white males over twenty-one years old, in the slave States, he was told, did not and never would own a slave: all these could go to the new territory—it would be still the South, "the sunny South" to them, like to the place of their birth and nativity, in all but slavery; and being relieved from its degrading associations in connection with labor, the privilege would be immense to them. If the owner of slaves cannot or will not go, he certainly will feel that he has "ample room and space enough" where *all* was left to the slave and his master. How can members from the South insist that this attempt to restriction looks to, and means, ultimate abolition of slavery? He said he was no abolitionist, but three-fifths of the soil of these States was now given up to slavery, and he would consent to no further extension. He did not propose to meddle with it where it was; but if limiting it to its present abodes will, as was insisted yesterday by the honorable member from Maryland, [Mr. GILES,] tend to swell the black tide till it ultimately overwhelms, either master or slave, he could not help it. Africa, from whence the fathers of the slaves were stolen by *our* fathers— British and Colonial—was open to receive back their black descendants. He did not propose this or any other scheme for emancipation—it was with those States where slavery was to find a remedy. He believed that He who inhabited the upper sanctuary and governed all things, would yet inspire the hearts of the slave owner with wisdom to devise means for the final extinction of slavery. He knew that southern men considered it a great evil—some so confess it—others fear to own that it is. . . .

14. Joshua Giddings (Whig, Ohio), February 13, 1847.[28]

Gentlemen from the South, with deep emotions, have solemnly warned us, that if we persist in our determination, the *"Union will be dissolved."* I do not doubt their sincerity. But I would rather see this Union rent into a thousand fragments than have my country disgraced, and its moral purity sacrificed, by the prosecution of a war for the extension of human bondage. Nor would I avoid this issue, were it in my power. For many years have I seen the rights of the North, and the vital principles of our Constitution, surrendered to the haughty vaporings of southern members. For many years have I exerted my humble influence to stimulate northern members to the maintenance of our honor and of the Constitution: And now I devoutly thank that God who has permitted me to witness the union of a portion of northern members of both political parties, upon a question so vital to our interests and honor, as well as to humanity. I also rejoice that

28. Joshua Giddings (1795–1864): attorney; Whig congressman (1838–1842, 1842–1859); resigned from Congress in 1842 after being censured for his motion in the House defending the slave mutineers in the *Creole* case (1842), but was returned to Congress by the voters one month later.

CHAPTER 9

SLAVERY AND
TERRITORIAL
EXPANSION: THE
WILMOT PROVISO
DEBATE,
FEBRUARY 1847

this is a question which admits of no compromise. Slavery and freedom are antagonisms. They must necessarily be at war with each other. There can be no compromise between right and wrong, or between virtue and crime. The conflicting interests of slave and free labor have agitated this Government from its foundation, and will continue to agitate it, until truth and justice shall triumph over error and oppression. Should the proposition now before us fail, it will surely succeed at the next session of Congress; for it is very evident that public sentiment in the free States is daily becoming more and more in favor of it. The legislatures in six of those States have instructed their Senators and requested their Representatives to vote for this measure. Few gentlemen on this floor will disregard those resolutions when we come to the vote. Whigs and Democrats will then be found acting together. Our party attachments will be disregarded, and the interests of the nation will receive our attention. Sir, for the first time in my life, I see northern Whigs and northern Democrats standing shoulder to shoulder in the cause of human rights. Would to God that such might be the case on all questions touching the interests, the honor, and the rights of the free States and of mankind! There is no good reason why northern Representatives should waste their political power by party divisions among themselves. Let them act irrespective of southern influence, and they will agree upon all the great questions so vitally interesting to our people. It is time that we should discard those counsels which have led to the sacrifice of nearly all our political interests. Before God and my country, I solemnly pledge myself never to place political confidence in any man who lacks the honesty, or the firmness to speak and act in favor of freedom and the Constitution. . . . I assure you, sir, that our people are becoming aroused to the dangers which threaten them; and although men of high character and of commanding talents may deem it bad policy to speak forth unwelcome truths, yet, sir, there are instrumentalities at work which will inform the public mind of the true political condition of the free States: and when the people of those States shall understand fully the manner in which their interests have been silently surrendered, and their constitutional rights subverted, they will take care to place more faithful sentinels upon the watchtowers of liberty. . . .

In the course of this debate, we have been told that *"a God of justice has ordained and established slavery;"* and "that the Scriptures of Divine Truth have furnished authority for holding men as *property*." I had hoped that our holy religion might have escaped this slaveholding sacrilege. Do gentlemen worship a God of oppression, of licentiousness, and of blood? It is a notorious fact that the average life of slaves, after entering the cotton plantations of the South, is but *seven years;* and on the sugar plantations, but *five years*—that is, the whole number of slaves on these plantations are driven so hard as to close their existence within those periods. Their places are supplied by new purchases from the slave-breeding States, and these in turn are also sacrificed to the master's cupidity. Is the taking of life in this manner less aggravated murder than it would be to slay them at once? Is there less crime in torturing a man so as to cause his death in five or seven years, than there would be in slaying him outright? Again, sir: look at yonder slave prison; view its gloomy walls; enter its cells; witness the sighs, and groans, and tears of its unhappy inmates, doomed to a southern slave market; note the unutterable agony of that mother, who has been torn from her home and family, and all she holds dear. Rumor speaks of one who, thus confined with two of her children, became frantic with her suffering, and, in a transport of horror, murdered her children, and then put a period to her own existence, rather than meet the doom that awaited her. Yet we are told, even by those who minister at slaveholding altars, that these "things are dictated by God himself." To me the doctrine appears impious. I would sooner be an infidel than render homage to such a Deity. I loath and detest such doctrines, whether they emanate from laymen or professed divines. The mind that can impute the moral corruptions, the reeking crimes of slavery, to a holy, just, and pure God, would, in my opinion, sustain the most horrid rites of Paganism; would worship in temples stained with blood, and minister at altars smoking with human sacrifice, if necessary to sustain the curse of slavery. I regard the devotees of Juggernaut far more consistent than such Christians. . . .

In conclusion, permit me to say to the country, that our political horizon is overcast; "clouds and darkness are round about us;" and impenetrable darkness shuts the future from our view. Foreign war, and internal strife, animosities, and heart-burnings, indicate that this nation is doomed to suffer the just penalty incurred by the oppression, outrage, and crime, which we have perpetrated upon our fellow men. If God deals out to offending nations, retributive justice, we cannot escape his displeasure.

❋ QUESTIONS TO CONSIDER ❋

As you examine and analyze the arguments for and against the expansion of slavery into what became the state of California (often called "Upper California" in the debate) and the New Mexico Territory, you will see

CHAPTER 9

SLAVERY AND
TERRITORIAL
EXPANSION: THE
WILMOT PROVISO
DEBATE,
FEBRUARY 1847

that most of the debate clusters around four central points:

1. *The constitutionality of slave expansion.* Most of the supporters of the Wilmot Proviso, including David Wilmot himself, recognized that the institution was imbedded in the Constitution (see Article I, Sections 2 and 9; Article IV, Section 1). But how did they interpret Article IV, Section 3 (on the admission of new states)? How did the proviso's opponents counter that interpretation? How did George Rathbun (Source 7) view the "three-fifths compromise" (Article I, Section 2)? What did he assert was the result of that 1787 compromise?

2. *The politics of the Wilmot Proviso.* A good deal of discussion took place over the *motives* of both the proponents and opponents of the Wilmot Proviso. What did Stephen Strong (Source 4) claim were the true motives of Wilmot and his allies? What did Rathbun (Source 7) assert were the motives of southerners? How did Thomas H. Bayly and James C. Dobbin (Sources 11 and 12) attempt to counter Rathbun's argument? Also on politics, what did James Dixon, Bradford R. Wood, and Joshua Giddings (Sources 9, 10, and 14, respectively) believe were the shifting political opinions of northern voters?[29]

3. *Slavery and the Bible.* As you can see, occasionally the debate shifted

from the *expansion* of slavery to slavery itself (as, for example, in Sources 5 and 12 on the capacity of slaves to be free people). How did both sides attempt to use the Bible in support of their respective positions?

4. *Slavery and the future of the West.* How did James Dixon (Source 9) and Paul Dillingham Jr. (Source 13) try to show that the growth and development of the West would take place better *without slavery?* Also, Dillingham offered the interesting observation regarding southerners who would *not* be prohibited from migrating to California and the New Mexico Territory. Who were those southerners?

5. *The fate of slavery where it existed.* What did each speaker think would happen to the well-established institution of slavery where it already existed if the Wilmot Proviso prevented the expansion of slavery into new territories?

6. *The roots of sectional conflict.* According to each speaker, who was responsible for the climate of mistrust that surrounded the debate over the Wilmot Proviso? In the opinion of each speaker, when did the spirit of compromise begin to dissolve?

In his classic essay on John C. Calhoun published over fifty years ago, historian Richard Hofstadter referred to Calhoun as the "Marx of the Master Class."[30] Hofstadter referred to Calhoun in this way because, in his defense of the institution of slavery, Calhoun used arguments very similar to those of his near-contemporary Karl

---

29. There is little question that the Wilmot Proviso had an important political aspect to it. On Febuary 1, 1847, the *New York Tribune* reported that the Polk administration was working hard behind the scenes to defeat the Proviso. Its tactic, the *Tribune* claimed, was to "carry the South by principle and the North by patronage."

30. Richard Hofstadter, *The American Political Tradition and the Men Who Made It* (New York, 1948), chap. 4.

Marx (1818–1883) to attack the "wage slavery" of the northern system of labor. In what ways might Representative R. W. Roberts (Source 2) also be referred to as a "Marx of the Master Class"?

Perhaps the most frightening aspect of the debate over the Wilmot Proviso had to do with the future of the Union itself. Which congressmen asserted that the northern states had given in to the South in the past but would not do so again? What did that infer? Which proponents of the Wilmot Proviso spoke openly about the threat of disunion? What was John Pettit's (Source 1) position? How many speakers whose excerpts are reproduced here agreed with Pettit? Which southern representatives addressed that issue, and how did they do so?

Now you are ready to answer the question: Why was compromise increasingly difficult? As noted earlier, be sure to consider the *tone* of the debate as well as the points that were made. Did either side have a "fallback" position? On what bases might compromise still have been possible? Remember that there actually *was* a compromise in 1850, although by then it is unclear how many people (at least in the North) sincerely intended to abide by it.

❋ EPILOGUE ❋

According to Wilmot's biographer Charles Buxton Going, on the morning of February 15, 1847 (the day the Wilmot Proviso and the "Three Million Dollar Bill" were to be voted on), President Polk called Wilmot to the White House, perhaps in a last-minute effort to derail the proviso.[31] But Wilmot allies Preston King (who had attempted to introduce the proviso as early as January 14, 1847), Jacob Brinkerhoff (who many believe was the true author of the proviso), and Hannibal Hamlin (Democratic representative from Maine who ultimately became Abraham Lincoln's first vice president), in Wilmot's absence, shepherded the proviso onto the floor and through a long series of parliamentary maneuvers to table or water down the amendment.[32] It is not clear whether Wilmot himself had reached the House in time to vote on the proviso that bore his name, but he was on the House floor by the time the appropriation bill, with the proviso approved and attached, was voted on. It passed 115–105.[33] Not surprisingly, the Senate later defeated the proviso by a vote of 21–31.

On one level, Representative Preston King summarized the main issue surrounding the Wilmot Proviso from the view of the average northern white. On the House floor, King

32. Technically, it was Hamlin who introduced the proviso on February 15, 1847.
33. *Congressional Globe,* 29th Congress, 2nd sess., p. 425.

31. Going, *David Wilmot,* p. 201. There is no record of such a meeting in Polk's diary.

CHAPTER 9

SLAVERY AND
TERRITORIAL
EXPANSION: THE
WILMOT PROVISO
DEBATE,
FEBRUARY 1847

warned that if "slavery is not excluded [from the territories] by law, the presence of the slave will exclude the laboring white man."[34] While ultimately the North would move toward a commercial-industrial economy, by the 1840s it was still primarily a section of free white farmers who, as population swelled due to natural increase and immigration, saw their collective future in new lands in the West. To those farmers, the Wilmot Proviso and King's remarks hit home. This was to be *their* West, one they saw as their heritage of the American Revolution—an uprising against aristocracy and tyranny from above.

Of course, white southerners also believed themselves to be heirs of the American Revolution for, in their view, the slavery of blacks allowed whites to be more free (see Roberts's attack on the "limited servitude" of the North in Source 2). In their minds, leadership from above guaranteed a republican form of government and prevented rule by a "mobocracy." And although most southern whites did not own slaves (see Dillingham's remarks in Source 13), they supported such an arrangement, in part hoping that planters would protect them from the slaves and in part because many hoped to migrate to western lands where they might become planter aristocrats themselves (as some of those who migrated to the Gulf states and to Texas had done).

On another level, however, the Wilmot Proviso signaled an end to meaningful compromise between the sec-

tions and their drifting ultimately toward disunion. One respected historian who has studied the period recently referred to the proviso as the beginning of "an immutable battle between North and South for control of the government and thus the ability to secure the fortunes of one or the other section."[35] In such an atmosphere, the second political party system could not survive. The increased antislavery sentiments of northern Whig party members caused the collapse of that party's southern wing until the Whigs, by the 1850s, were scarcely a national party at all. As for the Democrats, the controversy over slavery put enormous strain on moderates in that party. In the Twenty-ninth Congress (in which the Wilmot Proviso was first introduced and passed by the House of Representatives), almost 36 percent of the Democrats in the House could be classified as moderates on the slavery issue. By the Thirtieth Congress, only 8.4 percent could be designated as moderates.[36] By 1860, the Democrats could not even agree on a presidential nominee.

By then many of the northern Democrats had drifted into the new Republican party (founded in 1854). Preston King became a Republican and anticipated a political future in that party when he was drowned in a ferryboat accident in 1865. Jacob Brinkerhoff joined the Free-Soil party and then, in 1856, the Republicans. In

34. Quoted in Joseph G. Rayback, *Free Soil! The Election of 1848* (Lexington, Ky., 1970), p. 60.

35. Immutable: unchanging. See Michael A. Morrison, *Slavery and the American West: The Eclipse of Manifest Destiny and the Coming of the Civil War* (Chapel Hill, N.C., 1997), p. 6.

36. Joel H. Silbey, *The Shrine of Party: Congressional Voting Behavior, 1841–1852* (Pittsburgh, 1967), p. 96.

1872, he bolted the party over what he believed were the excesses and corruption of the Grant administration and became a Liberal Republican (see Chapter 11). He died in 1880.

For David Wilmot, the zenith of his political career came in 1846–1847, with the introduction of the proviso that, accurately or not, bears his name. Reelected to the House of Representatives in 1848, he bolted from the Democratic party in that year to support Martin Van Buren and the Free-Soilers. From there, like Brinkerhoff, he became a Republican, supported Lincoln in 1860, and was appointed to a federal judgeship in 1863. Interestingly, the Wilmot Proviso finally passed Congress on June 19, 1862. Wilmot died in 1868, at the age of fifty-four, and was buried in the Riverside Cemetary in Towanda, Pennsylvania (roughly thirty miles south of Elmira, New York). On his tombstone was carved a portion of the proviso that had made him famous.[37]

37. Going, *David Wilmot*, p. 642.

10

The Price for Victory:
The Decision to Use
African American Troops

✵ THE PROBLEM ✵

With the outbreak of war at Fort Sumter in April 1861, many northern African Americans volunteered for service in the Union army. President Abraham Lincoln initially rejected black petitions to become soldiers. On April 29, Secretary of War Simon Cameron wrote one of many letters to African American volunteers; it curtly stated that "this Department has no intention at present to call into the service of the Government any colored soldiers."[1] Later, in July 1862, when Congress passed the Confiscation Act (part of which authorized the presi-

dent to use escaped slaves for the suppression of the rebellion "in such manner as he may judge best") and the Militia Act (which authorized him to enroll African Americans for military service), Lincoln virtually ignored both laws, arguing that the two acts *authorized* him to recruit blacks but did not *require* him to do so.

Curiously, in the South, too, free blacks and some slaves petitioned to be included in the newly formed Confederate army, perhaps hoping that such service might improve their conditions or even win them freedom. Like Lincoln, Confederate president Jefferson Davis rejected African American volunteers for military service and consistently opposed their use. Yet ultimately both chief executives changed their minds and accepted Af-

---

1. The letter was addressed to "Jacob Dodson (colored)" and is in *The War of the Rebellion: A Compilation of the Official Records of the Union and Confederate Armies* (Washington, D.C.: U.S. Government Printing Office, 1899), Series III, Vol. I, p. 133.

rican Americans into the armed forces, although in Davis's case, the policy reversal came too late for black soldiers to serve on the Confederate side. And although the recruitment of African American soldiers by the South might have prolonged the conflict, it probably would not have altered the ultimate outcome. In this chapter, you will examine the evidence so as to answer the following questions:

1. What were the arguments in the North and South against arming African Americans and using them as regular soldiers? What were the arguments in favor of this move? How did the reasons in the North and South differ? How were they similar?

2. What do you think were the principal reasons that both the United States and the Confederate States of America changed their policies? How did the reasons in the North and South differ? How were they similar?

❋ BACKGROUND ❋

Although many leaders in both the North and South studiously tried to avoid public discussion of the issue, the institution of slavery unquestionably played a major role in bringing on the American Civil War. As slavery intruded into the important issues and events of the day (such as westward expansion, the Mexican War, the admission of new states to the Union, the course charted for the proposed transcontinental railroad, and the right of citizens to petition Congress), as well as into all the major institutions (churches and schools, for example), an increasing number of northerners and southerners came to feel that the question of slavery must be settled, and settled on the battlefield. Therefore, when news arrived of the firing on Fort Sumter, many greeted the announcement with relief. Lincoln's call for seventy-five thousand volunteers was answered with an enormous response. A wave of patriotic fervor swept across the northern states, as crowds greeted Union soldiers marching south to "lick the rebels." In the South, too, the outbreak of war was greeted with great enthusiasm. In Charleston, South Carolina, a day of celebration was followed by a night of parades and fireworks. Many southerners compared the upcoming war with the American Revolution, when, so the thinking went, an outnumbered but superior people had been victorious over the tyrant.

Yet for a number of reasons, most northern and southern leaders carefully avoided the slavery issue even after the war had begun. To Abraham Lincoln, the debate over the abolition of slavery threatened to divert northerners from what he considered the war's central aim: preserving the Union and denying the South's right to secede. In addition, Lincoln realized

CHAPTER 10

THE PRICE FOR
VICTORY: THE
DECISION TO
USE AFRICAN
AMERICAN
TROOPS

that a great number of northern whites, including himself, did not view African Americans as equals and might well oppose a war designed to liberate slaves from bondage. Finally, in large parts of Virginia, North Carolina, Kentucky, and Tennessee and in other pockets in the South, Union sentiment was strong, largely because of the antiplanter bias in these states. But anti-Negro sentiment also was strong in these same areas. With the border states so crucial to the Union both politically and militarily (as points of invasion into the South), it is not surprising that Lincoln purposely discouraged any notion that the war was for the purpose of emancipating slaves. Therefore, when influential editor Horace Greeley publicly called on Lincoln in August 1862 to make the Civil War a war for the emancipation of slaves, the president replied that the primary purpose of the war was to preserve the Union. "My paramount object in this struggle," Lincoln wrote, "is *not* either to save or destroy slavery" (italics added):

> If I could save the Union without freeing *any* slave I would do it, and if I could save it by freeing *all* the slaves I would do it; and if I could save it by freeing some and leaving others alone I would also do that. What I do about slavery, and the colored race, I do because I believe it helps to save the Union; and what I forbear, I forbear because I do *not* believe it would help to save the Union.[2]

Hence President Lincoln, in spite of his "*personal* wish that all men everywhere could be free" (italics added), strongly resisted all efforts to turn the Civil War into a moral crusade to, in his words, "destroy slavery."

On the Confederate side, President Jefferson Davis also had reasons to avoid making the preservation of slavery a primary war aim. Davis feared, correctly, that foreign governments would be unwilling to recognize or aid the Confederacy if the preservation of slavery was the most important southern reason for fighting. In addition, the majority of white southerners did not own slaves, often disliked people who did, and, Davis feared, might not fight if the principal war aim was to defend the peculiar institution. Therefore, while Lincoln was explaining to northerners that the war was being fought to preserve the Union, Davis was trying to convince southerners that the struggle was for independence and the defense of constitutional rights.

Yet as it became increasingly clear that the Civil War was going to be a long and costly conflict, issues concerning slavery and the use of African Americans in the war effort continually came to the surface. In the North, reports of battle casualties in 1862 caused widespread shock and outrage, and some feared that the United States would be exhausted before the Confederacy was finally subdued—if it was to be subdued at all.[3] Also, many

2. Lincoln to Greeley, August 22, 1862, in Roy P. Basler, ed., *The Collected Works of Abraham Lincoln* (New Brunswick, N.J.: Rutgers University Press, 1953), Vol. V, pp. 388–389. Italics added.

3. The following is an estimate of Union casualties (the sum of those killed, wounded, and missing) for the principal engagements of 1862: Shiloh (April, 13,000 casualties), Seven Pines (May, 6,000), Seven Days (June, 16,000), Antietam (September, 12,400), Fredericksburg (December, 12,000).

northerners came to feel that emancipation could be used as both a political and a diplomatic weapon. Those European nations—especially England, which had ended slavery throughout its own empire in 1833—that had been technically neutral but were leaning toward the Confederacy might, northerners reasoned, be afraid to oppose a government committed to such a worthy cause as emancipation. Some northerners also hoped that a proclamation of emancipation would incite widespread slave rebellions in the South that would cripple the Confederacy. Not to be overlooked, however, is the minority of northerners who sincerely viewed slavery as a stain on American society and whose eradication was a moral imperative.

Gradually, President Lincoln came to favor the emancipation of slaves, although never to the extent that the abolitionists wanted. In early 1862, the president proposed the gradual emancipation of slaves by the states, with compensation for the slave owners and colonization of the former slaves outside the boundaries of the United States. When Congress mandated that Lincoln go further than that, by passing the Confiscation Act of 1862, which explicitly called for the permanent emancipation of all slaves in the Confederacy, the president simply ignored the law, choosing not to enforce it.[4] But political and diplomatic considerations prompted Lincoln to alter his course and support the issuing of the Preliminary Emancipation Proclamation in September 1862. So that his action would not be

interpreted as one of desperation, the president waited until after the Union "victory" at the Battle of Antietam. Although the proclamation, scheduled to take effect on January 1, 1863, actually freed slaves only in areas still under Confederate control, hence immediately freeing no one, the act was a significant one regarding a shift in war aims. The final Emancipation Proclamation was issued on January 1, 1863.[5]

The second important issue that Lincoln and other northern leaders had to face was whether to arm African Americans and make them regular soldiers in the Union army. Blacks had seen service in the American Revolution and the War of 1812, prompting abolitionist Frederick Douglass, a former slave, to criticize the United States' initial policy of excluding African Americans from the army in the Civil War, saying in February 1862,

Colored men were good enough to fight under Washington. They are not good enough to fight under McClellan. They were good enough to fight under Andrew Jackson. They are not good enough to fight under Gen. Halleck. They were good enough to help win American Independence, but they are not good enough to help preserve that independence against treason and rebellion.[6]

4. It was this action by Lincoln that prompted the exchange between Greeley and the president in August 1862.

5. The Preliminary Emancipation Proclamation was issued to test public opinion in the North and to give southern states the opportunity to retain slavery by returning to the Union before January 1, 1863. No state in the Confederacy took advantage of Lincoln's offer, and the final proclamation was issued and took effect on January 1, 1863.
6. Quoted in James M. McPherson, *The Negro's Civil War: How American Negroes Felt*

CHAPTER 10

THE PRICE FOR
VICTORY: THE
DECISION TO
USE AFRICAN
AMERICAN
TROOPS

Emancipation of slaves in the South was one thing, but making blacks United States soldiers was another. Such a decision would imply that white northerners recognized African Americans as equals. Although most abolitionists preached the dual message of emancipation and racial equality, most northern whites did not look on African Americans as equals, a belief that they shared with their president. Would whites fight alongside blacks even in racially separated units? Were blacks, many northern whites asked, courageous enough to stand and hold their positions under fire? What would African Americans want as a price for their aid? Throughout 1862, northern leaders carried on an almost continual debate over whether to accept African Americans into the Union army, an issue that had a number of social, ideological, and moral implications.

In the Confederacy, the issue of arming African Americans for the southern war effort was also a divisive one. The northern superiority in population, supplemented by continued immigration from Europe, put the South at a terrific numerical disadvantage, a disadvantage that could be lessened by the enlistment of at least a portion of the approximately four million slaves. Southern battle casualties also had been fearfully high, in some battles higher than those of the Union.[7] How long could the Confederacy hold out as its numbers continually eroded? If the main goal of the war was southern independence, shouldn't Confederate leaders use all available means to secure that objective? It was known that some northern whites, shocked by Union casualty figures, were calling on Lincoln to let the South go in peace. If the Confederacy could hold out, many southerners hoped, northern peace sentiments might grow enough to force the Union to give up. If slaves could help in that effort, some reasoned, why not arm them? Yet, as in the North, the question of whether to arm African Americans had significance far beyond military considerations. Except for the promise of freedom, what would motivate the slaves to fight for their masters? If freedom was to be offered, then what, many would argue, was the war being fought over in the first place? Would southern whites fight with blacks? Would some African Americans, once armed, then turn against their masters? And finally, if southern whites were correct in their insistence that African Americans were essentially docile, childlike creatures, what conceivable support could they give to the war effort? Interestingly, there were some remarkable similarities in the points debated by the northern and southern policymakers and citizens.

and Acted During the War for the Union (New York: Pantheon Books, 1965), p. 163.

7. The following are estimates of Confederate casualties for the principal engagements of 1862–1863: Seven Days (June 1862, 20,000), Antietam (September 1862, 13,700), Fredericksburg (December 1862, 5,000), Gettysburg (July 1863, 28,000).

✳ THE METHOD ✳

In this chapter, you are confronted with two sets of evidence: private and official correspondence, reports, newspaper articles and editorials, and laws and proclamations. One set concerns the argument in the North over whether to arm blacks, and the other set deals with the same question in the South. Read and analyze each series separately. Take notes as you go along, always being careful not to lose track of your central objectives.

By now you should be easily able to identify and list the major points, pro and con, in a debate. Jotting down notes as you read the evidence is extremely helpful. Be careful, however, because some reports, articles, and letters contain more than one argument.

Several earlier chapters required that you read between the lines—that is, identify themes and issues that are implied though never directly stated.

What emotional factors can you identify on both sides of the question? How important would you say these factors were in the final decision? For example, you will see from the evidence that at no time in the debate being carried on in the North were battle casualties mentioned. Were casualties therefore of no importance in the debate? How would you go about answering this question?

In some cases, the identity of the author of a particular piece (if known) can give you several clues as to that person's emotions, fears, anxieties, and needs. Where the identity of the author is not known, you may have to exercise a little historical imagination. What might this person really have meant when he or she said (or failed to say) something? Can you infer from the context of the argument any emotions that are not explicitly stated?

✳ THE EVIDENCE ✳

NORTH

Source 1 from James M. McPherson, *The Negro's Civil War: How American Negroes Felt and Acted During the War for the Union* (New York: Pantheon Books, 1965), p. 33.

1. Petition of Some Northern Blacks to President Lincoln, October 1861.

We, the undersigned, respectfully represent to Your Excellency that we are native citizens of the United States, and that, notwithstanding much injustice and oppression which our race have suffered, we cherish a strong attachment for the land of our birth and for our Republican Government.

CHAPTER 10

THE PRICE FOR
VICTORY: THE
DECISION TO
USE AFRICAN
AMERICAN
TROOPS

We are filled with alarm at the formidable conspiracy for its overthrow, and lament the vast expense of blood and treasure which the present war involves. . . . We are anxious to use our power to give peace to our country and permanence to our Government.

We are strong in numbers, in courage, and in patriotism, and in behalf of our fellow countrymen of the colored race, we offer to you and to the nation a power and a will sufficient to conquer rebellion, and establish peace on a permanent basis. We pledge ourselves, upon receiving the sanction of Your Excellency, that we will immediately proceed to raise an efficient number of regiments, and so fast as arms and equipments shall be furnished, we will bring them into the field in good discipline, and ready for action.

Source 2 from Bell Irvin Wiley, *The Life of Billy Yank: The Common Soldier of the Union* (Baton Rouge: Louisiana State University Press, 1971), p. 109.

2. A. Davenport (a Union Soldier from New York) to His Home Folk, June 19, 1861.

I think that the best way to settle the question of what to do with the darkies would be to shoot them.

Source 3 from McPherson, *The Negro's Civil War*, p. 162.

3. Newspaper Editorial by Frederick Douglass, *Douglass' Monthly,* September 1861.

Our Presidents, Governors, Generals and Secretaries are calling, with almost frantic vehemence, for men—"Men! men! send us men!" they scream, or the cause of the Union is gone; . . . and yet these very officers, representing the people and Government, steadily and persistently refuse to receive the very class of men which have a deeper interest in the defeat and humiliation of the rebels, than all others. . . . What a spectacle of blind, unreasoning prejudice and pusillanimity[8] is this! The national edifice is on fire. Every man who can carry a bucket of water, or remove a brick, is wanted; but those who have the care of the building, having a profound respect for the feeling of the national burglars who set the building on fire,

8. Cowardice.

are determined that the flames shall only be extinguished by Indo-Caucasian[9] hands, and to have the building burnt rather than save it by means of any other. Such is the pride, the stupid prejudice and folly that rules the hour.

Why does the Government reject the negro? Is he not a man? Can he not wield a sword, fire a gun, march and countermarch, and obey orders like any other? . . . If persons so humble as we can be allowed to speak to the President of the United States, we should ask him if this dark and terrible hour of the nation's extremity is a time for consulting a mere vulgar and unnatural prejudice? . . . We would tell him that this is no time to fight with one hand, when both are needed; that this is no time to fight only with your white hand, and allow your black hand to remain tied. . . . While the Government continues to refuse the aid of colored men, thus alienating them from the national cause, and giving the rebels the advantage of them, it will not deserve better fortunes than it has thus far experienced.—Men in earnest don't fight with one hand, when they might fight with two, and a man drowning would not refuse to be saved even by a colored hand.

Source 4 from Roy P. Basler, ed., *The Collected Works of Abraham Lincoln* (New Brunswick, N.J.: Rutgers University Press, 1953), Vol. V, p. 222.

4. Lincoln's Proclamation Revoking General Hunter's Order of Military Emancipation of May 9, 1862.[10]

May 19, 1862

I, Abraham Lincoln, president of the United States, proclaim and declare, that the government of the United States, had no knowledge, information, or belief, of an intention on the part of General Hunter to issue such a proclamation; nor has it yet, any authentic information that the document is genuine. And further, that neither General Hunter, nor any other commander, or person, has been authorized by the Government of the United States, to make proclamations declaring the slaves of any State free; and that the supposed proclamation, now in question, whether genuine or false, is altogether void, so far as respects such declaration.

9. Douglass meant European American.
10. On April 12, 1862, General David Hunter organized the first official regiment of African American soldiers. On May 9, Hunter proclaimed that slaves in Georgia, Florida, and South Carolina were free. Lincoln overruled both proclamations, and the regiment was disbanded without pay. Observers reported that the regiment, composed of former slaves, was of poor quality. Do you think those reports influenced Lincoln's thinking? Lincoln also overruled similar proclamations by General John C. Frémont in Missouri.

CHAPTER 10

THE PRICE FOR
VICTORY: THE
DECISION TO
USE AFRICAN
AMERICAN
TROOPS

Sources 5 and 6 from *Diary and Correspondence of Salmon P. Chase,*[11] in *Annual Report of the American Historical Association for the Year 1902* (Washington, D.C.: U.S. Government Printing Office, 1903), Vol. II, pp. 45–46, 48–49.

5. Diary of Salmon P. Chase, Entry for July 21, 1862.

. . . I went at the appointed hour, and found that the President had been profoundly concerned at the present aspect of affairs, and had determined to take some definitive steps in respect to military action and slavery. He had prepared several Orders, the first of which contemplated authority to Commanders to subsist their troups in the hostile territory—the second, authority to employ negroes as laborers—the third requiring that both in the case of property taken and of negroes employed, accounts should be kept with such degrees of certainty as would enable compensation to be made in proper cases—another provided for the colonization of negroes in some tropical country.

A good deal of discussion took place upon these points. The first Order was universally approved. The second was approved entirely; and the third, by all except myself. I doubted the expediency of attempting to keep accounts for the benefit of the inhabitants of rebel States. The Colonization project was not much discussed.

The Secretary of War presented some letters from Genl. Hunter in which he advised the Department that the withdrawal of a large proportion of his troups to reinforce Genl. McClellan,[12] rendered it highly important that he should be immediately authorized to enlist all loyal persons without reference to complexion. Messrs. Stanton,[13] Seward[14] and myself, expressed ourselves in favor of this plan, and no one expressed himself against it. (Mr. Blair[15] was not present.) The President was not prepared to decide the question but expressed himself as averse to arming negroes. The whole matter was postponed until tomorrow. . . .

6. Diary of Salmon P. Chase, Entry for July 22, 1862.

. . . The question of arming slaves was then brought up and I advocated it warmly. The President was unwilling to adopt this measure, but proposed to issue a proclamation, on the basis of the Confiscation Bill, calling upon

11. Chase was Lincoln's secretary of the treasury from 1861 until 1864.
12. George McClellan (1826–1885) was commander of the Army of the Potomac in 1862. Lincoln removed him because of his excessive caution and lack of boldness.
13. Edwin Stanton (1814–1869), secretary of war.
14. William Seward (1801–1872), secretary of state.
15. Montgomery Blair (1813–1883), postmaster general.

the States to return to their allegiance—warning the rebels the provisions of the Act would have full force at the expiration of sixty days adding on his own part, a declaration of his intention to renew, at the next session of Congress, his recommendation of compensation to States adopting the gradual abolishment of slavery and proclaiming the emancipation of all slaves within States remaining in insurrection on the first of January, 1863.

I said that I should give to such a measure my cordial support: but I should prefer that no new expression on the subject of compensation should be made, and I thought that the measure of Emancipation could be much better and more quietly accomplished by allowing Generals to organize and arm the slaves (thus avoiding depredation and massacre on the one hand, and support to the insurrection on the other) and by directing the Commanders of Departments to proclaim emancipation within their Districts as soon as practicable; but I regarded this as so much better than inaction on the subject, that I should give it my entire support.

The President determined to publish the first three Orders forthwith, and to leave the other for some further consideration. The impression left upon my mind by the whole discussion was, that while the President thought that the organization, equipment and arming of negroes, like other soldiers, would be productive of more evil than good, he was not willing that Commanders should, at their discretion, arm, for purely defensive purposes, slaves coming within their lines.

Mr. Stanton brought forward a proposition to draft 50,000 men. Mr. Seward proposed that the number should be 100,000. The President directed that, whatever number were drafted, should be a part of the 3,000,000 already called for. No decision was reached, however.

Source 7 from Basler, ed., *The Collected Works of Abraham Lincoln,* Vol. V, p. 338.

7. Lincoln's Memorandum on Recruiting Negroes.

[July 22, 1862?]

To recruiting free negroes, no objection.

To recruiting slaves of disloyal owners, no objection.

To recruiting slaves of loyal owners, *with their consent,* no objection.

To recruiting slaves of loyal owners *without* consent, objection, *unless the necessity is urgent.*

To conducting offensively, while recruiting, and to carrying away slaves not suitable for recruits, objection.

CHAPTER 10

THE PRICE FOR
VICTORY: THE
DECISION TO
USE AFRICAN
AMERICAN
TROOPS

Source 8 from *Diary and Correspondence of Salmon P. Chase,* pp. 53–54.

8. Diary of Salmon P. Chase, Entry for August 3, 1862.

. . . There was a good deal of conversation on the connection of the Slavery question with the rebellion. I expressed my conviction for the tenth or twentieth time, that the time for the suppression of the rebellion without interference with slavery had passed; that it was possible, probably, at the outset, by striking the insurrectionists wherever found, strongly and decisively; but we had elected to act on the principles of a civil war, in which the whole population of every seceding state was engaged against the Federal Government, instead of treating the active secessionists as insurgents and exerting our utmost energies for their arrest and punishment;— that the bitternesses of the conflict had now substantially united the white population of the rebel states against us; that the loyal whites remaining, if they would not prefer the Union without Slavery, certainly would not prefer Slavery to the Union; that the blacks were really the only loyal population worth counting; and that, in the Gulf States at least, their right to Freedom ought to be at once recognized, while, in the Border States, the President's plan of Emancipation might be made the basis of the necessary measures for their ultimate enfranchisement;—that the practical mode of effecting this seemed to me quite simple;—that the President had already spoken of the importance of making of the freed blacks on the Mississippi, below Tennessee, a safeguard to the navigation of the river;—that Mitchell, with a few thousand soldiers, could take Vicksburgh;—assure the blacks freedom on condition of loyalty; organize the best of them in companies, regiments etc. and provide, as far as practicable for the cultivation of the plantations by the rest:—that Butler should signify to the slaveholders of Louisiana that they must recognize the freedom of their workpeople by paying them wages;—and that Hunter should do the same thing in South Carolina.

Mr. Seward expressed himself as in favor of any measures likely to accomplish the results I contemplated, which could be carried into effect without Proclamations; and the President said he was pretty well cured of objections to any measure except want of adaptedness to put down the rebellion; but did not seem satisfied that the time had come for the adoption of such a plan as I proposed. . . .

Source 9 from Basler, ed., *The Collected Works of Abraham Lincoln,* Vol. V, pp. 356–357.

9. President Lincoln, "Remarks to Deputation of Western Gentlemen," August 4, 1862. From an Article in the *New York Tribune,* August 5, 1862.

A deputation of Western gentlemen waited upon the President this morning to offer two colored regiments from the State of Indiana. Two members of Congress were of the party. The President received them courteously, but stated to them that he was not prepared to go the length of enlisting negroes as soldiers. He would employ all colored men offered as laborers, but would not promise to make soldiers of them.

The deputation came away satisfied that it is the determination of the Government not to arm negroes unless some new and more pressing emergency arises. The President argued that the nation could not afford to lose Kentucky at this crisis, and gave it as his opinion that to arm the negroes would turn 50,000 bayonets from the loyal Border States against us that were for us. . . .

Source 10 from McPherson, *The Negro's Civil War,* pp. 163–164.

10. Letter to the Editor, *New York Tribune,* August 16, 1862.[16]

I am quite sure there is not one man in ten but would feel himself degraded as a volunteer if negro equality is to be the order in the field of battle. . . . I take the liberty of warning the abettors of fraternizing with the blacks, that one negro regiment, in the present temper of things, put on equality with those who have the past year fought and suffered, will withdraw an amount of life and energy in our army equal to disbanding ten of the best regiments we can now raise.

16. This was a letter to the editor and did not reflect the opinion of Horace Greeley, editor of the *Tribune* and supporter of racial equality for African Americans.

CHAPTER 10

THE PRICE FOR
VICTORY: THE
DECISION TO
USE AFRICAN
AMERICAN
TROOPS

Source 11 from William Wells Brown,[17] *The Negro in the American Rebellion: His Heroism and His Fidelity* (Boston: Lee & Shepard, 1867), pp. 101–104.

11. Reminiscence of a Black Man of the Threat to Cincinnati, September 1862.[18]

The mayor's proclamation, under ordinary circumstances, would be explicit enough. "Every man, of every age, be he citizen or alien," surely meant the colored people. . . . Seeking to test the matter, a policeman was approached, as he strutted in his new dignity of provostguard. To the question, humbly, almost trembling, put, "Does the mayor desire colored men to report for service in the city's defence?" he replied, "You know d——d well he doesn't mean you. Niggers ain't citizens."—"But he calls on all, citizens and aliens. If he does not mean all, he should not say so."—"The mayor knows as well as you do what to write, and all he wants is for you niggers to keep quiet." This was at nine o'clock on the morning of the second. The military authorities had determined, however, to impress the colored men for work upon the fortifications. The privilege of volunteering, extended to others, was to be denied to them. Permission to volunteer would imply some freedom, some dignity, some independent manhood. . . .

If the guard appointed to the duty of collecting the colored people had gone to their houses, and notified them to report for duty on the fortifications, the order would have been cheerfully obeyed. But the brutal ruffians who composed the regular and special police took every opportunity to inflict abuse and insult upon the men whom they arrested. . . .

The captain of these conscripting squads was one William Homer, and in him organized ruffianism had its fitting head. He exhibited the brutal malignity of his nature in a continued series of petty tyrannies. Among the first squads marched into the yard was one which had to wait several hours before being ordered across the river. Seeking to make themselves as comfortable as possible, they had collected blocks of wood, and piled up bricks, upon which they seated themselves on the shaded side of the yard. Coming into the yard, he ordered all to rise, marched them to another part, then issued the order, "D—n you, squat." Turning to the guard, he added, "Shoot the first one who rises." Reaching the opposite side of the river, the same squad were marched from the sidewalk into the middle of the dusty road, and again the order, "D—n you, squat," and the command to shoot the first one who should rise. . . .

17. Brown was an African American who ultimately served in the Union army and recorded his experiences.
18. In early September 1862, the citizens of Cincinnati, Ohio, feared a raid on the city by Confederates. Mayor George Hatch issued a proclamation calling on "every man of every age" to take part in the defense of the city.

Calling up his men, he would address them thus: "Now, you fellows, hold up your heads. Pat, hold your musket straight; don't put your tongue out so far; keep your eyes open: I believe you are drunk. Now, then, I want you fellows to go out of this pen, and bring all the niggers you can catch. Don't come back here without niggers: if you do, you shall not have a bit of grog. Now be off, you shabby cusses, and come back in forty minutes, and bring me niggers; that's what I want." This barbarous and inhuman treatment of the colored citizens of Cincinnati continued for four days, without a single word of remonstrance, except from the "Gazette."

Source 12 from John G. Nicolay and John Hay, eds., *Abraham Lincoln— Complete Works* (New York: Century Co., 1894), Vol. II, pp. 234–235, 242–243.

12. Lincoln's Reply to a Committee from the Religious Denominations of Chicago, Asking the President to Issue a Proclamation of Emancipation, September 13, 1862.

The subject presented in the memorial is one upon which I have thought much for weeks past, and I may even say for months. I am approached with the most opposite opinions and advice, and that by religious men who are equally certain that they represent the divine will. I am sure that either the one or the other class is mistaken in that belief, and perhaps in some respects both. I hope it will not be irreverent for me to say that if it is probable that God would reveal his will to others on a point so connected with my duty, it might be supposed he would reveal it directly to me; for, unless I am more deceived in myself than I often am, it is my earnest desire to know the will of Providence in this matter. And if I can learn what it is, I will do it. These are not, however, the days of miracles, and I suppose it will be granted that I am not to expect a direct revelation. I must study the plain physical facts of the case, ascertain what is possible, and learn what appears to be wise and right. . . .

I admit that slavery is the root of the rebellion, or at least its *sine qua non*.[19] The ambition of politicians may have instigated them to act, but they would have been impotent without slavery as their instrument. I will also concede that emancipation would help us in Europe, and convince them that we are incited by something more than ambition. I grant, further, that it would help somewhat at the North, though not so much, I fear, as you

19. An essential element or condition; a necessary ingredient.

CHAPTER 10

THE PRICE FOR
VICTORY: THE
DECISION TO
USE AFRICAN
AMERICAN
TROOPS

and those you represent imagine. Still, some additional strength would be added in that way to the war, and then, unquestionably, it would weaken the rebels by drawing off their laborers, which is of great importance; but I am not so sure we could do much with the blacks. If we were to arm them, I fear that in a few weeks the arms would be in the hands of the rebels; and, indeed, thus far we have not had arms enough to equip our white troops. I will mention another thing, though it meet only your scorn and contempt. There are fifty thousand bayonets in the Union armies from the border slave States. It would be a serious matter if, in consequence of a proclamation such as you desire, they should go over to the rebels. I do not think they all would—not so many, indeed, as a year ago, or as six months ago—not so many to-day as yesterday. Every day increases their Union feeling. They are also getting their pride enlisted, and want to beat the rebels.

Sources 13 through 15 from Basler, ed., *The Collected Works of Abraham Lincoln,* Vol. V, pp. 444, 509, 28–30.

13. Lincoln to Vice President Hannibal Hamlin.

(Strictly private.) Executive Mansion,
Washington, September 28, 1862.

My Dear Sir:

Your kind letter of the 25th is just received. It is known to some that while I hope something from the proclamation,[20] my expectations are not as sanguine as are those of some friends. The time for its effect southward has not come; but northward the effect should be instantaneous.

It is six days old, and while commendation in newspapers and by distinguished individuals is all that a vain man could wish, the stocks have declined, and troops came forward more slowly than ever. This, looked soberly in the face, is not very satisfactory. We have fewer troops in the field at the end of six days than we had at the beginning—the attrition among the old outnumbering the addition of the new. The North responds to the proclamation sufficiently in breath; but breath alone kills no rebels.

I wish I could write more cheerfully; nor do I thank you the less for the kindness of your letter. Yours very truly,

A. LINCOLN

20. Lincoln was referring to his Preliminary Emancipation Proclamation, which he issued on September 22, 1862. Lincoln's hope was that the threat of emancipation would cause the South to surrender so as to keep slavery intact. See again Lincoln's letter to Horace Greeley, August 22, 1862, on page 246.

14. Lincoln to Carl Schurz.

Gen. Carl Schurz

Executive Mansion,
Washington, Nov. 24, 1862.

My dear Sir

I have just received, and read your letter of the 20th. The purport of it is that we lost the late elections,[21] and the administration is failing, because the war is unsuccessful; and that I must not flatter myself that I am not justly to blame for it. I certainly know that if the war fails, the administration fails, and that I *will* be blamed for it, whether I deserve it or not. And I ought to be blamed, if I could do better. You think I could do better; therefore you blame me already. I think I could not do better; therefore I blame you for blaming me. . . .

15. The Emancipation Proclamation.

January 1, 1863

By the President of the United States of America:
A Proclamation. . . .

Now, therefore I, Abraham Lincoln, President of the United States, by virtue of the power in me vested as Commander-in-Chief, of the Army and Navy of the United States in time of actual armed rebellion against authority and government of the United States, and as a fit and necessary war measure for suppressing said rebellion, do, on this first day of January, in the year of our Lord one thousand eight hundred and sixty three, and in accordance with my purpose so to do publicly proclaimed for the full period of one hundred days, from the day first above mentioned, order and designate as the States and parts of States wherein the people thereof respectively, are this day in rebellion against the United States, the following, to wit: . . .

[*Here Lincoln identified the geographic areas of the South still under the control of the Confederacy.*]

And by virtue of the power, and for the purpose aforesaid, I do order and declare that all persons held as slaves within said designated States, and

21. In the congressional elections of 1862, the Republicans lost three seats in the House of Representatives, although they were still the majority party. Senators were not elected by the people until the Seventeenth Amendment to the Constitution was ratified in 1913.

CHAPTER 10

THE PRICE FOR
VICTORY: THE
DECISION TO
USE AFRICAN
AMERICAN
TROOPS

parts of States, are, and henceforward shall be free; and that the Executive government of the United States, including the military and naval authorities thereof, will recognize and maintain the freedom of said persons.

And I hereby enjoin upon the people so declared to be free to abstain from all violence, unless in necessary self-defence; and I recommend to them that, in all cases when allowed, they labor faithfully for reasonable wages.

And I further declare and make known, that such persons of suitable condition, will be received into the armed services of the United States to garrison forts, positions, stations, and other places, and to man vessels of all sorts in said service.[22]

And upon this act, sincerely believed to be an act of justice, warranted by the Constitution, upon military necessity, I invoke the considerate judgment of mankind, and the gracious favor of Almighty God.

In witness whereof, I have hereunto set my hand and caused the seal of the United States to be affixed.

Done at the City of Washington, this first day of January, in the year of our Lord one thousand eight hundred and sixty three, and of the Independence of the United States of America the eighty-seventh. By the President:

ABRAHAM LINCOLN

Source 16 from George Washington Williams, *A History of the Negro Troops in the War of the Rebellion, 1861–65* (New York: Harper and Brothers, 1888), pp. 66–67, 90–91.

16. Reminiscence of a Former Black Soldier in the Union Army.

At first the faintest intimation that Negroes should be employed as soldiers in the Union Army was met with derision. By many it was regarded as a joke. The idea of arming the ex-slaves seemed ridiculous to most civil and military officers. . . .

Most observing and thoughtful people concluded that centuries of servitude had rendered the Negro slave incapable of any civil or military service. . . . Some officers talked of resigning if Negroes were to be called upon to fight the battles of a free republic. The privates in regiments from large cities and border States were bitter and demonstrative in their opposition. The Negro volunteers themselves were subjected to indignities from rebel civilians within the Union lines, and obtained no protection from the white troops. . . .

22. This paragraph was not part of the preliminary proclamation issued by Lincoln on September 22, 1862. See Basler, ed., *The Collected Works of Abraham Lincoln,* Vol. V, pp. 433–436.

Source 17 from Lawrence Frederick Kohl and Margaret Cosse Richard, eds., *Irish Green and Union Blue: The Civil War Letters of Peter Welsh, Color Sergeant, 28th Regiment, Massachusetts Volunteers* (New York: Fordham University Press, 1986), p. 62.

17. Fragment of a Letter from a Union Soldier, Early 1863.

I see by late papers that the governor of Massachusetts has been autheured to raise nigar regiments. i hope he may succeed but i doubt it very much if they can raise a few thousand and sent them out here i can assure you that whether they have the grit to go into battle or not if they are placed in front and any brigade of this army behind them they will have to go in or they will meet as hot a reception in their retreat as in their advance[.] The feeling against nigars is intensly strong in this army as is plainly to be seen wherever and whenever they meet them[.] They are looked upon as the principal cause of this war and this feeling is especially strong in the Irish regiments[.]

Source 18 from *The War of the Rebellion: A Compilation of the Official Records of the Union and Confederate Armies* (Washington, D.C.: Government Printing Office, 1899), Series III, Vol. III, p. 16.

18. L. Thomas to Governor of Rhode Island, January 15, 1863.

ADJUTANT-GENERAL'S OFFICE,
Washington, D.C., January 15, 1863.

GOVERNOR OF RHODE ISLAND
 Providence, R.I.:

 SIR: I am directed to say that the President will accept into the service of the United States an infantry regiment of volunteers of African descent, if offered by your State and organized according to the rules and regulations of the service.

 I am, very respectfully,

L. THOMAS,
Adjutant-General.

CHAPTER 10

THE PRICE FOR
VICTORY: THE
DECISION TO
USE AFRICAN
AMERICAN
TROOPS

Source 19 from Glenn W. Sunderland, *Five Days to Glory* (South Brunswick, N.J.: A. S. Barnes & Co., 1970), pp. 97–98.

19. Letter from Tighlman Jones (a Union Soldier) to Brother Zillman Jones, October 6, 1863.

You have heard of Negroes being enlisted to fight for Uncle Sam. If you would like to know what the soldiers think about the idea I can almost tell you. Why, that is just what they desire. There is some soldiers who curse and blow and make a great noise about it but we set him as a convalescent who is like a man who is afraid of the smallpox who curses the works of a power he can in no way avoid, but will kick and rail and act the part of a fool, but of no avail, nature will have its own course, or to say that this war will free the Negroes and that they will enlist and fight to sustain the Government. I think more of a Negro Union soldier than I do of all the cowardly Copperhead trash of the north[23] and there is no soldier but what approves of the course of the present administration and will fight till the Rebels unconditionally surrender and return to their allegiance.

Source 20 from Dudley Cornish, *The Sable Arm: Negro Troops in the Union Army, 1861–1865* (New York: W. W. Norton, 1966), pp. ix–x.

20. Editorial, *New York Times*, March 7, 1864.

There has been no more striking manifestation of the marvelous times that are upon us than the scene in our streets at the departure of the first of our colored regiments. Had any man predicted it last year he would have been thought a fool, even by the wisest and most discerning. History abounds with strange contrasts. It always has been an ever-shifting melo- drama. But never, in this land at least, has it presented a transition so extreme and yet so speedy as what our eyes have just beheld.

Eight months ago the African race in this City were literally hunted down like wild beasts.[24] They fled for their lives. When caught, they were shot down in cold blood, or stoned to death, or hung to the trees or the lamp- posts. Their homes were pillaged; the asylum which Christian charity had

23. Copperheads were northerners who opposed the war and advocated peace at any price.
24. In mid-1863, demonstrations against conscription in New York City turned into an ugly mob action against African Americans, partly because of their connection, through the Eman- cipation Proclamation of January 1, 1863, to the war and partly because of economic competi- tion with the poorer whites who constituted most of the rioters.

provided for their orphaned children was burned; and there was no limit to the persecution but in the physical impossibility of finding further material on which the mob could wreak its ruthless hate. Nor was it solely the raging horde in the streets that visited upon the black man the nefarious wrong. Thousands and tens of thousands of men of higher social grade, of better education, cherished precisely the same spirit. . . .

How astonishingly has all this been changed. The same men who could not have shown themselves in the most obscure street in the City without peril of instant death, even though in the most suppliant attitude, now march in solid platoons, with shouldered muskets, slung knapsacks, and buckled cartridge boxes down through our gayest avenues and our busiest thoroughfares to the pealing strains of martial music and are everywhere saluted with waving handkerchiefs, with descending flowers, and with the acclamations and plaudits of countless beholders. They are halted at our most beautiful square, and amid an admiring crowd, in the presence of many of our most prominent citizens, are addressed in an eloquent and most complimentary speech by the President of our chief literary institution, and are presented with a gorgeous stand of colors in the names of a large number of the first ladies of the City, who attest on parchment, signed by their own fair hands, that they "will anxiously watch your career, glorifying in your heroism, ministering to you when wounded and ill, and honoring your martyrdom with benedictions and with tears."

It is only by such occasions that we can at all realize the prodigious revolution which the public mind everywhere is experiencing. Such developments are infallible tokens of a new epoch.

SOUTH

Sources 21 and 22 from *The War of the Rebellion,* Series IV, Vol. I, pp. 482, 529.

21. Correspondence Between W. S. Turner and the Confederate War Department, July 17, 1861.

HELENA, ARK., *July 17, 1861.*

Hon. L. P. WALKER:[25]

DEAR SIR: I wrote you a few days since for myself and many others in this district to ascertain if we could get negro regiments received for Confederate service, officered, of course, by white men. All we ask is arms, clothing, and provisions, and usual pay for officers and not one cent pay for negroes.

25. Walker was the Confederate secretary of war from February to September 1861.

CHAPTER 10

THE PRICE FOR
VICTORY: THE
DECISION TO
USE AFRICAN
AMERICAN
TROOPS

Our negroes are too good to fight Lincoln hirelings, but as they pretend to love negroes so much we want to show them how much the true Southern cotton-patch negro loves them in return. The North cannot complain at this. They proclaim negro equality from the Senate Chamber to the pulpit, teach it in their schools, and are doing all they can to turn the slaves upon master, mistress, and children. And now, sir, if you can receive the negroes that can be raised we will soon give the Northern thieves a gorge of the negroes' love for them that will never be forgotten. As you well know, I have had long experience with negro character. I am satisfied they are easy disciplined and less trouble than whites in camp, and will fight desperately as long as they have a single white officer living. I know one man that will furnish and arm 100 of his own and his son for their captain. The sooner we bring a strong negro force against the hirelings the sooner we shall have peace, in my humble judgment. Let me hear from you.

Your old friend,

W. S. TURNER

22. Correspondence Between W. S. Turner and the Confederate War Department, August 2, 1861.

CONFEDERATE STATES OF AMERICA, WAR DEPARTMENT,

Richmond, August 2, 1861.

W. S. TURNER,

Helena, Ark.:

SIR: In reply to your letter of the 17th of July I am directed by the Secretary of War to say that this Department is not prepared to accept the negro regiment tendered by you, and yet it is not doubted that almost every slave would cheerfully aid his master in the work of hurling back the fanatical invader. Moreover, if the necessity were apparent there is high authority for the employment of such forces. Washington himself recommended the enlistment of two negro regiments in Georgia, and the Congress sanctioned the measure. But now there is a superabundance of our own color tendering their services to the Government in its day of peril and ruthless invasion, a superabundance of men when we are bound to admit the inadequate supply of arms at present at the disposal of the Government.

Respectfully,

A. T. BLEDSOE
Chief of Bureau of War.

Sources 23 through 26 from Robert F. Durden, *The Gray and the Black: The Confederate Debate on Emancipation* (Baton Rouge: Louisiana State University Press, 1972), pp. 30–31, 54–58, 61, 66–67.

23. *Montgomery* (Ala.) *Weekly Mail*, "Employment of Negroes in the Army," September 9, 1863.

. . . We must either employ the negroes ourselves, or the enemy will employ them against us. While the enemy retains so much of our territory, they are, in their present avocation and status, a dangerous element, a source of weakness. They are no longer negative characters, but subjects of volition as other people. They must be taught to know that this is peculiarly the country of the black man—that in no other is the climate and soil so well adapted to his nature and capacity. He must further be taught that it is his duty, as well as the white man's, to defend his home with arms, if need be.

We are aware that there are persons who shudder at the idea of placing arms in the hands of negroes, and who are not willing to trust them under any circumstances. The negro, however, is proverbial for his faithfulness under kind treatment. He is an affectionate, grateful being, and we are persuaded that the fears of such persons are groundless.

There are in the slaveholding States four millions of negroes, and out of this number at least six hundred thousand able-bodied men capable of bearing arms can be found. Lincoln proposes to free and arm them against us. There are already fifty thousand of them in the Federal ranks. Lincoln's scheme has worked well so far, and if no[t] checkmated, will most assuredly be carried out. The Confederate Government must adopt a counter policy. It must thwart the enemy in this gigantic scheme, at all hazards, and if nothing else will do it—if the negroes cannot be made effective and trustworthy to the Southern cause in no other way, we solemnly believe it is the duty of this Government to forestall Lincoln and proceed at once to take steps for the emancipation or liberation of the negroes itself. Let them be declared free, placed in the ranks, and told to fight for their homes and country. . . .

Such action on the part of our Government would place our people in a purer and better light before the world. It would disabuse the European mind of a grave error in regard to the cause of our separation. It would prove to them that there were higher and holier motives which actuated our people than the mere love of property. It would show that, although slavery is one of the principles that we started to fight for, yet it falls far short of being the chief one; that, for the sake of our liberty, we are capable

CHAPTER 10

THE PRICE FOR
VICTORY: THE
DECISION TO
USE AFRICAN
AMERICAN
TROOPS

of any personal sacrifice; that we regard the emancipation of slaves, and the consequent loss of property as an evil infinitely less than the subjugation and enslavement of ourselves; that it is not a war exclusively for the privilege of holding negroes in bondage. It would prove to our soldiers, three-fourths of whom never owned a negro, that it is not "the rich man's war and the poor man's fight," but a war for the most sacred of all principles, for the dearest of all rights—the right to govern ourselves. It would show them that the rich man who owned slaves was not willing to jeopardize the precious liberty of the country by his eagerness to hold on to his slaves, but that he was ready to give them up and sacrifice his interest in them whenever the cause demanded it. It would lend a new impetus, a new enthusiasm, a new and powerful strength to the cause, and place our success beyond a peradventure. It would at once remove all the odium which attached to us on account of slavery, and bring us speedy recognition, and, if necessary, intervention.

24. General Patrick Cleburne to General Joseph Johnston, January 2, 1864.

We have now been fighting for nearly three years, have spilled much of our best blood, and lost, consumed, or thrown to the flames an amount of property equal in value to the specie currency of the world. . . . Our soldiers can see no end to this state of affairs except in our own exhaustion; hence, instead of rising to the occasion, they are sinking into a fatal apathy, growing weary of hardships and slaughters which promise no results. In this state of things it is easy to understand why there is a growing belief that some black catastrophe is not far ahead of us, and that unless some extraordinary change is soon made in our condition we must overtake it. . . .

In view of the state of affairs what does our country propose to do? In the words of President Davis "no effort must be spared to add largely to our effective force as promptly as possible. The sources of supply are to be found in restoring to the army all who are improperly absent, putting an end to substitution, modifying the exemption law, restricting details, and placing in the ranks such of the able-bodied men now employed as wagoners, nurses, cooks, and other employees, as are doing service for which the negroes may be found competent.". . . [W]e propose, in addition to a modification of the President's plans, that we retain in service for the war all troops now in service, and that we immediately commence training a large reserve of the most courageous of our slaves, and further that we guarantee freedom within a reasonable time to every slave in the South who shall remain true to the Confederacy in this war. As between the loss of independence and the loss of slavery, we assume that every patriot will freely give up the latter—give up the negro slave rather than be a slave himself. If we are correct in this assumption it only remains to show how this great national sacrifice is, in all human probabilities, to change the current of success and sweep the invader from our country.

Our country has already some friends in England and France, and there are strong motives to induce these nations to recognize and assist us, but they cannot assist us without helping slavery, and to do this would be in conflict with their policy for the last quarter of a century. . . . But this barrier once removed, the sympathy and the interests of these and other nations will accord with their own, and we may expect from them both moral support and material aid. . . .

Will the slaves fight? . . . The negro slaves of Saint Domingo, fighting for freedom, defeated their white masters and the French troops sent against them.[26] The negro slaves of Jamaica revolted, and under the name of Maroons held the mountains against their masters for 150 years; and the experience of this war has been so far that half-trained negroes have fought as bravely as many other half-trained Yankees. If, contrary to the training of a lifetime, they can be made to face and fight bravely against their former masters, how much more probable is it that with the allurement of a higher reward, and led by those masters, they would submit to discipline and face dangers.

25. President Jefferson Davis to General Walker, January 13, 1864—Reaction to Cleburne's Proposal.

I have received your letter, with its inclosure, informing me of the propositions [Cleburne's proposal] submitted to a meeting of the general officers on the 2d instant, and thank you for the information. Deeming it to be injurious to the public service that such a subject should be mooted, or even known to be entertained by persons possessed of the confidence and

26. On August 23, 1791, thousands of slaves in the French colony of Saint Dominigue (in Spanish, Santo Domingo; now Haiti) revolted against their white masters. Ultimately led by Toussaint Louverture (often spelled L'Ouverture), the slaves overthrew their masters, beat back invasions from both Britain and France, and declared Haiti an independent republic in 1804. Whites who fled from Haiti to the United States reported atrocities that filled white southerners with alarm for years after. See especially Alfred N. Hunt, *Haiti's Influence on Antebellum America* (Baton Rouge: Louisiana State University Press, 1988).

CHAPTER 10

THE PRICE FOR
VICTORY: THE
DECISION TO
USE AFRICAN
AMERICAN
TROOPS

respect of the people, I have concluded that the best policy under the circumstances will be to avoid all publicity, and the Secretary of War has therefore written to General Johnston requesting him to convey to those concerned my desire that it should be kept private. If it be kept out of public journals its ill effect will be much lessened.

26. General Joseph Johnston to General Hardee et al., January 31, 1864—Reaction to Cleburne's Proposal.

Lieutenant-General Hardee, Major-Generals Cheatham, Hindman, Cleburne, Stewart, Walker, Brigadier-Generals Bate and P. Anderson:

GENERAL:

I have just received a letter from the Secretary of War in reference to Major-General Cleburne's memoir read in my quarters about the 2d instant. In this letter the Honorable Secretary expresses the earnest conviction of the President "that the dissemination or even promulgation of such opinions under the present circumstances of the Confederacy, whether in the Army or among the people, can be productive only of discouragement, distraction, and dissension." The agitation and controversy which must spring from the presentation of such views by officers high in the public confidence are to be deeply deprecated, and while no doubt or mistrust is for a moment entertained of the patriotic intents of the gallant author of the memorial, and such of his brother officers as may have favored his opinions, it is requested that you communicate to them, as well as all others present on the occasion, the opinions, as herein expressed, of the President, and urge on them the suppression, not only of the memorial itself, but likewise of all discussion and controversy respecting or growing out of it. . . .

Source 27 from Bell Irvin Wiley, ed., *Letters of Warren Akin, Confederate Congressman* (Athens: University of Georgia Press, 1959), pp. 32–33.

27. Letter from Warren Akin to Nathan Land, October 31, 1864.

As to calling out the negro men and placing them in the army, with the promise that they shall be free at the end of the war, I can only say it is a question of fearful magnitude. Can we prevent subjugation, confiscation, degradation and slavery without it? If not, will our condition or that of the negro, be any worse by calling them into service?

On the other hand: Can we feed our soldiers and their families if the negro men are taken from the plantations? Will our soldiers submit to having our negroes along side them in the ditches, or in line of battle? When the negro is taught the use of arms and the art of war, can we live in safety with them afterwards? Or if it be contemplated to send them off to another country, when peace is made, will it be right to force them to a new, distant and strange land, after they have fought for and won the independence of this? Would they go without having another war? Involving, perhaps a general insurrection of all the negroes? To call forth the negroes into the army, with the promise of freedom, will it not be giving up the great question involved by doing the very thing Lincoln is now doing? The Confederate States may take private property for public use, by paying for it; but can we ever pay for 300,000 negro men at present prices, in addition to our other indebtedness? The Confederate Government may buy the private negro property of the Citizens, but can it set them free among us, to corrupt our slaves, and place in peril our existence? These are some of the thoughts that have passed th[r]ough my mind on the subject. But I can not say that I have a definite and fixed opinion. If I were convinced that we will be subjugated, with the long train of horrors that will follow it, unless the negroes be placed in the army, I would not hesitate to enrol our slaves and put them to fighting. Subjugation will give us free negroes in abundance—enemies at that—while white slaves will be more numerous than free negroes. We and our children will be slaves, while our freed negroes will lord it over us. It is impossible for the evils resulting from placing our slaves in the army to be greater than those that will follow subjugation. We may (if necessary) put our slaves in the army, win our independence, and have liberty and homes for ourselves and children. But subjugation will deprive us of our homes, houses, property, liberty, honor, and every thing worth living for, leaving for us and our posterity only the chains of slavery, tenfold more galling and degrading than that now felt by our negroes. But I will not enlarge, I have made suggestions merely for your reflection.

Source 28 from McPherson, *The Negro's Civil War,* pp. 243–244.

28. Judah P. Benjamin (Secretary of War, Confederacy) to Fred A. Porcher (an Old Friend and Former Classmate), December 21, 1864.

For a year past I have seen that the period was fast approaching when we should be compelled to use every resource of our command for the defense of our liberties. . . . The negroes will certainly be made to fight against us

CHAPTER 10

THE PRICE FOR
VICTORY: THE
DECISION TO
USE AFRICAN
AMERICAN
TROOPS

if not armed for our defense. The drain of that source of our strength is steadily fatal, and irreversible by any other expedient than that of arming the slaves as an auxiliary force.

I further agree with you that if they are to fight for our freedom they are entitled to their own. Public opinion is fast ripening on the subject, and ere the close of the winter the conviction on this point will become so widespread that the Government will have no difficulty in inaugurating the policy [of recruiting Negro soldiers].

. . . It is well known that General Lee, who commands so largely the confidence of the people, is strongly in favor of our using the negroes for defense, and emancipating them, if necessary, for that purpose. Can you not yourself write a series of articles in your papers, always urging this point as the true issue, viz, is it better for the negro to fight for us or against us?

Source 29 from Durden, *The Gray and the Black,* pp. 89–91.

29. *Richmond Enquirer,* November 4, 1864, Letter to the Editor in Reply to the Editorial of October 6, 1864.

Can it be possible that you are serious and earnest in proposing such a step to be taken by our Government? Or were you merely discussing the matter as a something which might be done? An element of power which might be used—meaning thereby to intimidate or threaten our enemy with it as a weapon of offence which they may drive us to use? Can it be possible that a Southern man—editor of a Southern journal—recognizing the right of property in slaves, admitting their inferiority in the scale of being and also their social inferiority, would recommend the passage of a law which at one blow levels all distinctions, deprives the master of a right to his property, and elevates the negro to an equality with the white man?—for, disguise it as you may, those who fight together in a common cause, and by success win the *same* freedom, enjoy equal rights and equal position, and in this case, are distinguished only by color. Are we prepared for this? Is it for this we are contending? Is it for this we would seek the aid of our slaves? . . . When President Davis said: "We are not fighting for slavery, but independence," he meant that the question and subject of slavery was a matter settled amongst ourselves and one that admitted of no dispute—that he intended to be independent of all foreign influences on this as well as on other matters—free to own slaves if he pleased—free to lay our own taxes—free to govern ourselves. He never intended to ignore the question of slavery or to do aught else but express the determination to be *independent* in this as well as in all other matters. What has embittered the feelings of the two sections of the old Union? What has gradually driven them to the final separation? What is it that has made two nationalities of them, if it is not slavery?

The Yankee *steals* my slave, and makes a soldier and freeman of him to *destroy* me. You *take* my slave, and make a soldier and freeman of him to *defend* me. The difference in your intention is very great; but is not the practice of both equally pernicious to the slave and destruction to the country? And at the expiration of ten years after peace what would be the relative difference between my negro *stolen* and freed by the Yankee and my negro taken and freed by you? Would they not be equally worthless and vicious? How would you distinguish between them? How prevent the return of him whose hand is red with his master's blood, and his enjoyment of those privileges which you so lavishly bestow upon the faithful freedman?

Have you thought of the influence to be exerted by these half or quarter million of free negroes in the midst of slaves as you propose to leave them at the end of the war; these men constitute the bone and sinew of our slaves, the able-bodied between 18 and 45. They will be men who know the value and power of combination; they will be well disciplined, trained to the use of arms, with the power and ability of command; at the same time they will be grossly and miserably ignorant, without any fixed principle of life or the ability of acquiring one. . . .

Sources 30 and 31 from McPherson, *The Negro's Civil War,* p. 244.

30. Howell Cobb, Speech in the Confederate Senate, 1864.

. . . If slaves will make good soldiers our whole theory of slavery is wrong. . . . The day you make soldiers of them is the beginning of the end of the revolution.

31. Robert Toombs, Speech in the Confederate Senate, 1864.

. . . The worst calamity that could befall us would be to gain our independence by the valor of our slaves. . . . The day that the army of Virginia allows a negro regiment to enter their lines as soldiers they will be degraded, ruined, and disgraced.

CHAPTER 10

THE PRICE FOR
VICTORY: THE
DECISION TO
USE AFRICAN
AMERICAN
TROOPS

Source 32 from Durden, *The Gray and the Black,* pp. 93–94.

32. *Lynchburg* (Va.) *Republican,* November 2, 1864.

The proposition is so strange—so unconstitutional—so directly in conflict with all of our former practices and teachings—so entirely subversive of our social and political institutions—and so completely destructive of our liberties, that we stand completely appalled [and] dumfounded [*sic*] at its promulgation.

They propose that Congress shall conscribe two hundred and fifty thousand slaves, arm, equip and fight them in the field. As an inducement of them to be faithful, it is proposed that, at the end of the war, they shall have their freedom and live amongst us. "The conscription of negroes," says the *Enquirer,* "should be accompanied with freedom and the privilege of remaining in the States." This is the monstrous proposition. The South went to war to defeat the designs of the abolitionists, and behold! in the midst of the war, we turn abolitionists ourselves! We went to war because the Federal Congress kept eternally meddling with our domestic institutions, with which we contended they had nothing to do, and now we propose to end the war by asking the Confederate Congress to do precisely what Lincoln proposes to do—free our negroes and make them the equals of the white man! We have always been taught to believe that slaves are property, and under the exclusive control of the States and the courts. This new doctrine teaches us that Congress has a right to free our negroes and make them the equals of their masters. . . .

Source 33 from Wiley, ed., *Letters of Warren Akin,* p. 117.

33. Mary V. Akin to Warren Akin, January 8, 1865.

. . . Every one I talk to is in favor of putting negros in the army and that *immediately.* Major Jones speaks very strongly in favor of it. I think slavery is now gone and what little there is left of it should be rendered as serviceable as possible and for that reason the negro men ought to be put to fighting and where some of them will be killed, if it is not done there will soon be more negroes than whites in the country and they will be the free race. I want to see them *got rid of soon.* . . .

Sources 34 through 36 from Durden, *The Gray and the Black,* pp. 163, 195, 202–203.

34. *Macon* (Ga.) *Telegraph and Confederate,* January 11, 1865.

Mr. Editor:

A lady's opinion may not be worth much in such an hour as this, but I cannot resist the temptation of expressing my approbation of "The crisis—the Remedy," copied from the Mobile Register. Would to God our Government would act upon its suggestions at once. The women of the South are not so in love with their negro property, as to wish to see husbands, fathers, sons, brothers, slain to protect it; nor would they submit to Yankee rule, could it secure to them a thousand waiting maids, whence now they possess one. . . .

35. *Richmond Whig,* February 28, 1865.

Mobile, Feb. 14—One of the largest meetings ever assembled in Mobile was held at the Theatre last night, which was presided over by Hon. Judge Forsyth.

Resolutions were unanimously adopted declaring our unalterable purpose to sustain the civil and military authorities to achieve independence—that our battle-cry henceforth should be—"Victory or Death"—that there is now no middle-ground between treachery and patriotism—that we still have an abiding confidence in our ability to achieve our independence—that the Government should immediately place one hundred thousand negroes in the field—that reconstruction is no longer an open question.

36. Confederate Congress, "An Act to Increase the Military Force of the Confederate States," March 13, 1865.

The Congress of the Confederate States of America do enact, That in order to provide additional forces to repel invasion, maintain the rightful possession of the Confederate States, secure their independence, and preserve their institutions, the President be, and he is hereby, authorized to ask for and accept from the owners of slaves, the services of such number of able-bodied negro men as he may deem expedient, for and during the war, to perform military service in whatever capacity he may direct.

CHAPTER 10

THE PRICE FOR
VICTORY: THE
DECISION TO
USE AFRICAN
AMERICAN
TROOPS

Sec. 2. That the General-in-Chief be authorized to organize the said slaves into companies, battalions, regiments and brigades, under such rules and regulations as the Secretary of War may prescribe, and to be commanded by such officers as the President may appoint.

Sec. 3. That while employed in the service the said troops shall receive the same rations, clothing and compensation as are allowed to other troops in the same branch of the service.

Sec. 4. That if, under the previous sections of this act, the President shall not be able to raise a sufficient number of troops to prosecute the war successfully and maintain the sovereignty of the States and the independence of the Confederate States, then he is hereby authorized to call on each State, whenever he thinks it expedient, for her quota of 300,000 troops, in addition to those subject to military service under existing laws, or so many thereof as the President may deem necessary to be raised from such classes of the population, irrespective of color, in each State, as the proper authorities thereof may determine: *Provided,* that no more than twenty-five per cent of the male slaves between the ages of eighteen and forty-five, in any State, shall be called for under the provisions of this act.

Sec. 5. That nothing in this act shall be construed to authorize a change in the relation which the said slaves shall bear toward their owners, except by consent of the owners and of the States in which they may reside, and in pursuance of the laws thereof.

Approved March 13, 1865.

✳ QUESTIONS TO CONSIDER ✳

Begin by examining the evidence from the North. For each piece of evidence, answer the following questions:

1. Is the writer for or against using African Americans as soldiers?
2. What are the principal reasons for taking this position? (A piece of evidence may have more than one reason, as does Lincoln's September 13, 1862, reply to a delegation of Chicago Christians, Source 12.)

At this point, you will confront your first problem. Some pieces of evidence

do not speak directly to the issue of enlisting African Americans as soldiers (two such examples are A. Davenport's letter and William Wells Brown's recollections, Sources 2 and 11, respectively). Yet are there implied reasons for or against arming African Americans? Included in these reasons may be unstated racial feelings (look again at Lincoln's September 13, 1862, remarks in Source 12), casualty figures (note when the casualties were suffered and consult the evidence for any shifts in the argument at that time), or political considerations.

The central figure in the decision of whether the United States should arm African Americans was Abraham Lincoln. In July 1862, Congress gave the president the authority to do so, yet Lincoln hesitated. How did members of Lincoln's cabinet attempt to influence his opinion in July and August 1862? What was Lincoln's reply?

President Lincoln's memorandum (Source 7), probably written after the July 22 cabinet meeting, appears to show a shift in his opinion. How does this compare with his remarks on August 4, 1862 (Source 9), and September 13, 1862 (Source 12)? How would you explain this shift?

By January 1, 1863, the president had changed his public stance completely and was on record as favoring taking African Americans into the United States Army (Source 15). Because President Lincoln did not live to write his memoirs and kept no diary,

we are not sure what arguments or circumstances were responsible for the shift in his position. Yet a close examination of the evidence and some educated guesswork will allow you to come very close to the truth. Do Lincoln's letters to Hamlin and Schurz (Sources 13 and 14) provide any clues?

The remaining evidence from the North deals with northern reactions to Lincoln's decision (Sources 16 through 20). Was the decision a popular one in the army? Among private citizens? Can you detect a shift in northern white public opinion? Can you explain this shift?

Now repeat the same steps for the South (Sources 21 through 36). In what ways was the debate in the South similar to that in the North? In what ways was it different? Which reasons do you think were most influential in the Confederacy's change of mind about arming African Americans? How would you support your evaluation?

❋ EPILOGUE ❋

Even after northern leaders adopted the policy that blacks would be recruited as soldiers in the Union army, many white northerners still doubted whether blacks would volunteer and, if they did, whether they would fight. Yet the evidence overwhelmingly demonstrates that African Americans rushed to the colors and were an effective part of the Union war effort. By the end of the Civil War, approximately 190,000 African American men had served in the United States army

and navy, a figure that represents roughly 10 percent of all the North's fighting men throughout the war. Former slaves who had come within the Union lines during the war made up the majority of African American soldiers, and Louisiana, Kentucky, and Tennessee contributed the most African American soldiers to the Union cause (approximately 37 percent of the total), probably because these states had been occupied the longest by Union troops.

CHAPTER 10

THE PRICE FOR
VICTORY: THE
DECISION TO
USE AFRICAN
AMERICAN
TROOPS

Although, as we have seen, Lincoln initially opposed the use of black soldiers, once he changed his mind, he pursued the new policy with vigor. Moreover, the president was determined to be fair to those African Americans who had volunteered to serve the Union. In an August 19, 1864, interview, Lincoln said, "There have been men who have proposed to me to return to slavery the black warriors . . . to their masters to conciliate the South. I should be damned in time & in eternity for so doing. The world shall know that I will keep my faith."[27]

Black soldiers were employed by the Union largely in noncombat roles such as to garrison forts, protect supply dumps and wagons, load and unload equipment and supplies, guard prison camps, and so on. In addition, a number of black regiments saw combat, participating in approximately four hundred engagements, including thirty-nine major battles. One of the most famous battles was the ill-fated assault on Fort Wagner (near Charleston, South Carolina), led by the 54th Massachusetts Infantry, the first black regiment recruited in the North. Almost half the regiment, including its commander, Colonel Robert Gould Shaw, was lost in the frontal attack, but the troops fought valiantly in the losing effort. The *Atlantic Monthly* reported, "Through the cannon smoke of that dark night, the manhood of the colored race shines before many eyes." Over a century later, the regiment was immortalized in the film *Glory*.[28]

27. Basler, ed., *The Collected Works of Abraham Lincoln,* Vol. VII, pp. 506–508.
28. The Confederates refused to return Shaw's body to his parents for burial, saying, "We have buried him with his niggers."

Overall, African American casualties were high: more than one-third of the African American soldiers were killed or wounded, although the majority of deaths, as with white soldiers, came from disease rather than battle wounds. The percentage of desertions among African Americans was lower than for the army as a whole. Moreover, twenty-one black soldiers and sailors were awarded the Congressional Medal of Honor, the nation's most distinguished award to military personnel.

Yet there is another side to the story of African American service in the Union army and navy. African American volunteers were rigidly segregated, serving in all-black regiments, usually under white officers. At first, black troops received less pay than their white counterparts. However, after many petitions and protests by African American soldiers, Congress at last established the principle of equal pay for African American soldiers in June 1864. Unfortunately, racial incidents within the Union army and navy were common.

Confederate reaction to the Union's recruitment of African American troops was predictably harsh. The Confederate government announced that any blacks taken as prisoners of war would be either shot on the spot or returned to slavery. In retaliation, Lincoln stated that he would order a Confederate prisoner of war executed for every African American prisoner shot by the South and would order a southern prisoner to do hard labor for every African American prisoner returned to slavery. Confederates sometimes treated black prisoners of war the same as they did whites. Nevertheless, in several instances, surrendering African Americans were murdered, the most notable instance occurring at Fort Pillow, Tennessee, where apparently several dozen African American prisoners of war and their white commander, Major William Bradford, were shot "while attempting to escape." After another engagement, one Confederate colonel bragged, "I then ordered every one shot, and with my Six Shooter I assisted in the execution of the order." Yet in spite of his warning, Lincoln did not retaliate, even though a United States Senate investigating committee charged that about three hundred African American Union soldiers had been murdered. The president probably felt that any action on his part would only further inflame the Confederates.

Within the Confederacy, the adoption of the policy to recruit African American soldiers came much too late, the last gasp of a dying nation that had debated too long between principle and survival. In the month between the approval of the policy and the end of the war at Appomattox Court House, a few black companies were organized, but there is no record that they ever saw action. In spite of this lack of evidence, stories about black Confederate soldiers occasionally still circulate.

The debate over the use of African American troops points out what many abolitionists had maintained for years: Although slavery was a moral concern that consumed all who touched it, the institution of slavery was but part of the problem facing black—and white—Americans. More insidious and less easily eradicated was racism, a set of assumptions, feelings, and emotions that has survived long after slavery was destroyed. The debate in both the North and the South over the use of African American troops clearly demonstrates that the true problem confronting many people of the Civil War era was their own feelings, anxieties, and fears.

CHAPTER

11

Grant, Greeley, and the Popular Press: The Presidential Election of 1872

✳ THE PROBLEM ✳

By 1872, it appeared that Reconstruction was in serious trouble. Although Congress had increased the powers of military governors in the states of the former Confederacy, many southern whites remained fiercely unrepentant and resisted—sometimes violently—efforts to grant citizenship and voting rights to former slaves. For the most part African Americans remained landless and uneducated, making them highly vulnerable to white landowners and unscrupulous election officials. More serious, among northern white voters the zeal for reconstructing the South was beginning to wane, as new issues and concerns, such as government corruption, civil service reform, continued westward expansion and conflict with Native Americans, currency inflation, and the

rise of industry, vied with one another for people's attention.

In May 1872, a group of disillusioned men broke with the Grant administration and the Republican party and held their own convention in Cincinnati, Ohio. Calling themselves Liberal Republicans, they formally nominated the widely known and controversial New York *Tribune* editor Horace Greeley as the party's presidential candidate and Missouri Governor B. Gratz Brown as his running mate. In a letter accepting the convention's nomination, Greeley called for an end to the failed experiment of Reconstruction, asserting that he had "the confident trust that the masses of our countrymen North and South are eager to clasp hands across the bloody chasm which has too long divided them. . . ."[1] Hoping to turn the Grant administration out of office, the Democrats also nominated Greeley and Brown.

What began as a contest over opposing philosophies and stands on issues such as Reconstruction, however, soon turned into one of the most vicious and personal presidential campaigns in American history. To be sure, some previous presidential contests had been ugly affairs as well (especially those of 1800 and 1828), but the campaign of 1872 seemed to descend to a new low in political vituperation and smear tactics. By November 1872, no office seeker was left unscathed.[2]

Although no one who participated in the 1872 presidential race escaped blame, two people in particular were among the most responsible: Thomas Nast and Matthew Somerville (Matt) Morgan. Nast (1840–1902) was the chief political cartoonist for the popular *Harper's Weekly,* while Morgan (1839–1890) was Nast's opposite on the rival *Frank Leslie's Illustrated Newspaper.* Two of the most talented illustrators of their time, Nast and Morgan were in large part responsible for their respective weekly publications reaching circulations of 100,000 by 1872, the year that both men were at the zeniths of their power and influence.

Your tasks in this chapter are to analyze the political cartoons of both Thomas Nast and Matt Morgan, and then, using those cartoons, to answer the following questions:

1. How did each side attempt to portray the other? the respective presidential candidates (Grant and Greeley)?
2. What were the principal issues the cartoons attempted to address? Which issues did they *not* address or avoid addressing?
3. How did each side attempt to deal with Reconstruction in the presidential election of 1872?

For those who maintain that recent presidential contests have reached a new level of personal attacks and general nastiness, the 1872 election is a much-needed corrective.

1. For Greeley's acceptance letter see William Gillette, "Election of 1872," in Arthur M. Schlesinger Jr., ed., *History of American Presidential Elections* (New York: Chelsea House, 1971), Vol. II, p. 1359.
2. An excellent book on the earliest "nasty" election is Bernard A. Weisberger's *America Afire: Jefferson, Adams, and the Revolutionary Election of 1800* (New York: William Morrow, 2000).

CHAPTER 11

GRANT, GREELEY,
AND THE POPULAR
PRESS: THE
PRESIDENTIAL
ELECTION OF 1872

✤ BACKGROUND ✤

Although Radical Republicans[3] outdid each other in oratorical eulogies to Abraham Lincoln, secretly they were not altogether displeased by the death of the president. Not only could the Radical Republicans then use Lincoln as a martyr for their own cause, but also they had reason to believe that Lincoln's successor, Andrew Johnson of Tennessee, would be more sympathetic to their plans than the late president had been. After all, Johnson had been a harsh military governor of Tennessee (1862–1864) who had said many times that treason "must be made odious, and the traitors must be punished and impoverished."[4]

Yet it did not take Radical Republicans long to realize that President Andrew Johnson was not one of them. Although he had spoken harshly, he pardoned around 13,000 former Confederates, who quickly captured control of southern state governments and congressional delegations. Many northerners were shocked to see former Confederate officers and officials, and even former Confederate Vice President Alexander Stephens, returned to Washington. At the same time, the new southern state legislatures passed a series of laws, known collectively as black codes, that so se-

3. The Radical Republicans were the left wing of the Republican party. They favored the abolition of slavery, a harsher policy against the defeated South, and full equality for African Americans.

4. See his remarks on the fall of Richmond, April 3, 1865, in LeRoy P. Graf, ed., *The Papers of Andrew Johnson* (Knoxville: University of Tennessee Press, 1986), Vol. VII, p. 545.

verely restricted the rights of former slaves that they were all but slaves again. Moreover, Johnson privately told southerners that he opposed the Fourteenth Amendment to the Constitution, intended to confer full civil rights on the newly freed slaves. When Radical Republicans in Congress attempted to enact harsher measures, Johnson vetoed them and, simultaneously, appeared to do little to combat the widespread defiance of white southerners, including insulting federal troops, desecrating the American flag, and participating in organized resistance groups such as the Ku Klux Klan.

The congressional elections of 1866 gave Radical Republicans enough seats in Congress to override Johnson's vetoes. Beginning in March 1867, Congress passed a series of Reconstruction acts that divided the South into five military districts, to be ruled by military commanders under martial law. Southern states had to ratify the Fourteenth Amendment and institute African American suffrage before being allowed to take their formal places in the Union. The Freedmen's Bureau, founded in 1865, was given additional federal support to set up schools and hospitals for African Americans, negotiate labor contracts, and, with military assistance, monitor elections. When President Johnson attempted to block these acts and purposely violated the Tenure of Office Act and the Command of the Army Act (both of which were Radical Republican measures passed over his vetoes), he was impeached by Congress in 1868, but fell one vote short of the two-thirds required to remove him.

With the impotent Johnson left to serve out the final months of his term, Radical Republicans picked the popular war hero General Ulysses Grant as the Republican party's 1868 presidential nominee. Although it was not widely known at the time, Grant had harbored presidential ambitions as early as 1863. At war's end, he set out on a series of national tours on which he attended celebrations in his honor, received honorary degrees, delivered carefully written noncontroversial speeches, and attended funerals of his comrades. A far more wily politician than he was credited with being, Grant simultaneously stayed on good terms with Andrew Johnson while privately cultivating the president's enemies. Only in early 1868 did Johnson fully realize what Grant was doing. In a conversation with Gideon Welles, Welles told Johnson that "Grant is going over." Ruefully, Johnson replied, "Yes." The open break came in January of 1868.[5] After Grant won the 1868 presidential race in a very close vote (versus the Democratic governor of New York, Horatio Seymour), Johnson bitterly refused to attend the new president's inauguration.

The political skills that helped Grant reach the presidency seemed to abandon him once he got there. A series of scandals rocked the administration, two of the most prominent occurring before 1872 and involving the president's brother-in-law in a scheme to corner the gold market and his vice president Schuyler Colfax who, along with some Republican congressmen, was linked to a fraudulent construction company (the Credit Mobilier) designed to skim off government funds appropriated for the Union Pacific Railroad (Colfax was dropped from the Republican ticket in 1872). In addition, the Grant administration increased tariff rates in 1870 (thus driving up the prices for certain goods), reinstituted paper money in 1871 (to inflate the currency), opposed civil service reform, and advocated what one historian called a "farcical plan" to annex the Dominican Republic. As one disillusioned Republican said of Grant, the "rascals . . . know they can twist him around their thumb by flattering him."[6] Reconstruction in the South seemed as if it would never end.

By early 1872, a diverse group of editors, professional men, businessmen, disappointed office seekers, upper-class intellectuals, and reform-minded Republicans was determined to overthrow the Grant administration. Calling themselves Liberal Republicans, they gathered in Cincinnati in May 1872 to establish a new political party to oust the "stalwart" Republicans.

Deciding who would be the standard bearer of such a disparate conglomeration was no easy matter. U.S. Supreme Court Chief Justice Salmon P. Chase was available and eager, but he had been a perennial candidate who, it was felt, could never beat Grant. Venerable Senator Charles Sumner of Mas-

5. See William S. McFeely, *Grant: A Biography* (New York: Norton, 1981), p. 263. Gideon Welles (1802–1878) was U.S. Secretary of the Navy, 1861–1869.

6. Gillette, "Election of 1872," pp. 1303, 1307.

CHAPTER 11

GRANT, GREELEY,
AND THE POPULAR
PRESS: THE
PRESIDENTIAL
ELECTION OF 1872

sachusetts was in poor health and former Minister to Great Britain Charles Francis Adams (son of former President John Quincy Adams) was considered a poor campaigner and too aristocratic (he had opposed universal suffrage). Senator Carl Schurz of Missouri was one of the original founders of the Liberal Republicans, but he was ineligible because of his foreign birth (Germany). Missouri Governor B. Gratz Brown was widely known to be a heavy drinker, and U.S. Supreme Court Associate Justice David Davis had written some court decisions that were unpopular. Finally, on the sixth ballot, the Cincinnati convention nominated New York *Tribune* editor Horace Greeley.

Horace Greeley had made no secret of the fact that he yearned to be the Liberal Republicans' presidential candidate. Born into a poor New Hampshire family in 1811, Greeley was considered a child prodigy in the tiny community of Amherst. But the family was evicted from its farm when Horace was nine years old, and he was unable to attend school past the age of thirteen. Apprenticed to a printer, he worked his way up from apprentice to journeyman to printer and finally to editor of a number of newspapers, most of which folded for lack of readers. In 1841, his fortune turned, as he became editor of the New York *Tribune* and built that paper into one of the largest and most influential in the nation. Greeley knew great talent when he saw it, employing at various times Charles Dana, Margaret Fuller, and George Ripley. Authors whose work was accepted for inclusion in the *Tribune* included Ralph Waldo Emerson, Nathaniel Hawthorne, Walt Whit-

man (first published in the *Tribune*), and Karl Marx (on the revolutions of 1848). A three-month term in the U.S. House of Representatives (filling out the term of a congressman removed from office) was the only office Greeley had held previously, although he had sought a seat in the U.S. Senate and the governorship of New York.

The Greeley candidacy had several liabilities. To begin with, over the years Greeley's editorials in the *Tribune* had made him many enemies. As early as 1853, he had confessed to William Seward that a man "says so many things in the course of thirty years that may be quoted against him. . . ."[7] In addition, in his years at the *Tribune*, Greeley had advocated a number of causes, including prohibition (his father almost certainly was an alcoholic), vegetarianism, changing the name of the United States to Columbia, opposing women's corsets, and other ideas that made him appear to some people as an eccentric. Finally, Greeley was on record as criticizing the Democratic party, whose support he certainly would need to overthrow Grant, and being at odds with key provisions of his own party's platform. Hearing of Greeley's nomination, one politician exclaimed, "Six weeks ago I did not suppose that any considerable number of men, outside of a Lunatic Asylum, would nominate Greeley for President."[8]

No sooner had the Liberal Republicans' Cincinnati convention concluded than the nation's newspapers and

7. Glyndon G. Van Deusen, *Horace Greeley, Nineteenth-Century Crusader* (Philadelphia: University of Pennsylvania Press, 1953), p. 414.
8. Gillette, "Election of 1872," p. 1316.

newsmagazines began to take aim at one presidential candidate or the other. By 1872, the illustrated weekly newspaper or newsmagazine was the most influential medium in the United States, and the editorial cartoonists or illustrators were the crown princes of that medium.

The first successful illustrated weekly newspaper in the United States was *Frank Leslie's Illustrated Newspaper,* whose first issue was published on December 15, 1855. The newspaper's founder, whose real name was Henry Carter, was born near London, England, in 1821. According to legend, Carter signed his illustrations with the pseudonym "Frank Leslie" so that his disapproving father would not discover that he had taken up a career in illustration. Immigrating to the United States in 1848 in search of more economic opportunity, Frank Leslie (as he now called himself) made a fortune publishing *Frank Leslie's Illustrated Newspaper* and other papers and magazines. At one time employing over a hundred artists, engravers, and printers, Leslie set the standards for illustrated newspapers and magazines that others followed. He brought in illustrator-cartoonist Matt Morgan from Great Britain specifically for the paper's coverage of the 1872 election.

Harper's Weekly was the brainchild of Fletcher Harper, one of four brothers who founded and operated Harper Brothers printing and publishing company.[9] By 1830, Harper Brothers was the largest book publisher in the United States. In 1857, Fletcher Harper established *Harper's Weekly* and

in 1859, he lured illustrator-cartoonist Thomas Nast from rival Frank Leslie.

Born in the German Palatinate (one of the German states) in 1840, Nast immigrated with his family to New York City in 1846, and by the age of fifteen he was among Leslie's "stable" of artists. Throughout his career, Nast produced more than three thousand cartoons, book illustrations, and printings (he did 150 drawings for *Harper's Weekly* in 1872 alone). He is credited with originating the modern depiction of Santa Claus, the Republican elephant, and the Democratic donkey. Paid the princely sum of $18,000 by *Harper's Weekly* in 1872, Nast had the complete support of owner-publisher Fletcher Harper, even when editor George William Curtis "begged the artist to hold his fire."[10] When it came to holding his fire, Thomas Nast never did.

As you examine and analyze the political cartoons by Matt Morgan from *Frank Leslie's Illustrated Newspaper* and Thomas Nast from *Harper's Weekly*, consider the following questions:

1. How did each side attempt to portray the other? the respective presidential candidates (Grant and Greeley)?

2. What were the principal issues the cartoons attempted to address? Which issues did they *not* address or avoid addressing?

3. How did each side attempt to deal with Reconstruction in the presidential election of 1872?

Be sure to take notes as you go along.

9. The Harper firm was founded in 1817. Fletcher Harper joined Harper Brothers in 1825.

10. J. Chal Vinson, *Thomas Nast, Political Cartoonist* (Athens, Ga.: University of Georgia Press, 1967), p. 24.

CHAPTER 11

GRANT, GREELEY,
AND THE POPULAR
PRESS: THE
PRESIDENTIAL
ELECTION OF 1872

✳ THE METHOD ✳

Although the presidential election of 1872 perhaps represents the zenith of the political cartoon as an influential art form, cartoons and caricatures had a long tradition of influence in both Europe and America before 1872. English artists established the cartoon style that eventually made *Punch* (founded in 1841) one of the liveliest periodicals on both sides of the Atlantic. In America, Benjamin Franklin is traditionally credited with publishing the first newspaper cartoon in the colonies, in 1754—the multidivided snake, each part of the snake representing one colony, with the ominous warning "Join or Die." By the time Andrew Jackson sought the presidency in the 1820s, the political cartoon had become a regular and popular feature of American political life. Lacking modern sophistication, these cartoons nonetheless influenced people far more than the printed word.

Like the newspaper editorial, the political cartoon is intended to do much more than objectively report events. Instead, the political cartoon is meant to express an opinion, a point of view, an approval or disapproval. Political cartoonists want to catch people's attention, make them laugh or feel angry, move them to action. In short, political cartoons do not depict exactly what is happening, but rather try to make people see what is happening from a particular point of view.

How can we hope to analyze political cartoons that deal with issues, events, and people from over 125 years ago? To begin with, using your text,

The Problem and Background sections of this chapter, and assistance from your instructor, make a list of the most important issues having to do with the Reconstruction of the South, the Grant administration, the Liberal Republican revolt, and Horace Greeley himself. As you examine each of the cartoons in this chapter (seven cartoons from *Frank Leslie's Illustrated Newspaper* and seven from *Harper's Weekly*), try to determine what the artist is trying to say, what issue or event (or pseudo-issue or pseudo-event)[11] is being portrayed, and how the individuals are depicted. Sometimes a cartoon's caption, dialogue, or other words or phrases can help you determine the cartoon's focus.

Next, look closely at each cartoon for clues that will help you understand what Morgan or Nast was trying to say. People who saw these cartoons in 1872 did not have to study them so carefully—just as you do not have to spend a great deal of time studying contemporary political cartoons in today's newspapers or newsmagazines. The individuals and events depicted in each cartoon were immediately familiar to people in 1872, and the messages were obvious. But you are a *historian,* and you will be using these cartoons as historical evidence to help

11. A pseudo-event is a sham event, one that never actually took place or took place as a staged event for the press. Both sets of cartoons are replete with such pseudo-events. Similarly, a pseudo-issue is a false issue, one that may have been created by the cartoonist or by other political partisans.

you understand the presidential election of 1872.

As you will see, both Matt Morgan and Thomas Nast were talented artists. Both cartoonists often used *symbolism* to make their respective points, sometimes in the form of *allegory*. In an allegory, familiar figures (such as Grant or Greeley) are portrayed in a setting or situation that everyone knows—see, for example, Sources 4 and 10 in the Evidence section of this chapter. Thus, by placing these familiar figures in a well-known setting (a Bible story, a piece of mythology, Aesop's fables, and so forth) a deeper meaning or depiction of the figures is communicated.

Other, less complicated symbolism was employed in the 1872 cartoons as well. Both the American flag and military uniforms were powerful images that could be used by each cartoonist. Similarly, Columbia (a tall woman wearing a long classical dress) was a common representation of the United States itself, as was the emerging figure of Uncle Sam when it was used in cartoons in juxtaposition with such figures as Grant, Greeley, and others.

Both President Ulysses Grant and Liberal Republican-Democratic challenger Horace Greeley were instantly recognizable in both Morgan's and Nast's cartoons. How the two candidates were depicted in the cartoons will be crucially important to you as you attempt to analyze each cartoonist's approach to the presidential election of 1872. Other caricatures, however, will be less familiar to you. When identification of a caricatured individual is necessary for you to "read" a cartoon, it is provided in a footnote.

As you can see, a political cartoon must be analyzed in detail to get the full meaning the cartoonist was trying to convey. If you proceed with patience and care, you will be able to analyze the fourteen 1872 political cartoons and thereby to answer the three questions this chapter asks.

❈ THE EVIDENCE ❈

Sources 1 through 7 from *Frank Leslie's Illustrated Newspaper*, April 6, May 4, May 25, June 29, August 10, August 24, and November 2, 1872. Source 1: The Granger Collection. Sources 2 through 7: Courtesy of The University of Tennessee, Knoxville.

CHAPTER 11

GRANT, GREELEY,
AND THE POPULAR
PRESS: THE
PRESIDENTIAL
ELECTION OF 1872

Political Cartoons by Matt Morgan

1. A Drunken Despot, April 6, 1872.

12. Roscoe Conkling (Republican, N.Y.), U.S. Senator.
13. President Ulysses Grant.

2. Uncle Sam in Danger, May 4, 1872.

14. Carl Schurz (Liberal Republican, Mo.), U.S. Senator.
15. Horace Greeley.

CHAPTER 11

GRANT, GREELEY,
AND THE POPULAR
PRESS: THE
PRESIDENTIAL
ELECTION OF 1872

3. Swords into Plowshares, May 25, 1872.

16. Schurz.
17. Greeley.

4. Our King Canute, June 29, 1872.

OUR KING CANUTE-AND THE RISING TIDE.

"King Canute caused his throne to be placed on the verge of the sands, on the seashore, when the tide was rolling in, and said to the Ocean: 'Thus far shalt thou go, and no further.' Finding that it did not obey him, he took off his crown, and never wore it again."

CHAPTER 11

GRANT, GREELEY,
AND THE POPULAR
PRESS: THE
PRESIDENTIAL
ELECTION OF 1872

5. The Bribe Refused, August 10, 1872.

THE BRIBE REFUSED.

"Notwithstanding the large sums of money which have been sent by the Administration to North Carolina (under the pretense that it was to pay Court expenses), the more intelligent portion of the Blacks are very enthusiastic for Mr. Greeley, and have succeeded in making many converts. They exercise a very controlling influence among their associates, which is one of the most encouraging signs of the campaign."—Ex-Senator Doolittle.

6. Sumner as a Modern Moses, August 24, 1872.

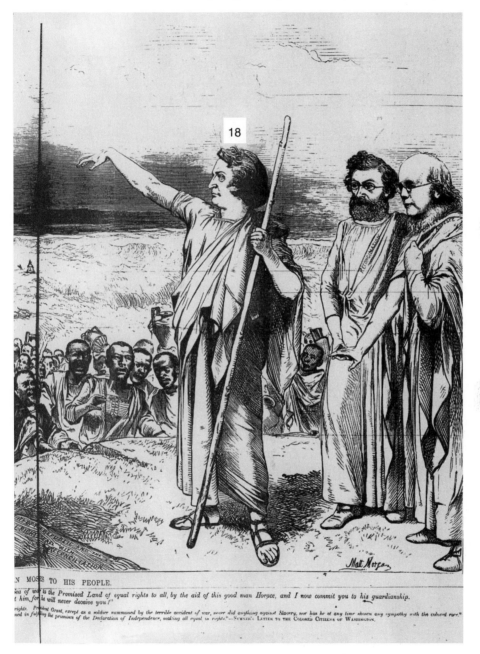

18. Charles Sumner (Republican, Mass.), Radical Republican; broke with Grant. To the right of Sumner are Schurz and Greeley.

CHAPTER 11

GRANT, GREELEY,
AND THE POPULAR
PRESS: THE
PRESIDENTIAL
ELECTION OF 1872

7. A Useless Appeal, November 2, 1872.

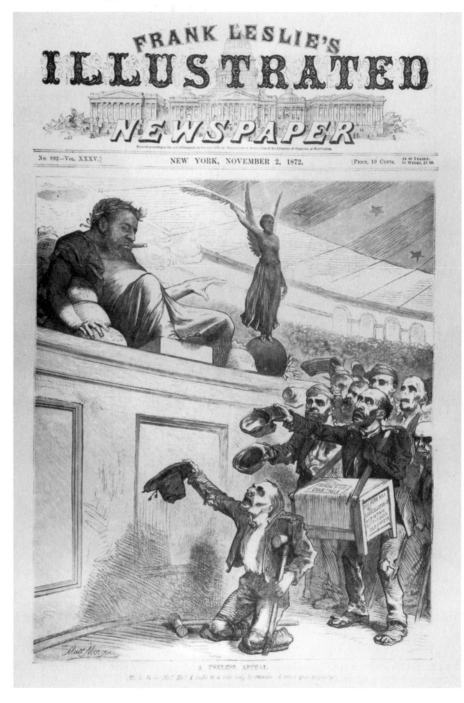

Sources 8 through 14 from *Harper's Weekly,* April 13, April 20, August 10, September 14, September 21, and October 12, 1872. Courtesy of The University of Tennessee, Knoxville.

Political Cartoons by Thomas Nast

8. The Republic Is Not Ungrateful, April 13, 1872.

CHAPTER 11

GRANT, GREELEY,
AND THE POPULAR
PRESS: THE
PRESIDENTIAL
ELECTION OF 1872

9. Sumner as Robinson Crusoe, April 20, 1872.

10. Any Thing to Get In, August 10, 1872.

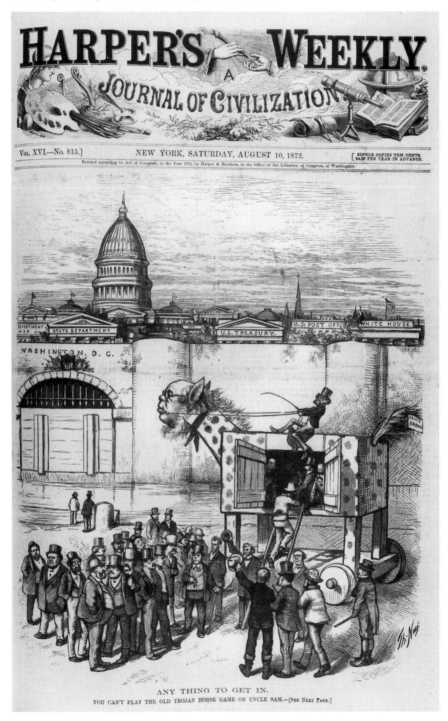

CHAPTER 11

GRANT, GREELEY,
AND THE POPULAR
PRESS: THE
PRESIDENTIAL
ELECTION OF 1872

11. Greeley and Booth, September 14, 1872.

19. John Wilkes Booth (1838–1865), assassin of President Lincoln.

12. General Orders, September 21, 1872.

CHAPTER 11

GRANT, GREELEY,
AND THE POPULAR
PRESS: THE
PRESIDENTIAL
ELECTION OF 1872

13. "Let Us Clasp Hands over the Bloody Chasm," September 21, 1872.

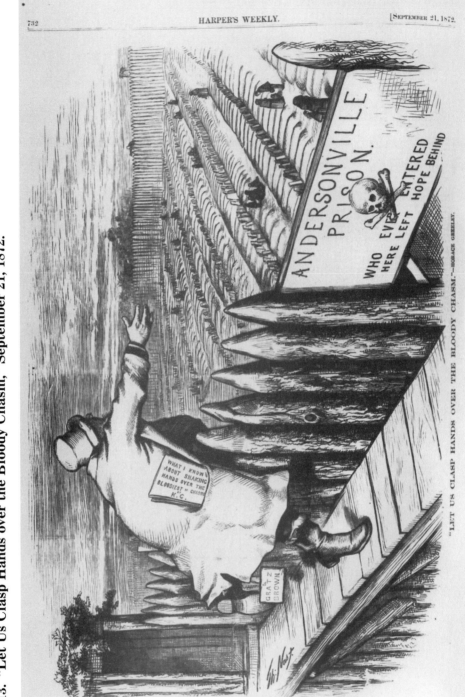

14. More Secession Conspiracy, October 12, 1872.

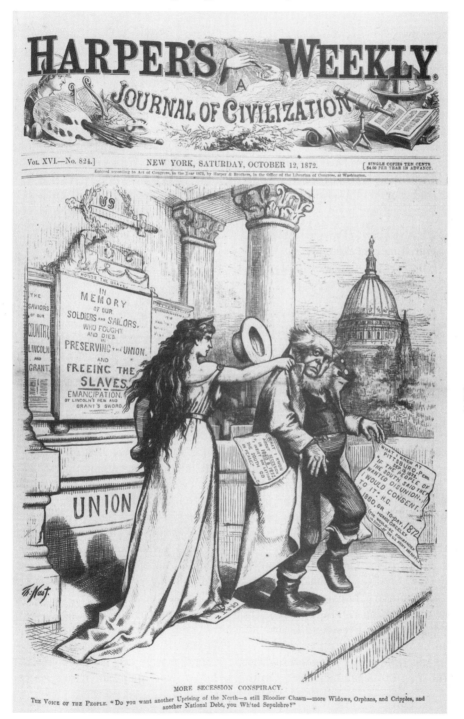

MORE SECESSION CONSPIRACY.

THE VOICE OF THE PEOPLE. "Do you want another Uprising of the North—a still Bloodier Chasm—more Widows, Orphans, and Cripples, and another National Debt, you Wh'ted Sepulchre?"

QUESTIONS TO CONSIDER

Begin by reviewing your list of important issues having to do with Reconstruction, the Grant administration, the Liberal Republican revolt, and Horace Greeley himself. Then, starting with the seven Morgan cartoons from *Frank Leslie's Illustrated Newspaper* (Source 1 through 7) and moving on to the seven Nast cartoons from *Harper's Weekly* (Sources 8 through 14), answer the following questions for each cartoon:

1. What issue (or event) is represented by this cartoon?
2. Who are the principal figures, and how are they portrayed?
3. What *imagery* is used?
4. Is the cartoon an *allegory*? If so, what is the basis of that allegory?
5. What *symbols* (flag, Columbia, and Uncle Sam, for example) are used, and how are they used?
6. How were Morgan and Nast trying to influence public opinion through their respective cartoons?

You may find that making a chart is the easiest way to sort your answers.

Morgan's cartoons in Sources 3, 5, and 6 deal with Greeley's, Liberal Republicans', and the Democratic party's views of Reconstruction. With regard to Reconstruction, what do these three cartoons advocate? How is Greeley portrayed in each cartoon (notice, in Source 5, he is standing behind the glass voting receptacle to the far left)? How are President Grant and the stalwart Republicans portrayed? Sources 4, 6, and 7 are all allegories. Who was the legendary King Canute (Source 4)? Why is Grant portrayed as Canute? What is the allegory represented in Source 6 (from left to right, the caricatures depict Sumner, Schurz, and Greeley)? What is the message of this cartoon? Source 7 portrays Grant as a Roman emperor, apparently dispensing charity. Who are the beggars? What is the cartoon's message?

Grant is depicted in all but one of the Morgan cartoons (Source 6). How is he portrayed? Conversely, how is Greeley portrayed (see, especially, Sources 2, 3, 5, and 6)? What reasons does Morgan infer that voters should choose Greeley?

Now move on to the seven Nast cartoons from *Harper's Weekly* (Sources 8 through 14), again using the preceding six questions.

Nast's cartoons in Sources 9, 12, and 14 deal directly with Reconstruction (Sources 11 and 13 do so as well, albeit indirectly). Begin by examining Source 9, an allegory based on Daniel Defoe's 1719 novel *Robinson Crusoe.* You should notice almost immediately that Nast's cartoons are more filled with details than those of Morgan. In Source 9, Greeley is leading a party that is trying to lure respected abolitionist Charles Sumner of Massachusetts (Crusoe) away from the freed man (Friday) and into a rowboat that will take them to the ship "Democrat." Note that the original name of the ship, "Slavery," is crossed out. What do the four flags on the ship represent? Notice, too, that the papers in the African American man's hat are titled "Emancipated by A. Lincoln" and "Protected by U.S. Grant," and that the schoolhouse in the background is named "Lincoln School." What is Nast saying in Source 9 about Greeley's stand on Reconstruction? See Sources 12 and 14 as well.

In addition to the Robinson Crusoe allegory in Source 9, Nast makes use of allegory in Source 10. What does the Trojan horse represent in Virgil's account of the war between Greece and Troy? What does the Trojan horse represent here? Who is getting into the Trojan horse? Notice that B. Gratz Brown, Greeley's running mate, is portrayed as a slip of paper attached to Greeley's tail (see also Sources 11 through 14). It was said at the time that Nast had no photograph of Brown from which to draw a caricature, so he portrayed him as an insignificant slip of paper.

Nast's portrayals of Greeley are vicious and withering. In Sources 11 and 13, he distorts a phrase from Greeley's acceptance letter beyond recognition: Greeley is shown "clasp[ing] hands over the bloody chasm," a comment Greeley intended as an offer of reconciliation between the North and South. How does Nast use Greeley's phrase? In an 1869 essay titled "What I Know of Farming," Greeley celebrated life in rural America. How does Nast twist that as well (see Sources 9, 11, 12, and 14)?

Like Morgan, Nast uses symbolism in his cartoons. How does Nast employ the symbols of the flag (in Sources 9 and, especially, 12) and Columbia (in Sources 8 and 14)? How does he use other symbols?

Grant is depicted in only one of the Nast cartoons (Source 8). How is he portrayed? What is the bust of Abraham Lincoln meant to represent? The feathers on the arrows aimed at Grant are labeled "slander," "malice," "misrepresentations," "insinuations," and "lies." How is Columbia protecting Grant? How, then, is Grant depicted by Nast?

Now put all your notes together to answer the three central questions of this chapter:

1. How did each side attempt to portray the other? the respective presidential candidates (Grant and Greeley)?
2. What were the principal issues the cartoons attempted to address? Which issues did they *not* address or avoid addressing?
3. How did each side attempt to deal with Reconstruction in the presidential election of 1872?

❋ EPILOGUE ❋

For Horace Greeley and Liberal Republicanism, the 1872 election campaign was a fiasco. As he himself had predicted, Greeley's comments in earlier speeches and writings (especially his willingness in 1860 to let the South secede rather than fight a war, his 1867 offer to post a bond for Jefferson

CHAPTER 11

GRANT, GREELEY,
AND THE POPULAR
PRESS: THE
PRESIDENTIAL
ELECTION OF 1872

Davis, and his advocacy of a quick and gentle reconstruction of the South) virtually doomed his candidacy in the northern states. For its part, the Republican party hired three hundred researchers to dig up material against Greeley and then feed that material to people such as Thomas Nast.

Realizing his candidacy was in deep trouble, Greeley embarked on a physically punishing speaking tour through New Jersey, Pennsylvania, Ohio, Indiana, and Kentucky, delivering around two hundred speeches in ten days. Increasingly intemperate, in a speech in Jeffersonville, Indiana, on September 23, he lashed out at African Americans for supporting Grant, even asserting that his opposition to slavery "might have been a mistake!"[20]

The behavior of Greeley's running mate, B. Gratz Brown, did little to help the campaign. At a picnic, Brown became so intoxicated that he attempted to butter a watermelon. During a commencement address at Yale, his alma mater, Brown insulted the college, claimed he didn't know why he had gone there, and urged the graduates to vote for Greeley because "I believe he has the largest head in America."[21] Later in the campaign, the inebriated Brown passed out while delivering a speech in New York City.

The election was a rout of Greeley. Backed by the interests of new businessmen, the Grand Army of the Republic (a group of northern Civil War veterans), African Americans, and voters outraged by Greeley, Grant won the election with almost 56 percent of the popular vote and the electoral votes in all but six states (Georgia, Kentucky, Maryland, Missouri, Tennessee, and Texas).

Although the voters appeared to reject the Reconstruction plans of Greeley and embrace Grant and the Radical Republicans, after the 1872 presidential race, Radical Reconstruction deteriorated rapidly. The Amnesty Act of 1872, passed by Congress and signed by Grant to deprive Greeley of a campaign issue, restored the rights to vote and hold office to all but a handful of former Confederates. With northern support of Reconstruction declining and the Grant administration (in spite of its 1872 promises) losing interest in forcing the white South to respect the Fourteenth Amendment, southern Democrats quickly regained control of southern states. By late 1876, only Florida, Louisiana, and South Carolina had not been "redeemed," as southern Democrats referred to their recapture of the South. By the presidential election of 1876, it was clear that Reconstruction was almost over, as both major party candidates pledged to end it in 1877.

Greeley returned to New York from his speaking tour a physically and mentally exhausted man. Then, on October 30, one week before the election, his wife died after a lingering illness. It was the final blow, and Greeley himself died on November 29, two weeks after the election. In its eulogy to Greeley, *Frank Leslie's Illustrated Weekly* mourned that "his life was worn out in his struggle to restore love between the sections." In a final touch of irony, the paper predicted that over

---

20. Gillette, "Election of 1872," p. 1326.
21. *Ibid.,* p. 1327.

Greeley's grave "the sections 'will clasp hands.'"[22]

As a gesture of good will and reconciliation, President Grant attended Greeley's funeral. But reconciliation would be long in coming. When Grant yearned for a third term in 1876, the abandonment of the Republican party by Greeley's supporters, combined with a fresh batch of second-term scandals, denied Grant the prize he so desperately sought. In retirement, he rushed to finish his memoirs (to provide for his wife Julia) before the throat cancer he had been diagnosed as having ultimately killed him. Grant died on July 23, 1885, and was interred in Central Park in New York City. In 1897, a magnificent tomb was dedicated to Grant and his remains were relocated there. When Julia died in 1902, President Theodore Roosevelt attended her funeral, and she was laid to rest in what grammatically should be called Grants' Tomb.[23]

Fletcher Harper died in 1877, but his brothers and heirs continued *Harper's Weekly* and, later, *Harper's* magazine. For his part, Frank Leslie created a scandal of his own when in 1873 he divorced his wife to marry a woman who simultaneously had divorced her husband. And when Leslie died in 1880 (like Grant, of throat cancer), his wife Miriam had her name legally changed to Frank Leslie. Soon after that, she married William Charles Wilde, the brother of Oscar Wilde, but they were divorced in 1893. When "Frank Leslie" (Miriam) died in 1914, she left her considerable estate to the cause of women's suffrage.

We know almost nothing about cartoonist-illustrator Matt Morgan after 1872, except that he died in 1890. But Thomas Nast is a different story. After the 1872 presidential election, Mark Twain told Nast that "you more than any other man have won a prodigious victory for Grant. . . . Those pictures were simply marvelous."[24] Taking advantage of his celebrity, Nast renegotiated his contract with *Harper's Weekly* and then went on a speaking tour that brought in $40,000 in seven months.[25]

But Nast was a spendthrift. Financially struggling, he appealed to friends, who ultimately influenced President Theodore Roosevelt to appoint him to a minor consular post in Ecuador. Nast died there of yellow fever in 1902.

22. *Frank Leslie's Illustrated Newspaper,* December 14, 1872.

23. In 1913 the Grants's son, Ulysses S. Grant, Jr., married a woman named America Mills. They were constantly introduced as "U.S. and America Grant." McFeely, *Grant,* p. 520.

24. Morton Keller, *The Art and Politics of Thomas Nast* (New York: Oxford Univ. Press, 1968), pp. 77–78.

25. $40,000 in 1873 would be approximately $452,000 in 1991 dollars.

TEXT CREDITS

CHAPTER ONE

Source 10: From *The Broken Spears* by Miguel Leon-Portilla. © 1962, 1990 by Beacon Press. Used by permission of Beacon Press, Boston.

CHAPTER TWO

Source 1: The Threat of Mrs. Anne Hutchinson. Reprinted by permission of the publisher from *The History of the Colony and Province of Massachusetts,* Vol. 2, by Thomas Hutchinson, Cambridge, Mass.: Harvard University Press, Copyright © 1936 by the President and Fellows of Harvard College.

CHAPTER THREE

Sources 2, 4–6, 12, 15–17: Reprinted from Philip J. Greven, Jr., *Four Generations: Population, Land and Family in Colonial Andover, Massachusetts.* Copyright © 1970 by Cornell University. Used by permission of the publisher, Cornell University.

Sources 3, 6, 8–10, 14, 17, 19: Excerpts from *The Minutemen and Their World* by Robert A. Gross. Copyright © 1976 by Robert A. Gross. New York: Hill and Wang, a division of Farrar, Straus & Giroux, Inc.

Source 7: From *Slave Counterpoint: Black Culture in the Eighteenth-Century Chesapeake and Low Country* by Philip D. Morgan. Copyright © 1998 by The University of North Carolina Press. Used by permission of the publisher.

Sources 7, 11, 13: Data from *The Evolution of American Society, 1700–1815* by James A. Henretta. Copyright © 1973 by D.C. Heath and Company. Reprinted by permission of the publisher.

Sources 12–13: From Paul G.E. Clemens, *The Atlantic Economy and Colonial Maryland's Eastern Shore: From Tobacco to Grain* (Ithaca: Cornell University Press, 1980, pp. 194–195).

Sources 18, 20–22: Reprinted from *The Journal of Interdisciplinary History,* VI (1976), 549, 557, 564, with permission of the editors of *The Journal of Interdisciplinary History* and The MIT Press, Cambridge, MA. © 1976 by the Massachusetts Institute of Technology and the editors of *The Journal of Interdisciplinary History.*

CHAPTER FOUR

Source 3: The Trial of Capt. Thomas Preston. Reprinted by permission of the publisher from *The Legal Papers of John Adams,* Vol. III by John Adams, Cambridge, Mass.: Harvard University Press, Copyright © 1965 by the Massachusetts Historical Society.

Source 4: From Anthony D. Darling, *Red Coat and Brown Bess,* Historical Arms Series, No. 12 (Bloomfield, Ontario). Courtesy of Museum Restoration Service, © 1970, 1981.

Source 5: From *Age of Firearms* by Robert Helm, p. 93, 1957. Drawing by Nancy Jenkins. Reprinted by permission of the author.

CHAPTER FIVE

Sources 10–11: Adapted from Billy G. Smith: *The "Lower Sort": Philadelphia's Laboring People, 1750–1800.* Copyright © 1990 by Cornell University. Used by permission of the publisher, Cornell University Press.

Sources 13–14: Excerpts from *Letters of Benjamin Rush,* Vol. II, edited by L.H. Butterfield, American Philosophical Society, 1951, pp. 644–645, 657–658. Reprinted by permission.

CHAPTER SIX

Map 1: From Grace Steele Woodward, *The Cherokees* (Norman: University of Oklahoma Press, 1963), pp. 206–207. Copyright © 1963 by the University of Oklahoma Press, Norman, Publishing Division of the University of Oklahoma. Reprinted by permission.

Map 2: From Duane H. King, ed., *The Cherokee Nation: A Troubled History,* (Knoxville: University of Tennessee Press, 1979), p. 50. Reprinted by permission.

CHAPTER EIGHT

Sources 1–16: From *Lay My Burden Down: A Folk History of Slavery* from Federal Writer's Project, by B. A. Botkin. Copyright 1945. Reprinted by permission.

Sources 22–23: Songs from S. Stuckey, "Through the Prism of Folklore," *Massachusetts Review,* 1968, reprinted by permission of the Editors of *Massachusetts Review.*

Source 24: From *Narrative of the Life of Frederick Douglass* by Frederick Douglass, pp. 1–3, 13–15, 36–37, 40–41, 44–46, and 74–75. Copyright 1963 by Doubleday. Reprinted by permission of Doubleday, a division of Bantam, Doubleday, Dell Publishing Group, Inc.

Source 25: Excerpts from *Incidents in the Life of a Slave Girl* by Linda Brent, Edited by Walter Magnes Teller, Introduction and Notes copyright © 1973 by Walter Magnes Teller, reprinted by permission of Harcourt Brace & Company.

CHAPTER TEN

Sources 4, 7, 9, 13–15: *The Collected Works of Abraham Lincoln,* Roy P. Basler, ed., copyright © 1953 by the Abraham Lincoln Association. Reprinted by permission of Rutgers University Press.

Source 20: Selections are reprinted from *The Sable Arm: Negro Troops in the Union Army, 1861–1865,* by Dudley Taylor Cornish, by permission of W. W. Norton & Company, Inc. Copyright © 1966 by W. W. Norton & Company, Inc. Copyright © 1956 by Dudley Taylor Cornish.

Sources 23–26, 29, 32, 34–36: From Robert F. Durden, *The Gray and the Black.* Reprinted by permission of the publisher, Louisiana State University Press.